Magical Consciousness

C000113199

How does a mind think magically? The research documented in this book is one answer that allows the disciplines of anthropology and neurobiology to come together to reveal a largely hidden dynamic of magic. Magic gets to the very heart of some theoretical and methodological difficulties encountered in the social and natural sciences, especially those having to do with issues of rationality. This book examines magic head-on, not through its instrumental aspects, but as an orientation of consciousness. Magical consciousness is affective, associative, and synchronistic, shaped through individual experience within a particular environment. This work focuses on an in-depth case study that uses the anthropologist's own experience gained through years of anthropological fieldwork with British practitioners of magic. As an ethnographic view, it is an intimate study of the way in which the cognitive architecture of a mind engages the emotions and imagination in a pattern of meanings related to childhood experiences, spiritual communications, and the environment. Although the detail of the involvement in magical consciousness presented here is necessarily specific, the central tenets of *modus operandi* is common to magical thought in general, and can be applied to cross-cultural analyses to increase understanding of this ubiquitous human phenomenon.

Susan Greenwood is a past lecturer at Goldsmiths College and the University of Sussex.

Erik D. Goodwyn is an Assistant Professor at the University of Louisville.

Routledge Studies in Anthropology

Magical Consciousness

An Anthropological and
Neurobiological Approach

**Susan Greenwood and
Erik D. Goodwyn**

 Routledge
Taylor & Francis Group

NEW YORK AND LONDON

First published 2016
by Routledge
711 Third Avenue, New York, NY 10017

and by Routledge
2 Park Square, Milton Park, Abingdon, Oxon OX14 4RN

First issued in paperback 2017

*Routledge is an imprint of the Taylor & Francis Group,
an informa business*

© 2016 Taylor & Francis

The right of Susan Greenwood and Erik D. Goodwyn to be identified as authors of this work has been asserted in accordance with sections 77 and 78 of the Copyright, Designs and Patents Act 1988.

All rights reserved. No part of this book may be reprinted or reproduced or utilised in any form or by any electronic, mechanical, or other means, now known or hereafter invented, including photocopying and recording, or in any information storage or retrieval system, without permission in writing from the publishers.

Trademark notice: Product or corporate names may be trademarks or registered trademarks, and are used only for identification and explanation without intent to infringe.

Library of Congress Cataloging-in-Publication Data
CIP data has been applied for.

ISBN 13: 978-0-8153-4670-8 (pbk)
ISBN 13: 978-1-138-85036-1 (hbk)

Typeset in Sabon
by Apex CoVantage, LLC

For Ryder and India Greenwood, and all those past, present, and to come

Contents

PART THREE
Conclusions

Figures

Tables

Preface

The process of magic as an aspect of the mind has been rendered largely invisible, except in a negative sense as irrational and "other" to the logical reasoning of science. An important part of this work is to explore new avenues of investigation through the building of bridges between anthropology and neuroscience to highlight what we believe is an important aspect of human thinking. We draw on our previous research—specifically, Greenwood's *Magic, Witchcraft and the Otherworld* (2000), *The Nature of Magic* (2005), and *The Anthropology of Magic* (2009), and Goodwyn's *The Neurobiology of the Gods* (2012) and *A Psychological Reading of the Anglo-Saxon Poem Beowulf* (2014)—to create an interdisciplinary dialogue of scholarly analyses of what we term *magical consciousness*. Above all, as we aim to show, magical consciousness is always affective, associative, and synchronistic in its mode of operation, and it is shaped through an individual's experience within a particular environment through which meanings are gained. A primary aim is to address the question, "What would an ethnography of a mind involved in magic be like?" The research documented in this work is one answer. Rather than the more usual focus on the many cultural contexts in which beliefs in magic may be found, this investigation highlights some of the attributes of magic as a process of thought as demonstrated by Greenwood's own research into the process of magic. Too often, magic is viewed in its instrumental aspects rather than as a mode of thinking, and a primary aim of this volume is to offer an additional perspective. From an ethnographic view, it is an intimate study of the way in which the cognitive architecture of a mind engages the emotions and imagination of an alternative perception in a pattern of meanings. Magical consciousness is as intensely personal as it is universal in some of its fundamental features. While there are many different cultural expressions of magic, there are some underlying fundamental aspects that are shared by all. Thus, although the detail of the involvement in magical consciousness presented here is necessarily specific, the *modus operandi* is common to magical thought processes in general. The tenets of this mode of thinking, can be applied to a cross-cultural analysis to increase understanding of this ubiquitous human phenomenon.

A relational and holistic aspect of the mind in which spiritual entities are experienced as pervading the universe, magical consciousness, as we are using the term, differs from logical, abstract, and analytical thinking, the more usual focus of cognitive science. The latter is a loose affiliation of disciplines of neuroscience and anthropology, as well as linguistics, psychology, and philosophy, each with its own particular view of the "mind." Thus, cognitive science represents a diversity of visions.[1] Being inextricably linked to new technologies, a central branch of study has been based on the view that human cognition is a manipulation of symbols after the fashion of a digital computer, independent of neurobiology and anthropology.[2] In this perspective, a sense of "embodiment," a notion of the body as a lived experiential being as well as a context of cognitive mechanisms, is largely absent. Consequentially, cognitive science has virtually nothing to say about what it means to be human in the situations that are lived every day. More reflective dimensions of human experience are treated with little more than a cursory, matter-of-fact manner that has no depth or the sophistication of scientific analysis.[3] In addition, in the past, some of the complex workings of the mind have been obscured by an historical separation of the disciplines, and this has led to differences that obscure important insights, and a tendency of each to misunderstand or even ignore the other. Although cognitive science is "unavoidably an ethnographic enterprise,"[4] there are far-reaching implications for how culture and the mind are generally conceptualised between disciplines. This results in a rather intractable division between the ideas of culture and the ideas of the mind, and has left a legacy that has frequently marginalised anthropology from cognitive research. This is particularly so in relation to studies of magic.[5] With regard to anthropology and neuroscience, anthropologists are more comfortable looking at the social and cultural dimensions of human life, while neurobiologists concentrate more on individuals and the functioning of the brain. Biogenetic structuralism has been developed as a perspective in anthropology that focuses on the brain, consciousness, and culture—as "a neuroanthropology" that integrates anthropology with neuroscience, phenomenology, and quantum physics.[6] However, in this present work, we seek a creative, experimental place of amelioration between anthropology and neuroscience to reveal a hitherto largely hidden dynamic of magical thinking.

This hidden dimension of magic has been generally obscured in anthropology and neuroscience by a perhaps overzealous emphasis on certain notions of analytical reasoning in the pursuit of knowledge. A "magical" affective aspect of research on cognition is a result of many centuries of academic focus on abstract and emotionally detached thought;[7] an effect of this thinking is that certain perceptions of logical, analytical thought are valued above the sensory and subjective experience of magic. An eighteenth-century Enlightenment ideal grounded notions of rationality on the universality of analytical reasoning, and this has divided the human mind not only from emotions and sensory experience, including that with non-human beings, but has crystallised into a dichotomy between so-called rational and irrational modes of thought. Analytical reasoning has become the basis for science, and magical thought relegated to superstition or primitive, erroneous beliefs. This exposes a modern Western cultural bias in the privileging of one mode of thought over another. As David J. Hufford notes, science is not the problem, but the cultural bias of scientism is.[8] Although scientific attitudes are now changing, especially in the opening up of studies of emotion,[9] there has been comparatively little work done on the neglected process of emotionally driven magical thought, the subject of this study. Consequently, many social-scientific theories have made implicit assumptions about the inferiority of magic compared to science.[10] This attitude has been detrimental to a study of the process of magical thinking. Apart from understanding the fascinating and ubiquitous phenomenon of "magic," another reason for exploring this issue is that it enables a consideration of the very heart of some of the theoretical and methodological difficulties encountered in the social and natural sciences, especially those having to do with issues of "rationality" and "reason."

We each came to be involved in this project on magical consciousness in different ways. For Greenwood, the possibility of such an interdisciplinary study was finally crystallised in a moment at the University of California, Berkeley Art Museum's exhibition on Deities, Demons, and Teachers of Tibet, Nepal, and India, with friend and colleague Geoffrey Samuel, author of *The Origins of Yoga and Tantra: Indic Religions to the Thirteenth Century* (2010). Trying to get a sense of the essence of the Buddha's teaching on the mind and liberating insight in relation to her own work amongst Western practitioners of magic, Greenwood studied the figures of Indian deities and dancers and the images of enlightened beings from Tibet and Nepal. Having visited the Asian Art Museum in San Francisco some days before, and amid various conversations with Geoffrey Samuel, Greenwood thought about what the figures in the museums might mean in terms of human thinking and meaning in a universal dimension. Greenwood and Samuel were preparing to attend an invited seminar at The Esalen Institute's Center for Theory and Research on Anthropology and the Paranormal in Big Sur, further south down the Californian coast. Ideas about connection were on Greenwood's mind. Esalen was Gregory Bateson's final home at the end of his life; Bateson was a pioneer in the interrelationships of different forms of knowledge.[11] Studying communications from subjects as diverse as mental health, cybernetics, and the language of dolphins, Bateson's work had inspired Greenwood's research on magic as an associative process of the mind. Greenwood decided to try an experiment in making a narrative out of her own experience of magic as a process of the communication of the mind, the basis of the experiential chapters of this volume.

Some time previously, Erik Goodwyn had contacted her about the possibility of writing a paper together, and when Greenwood read his *The*

Neurobiology of the Gods, she was prompted to write on the inside front cover: "[T]his book gave me the keys to a previously locked room." Goodwyn's work in this study took a neuropsychiatric perspective in seeking to address what religious ideas meant in cognitive terms, and his aim was to understand gods and spirits as subsets of ideas formalised as symbols; however, he did not reduce the gods to ideas. The gods were metaphorical representations of thoughts, feelings, actions, and environments, a fundamental part of existence. Symbols, Goodwyn argued, "[C]arry the weight of the gods in the human heart, and are very real and potent forces acting on us." Of deep-rooted and innate predispositions, symbols interact with the environment and are highly charged with emotion.[12] From reading this work, Greenwood saw a whole new dimension to magic that corresponded with her own research.[13] She decided to offer her narrative on her research experience of magical thinking to Goodwyn to examine as co-author in this present study. Thus, Goodwyn's work on the neurobiological, evolutionary, and cognitive perspectives on thinking about gods and magic provided another window through which to look at the extraordinarily complex mental-spiritual-physical-cultural activity that occurs during magical thinking. To be truly "scientific," meaning to observe with as little preconceived bias as possible and with an eye toward discovering deeper truths, requires us to look from multiple angles to find what is actually going on in this heretofore largely forgotten style of thought—the inclusive, story telling, holistic, non-verbal, physical, and emotional "language" of magical thought. Such a mode of thought was felt to be absolutely essential to some of the deepest thinkers in the West, and the present work seeks to update that line of inquiry with newer disciplines, acquired data, and also insights from Asian, particularly Buddhist, perspectives.

This study is a move, therefore, from the counterproductive premise that we are all living in a world best described and apprehended by a certain "scientific" view that marginalises emotion and intuition, and where magic is ignored or passed off as being irrational.[14] The result is a poly-vocal narrative study in which the voices of the neurobiologist, anthropologist as anthropologist, anthropologist as "native," and various spirit beings and entities weave an alternative story that displays a largely hidden dynamic process of magic.

A collaborative work such as this has drawn on the support and expertise of many individuals, and Susan Greenwood would particularly like to thank Brian Bates for his comments and helpful advice on draft chapters, Geoffrey Samuel for continued conversations, Liz Puttick for her constructive criticism of some early dragon material, and the past and present students in the Shamanic Consciousness Course. Inspiration has come from Michael Murphy, Jeffrey J. Kripal, David J. Hufford, Ed Kelly, Paul Stoller, Edith Turner, Stanley Krippner, Jack Hunter, Mark Schroll, Øyvind Eikrem, and, as ever, Pat Caplan and her daughter Lauren Greenwood.

NOTES

1. Francisco Varela, Evan Thompson, and Eleanor Rosch *The Embodied Mind: Cognitive Science and Human Experience* (Cambridge, Massachusetts: MIT Press, [1991] 1993): 4–6.
2. Francisco Varela et al. *"Embodied Mind"*, 8.
3. Francisco Varela et al. *"Embodied Mind"*, xv–xviii.
4. Bradd Shore, *Culture in Mind: cognition, culture, and the problem of meaning*, (Oxford: Oxford University Press, 1998): 8.
5. Edward Bever "Current Trends in the Application of Cognitive Science to Magic" in *Magic, Ritual and Witchcraft* (Summer 2012, University of Pennsylvania Press).
6. Charles D. Laughlin http://www.biogeneticstructuralism.com/index2.htm, accessed 27 Sep. 14.
7. Christina Toren "The Child in Mind" in Harvey Whitehouse (ed.) *The Debated Mind: evolutionary psychology versus ethnography* (Oxford: Berg: 2001): 155.
8. Hufford, D.J. 2003. "Evaluating Alternative and Complementary Medicine: The Limits of Science and of Scientists." (*Journal of Law, Medicine & Ethics.* 2003); *The Terror That Comes in the Night: An Experience-Centered Study of Supernatural Assault Traditions.* (Philadelphia, University of Pennsylvania Press, 1982).
9. C. Lutz, and G.M. White The Anthropology of Emotions" (*Annual Review of Anthropology*, Vol. 15) 405; Anna Wierzbicka "Human Emotions: Universal or Culture-Specific?"(*American Anthropologist*, New Series, Vol. 88, No. 3.1986) 584–594. Kay Milton and Maruška Svašek *Mixed Emotions: anthropological studies of feeling* (Oxford: Berg, 2005).
10. Susan Greenwood "Magical Consciousness: A Legitimate Form of Knowledge" in *Defining Magic: A Reader* Bernd-Christian Otto & Michael Stausberg (eds.) (London: Equinox, 2013) 201; Susan Greenwood *The Anthropology of Magic* (Oxford: Berg, 2009).
11. Jeffrey J. Kripal *Esalen: America and the Religion of No Religion* (Chicago: University of Chicago Press, 2007): 307–308.
12. Erik D. Goodwyn *The Neurobiology of the Gods: How Brain Physiology Shapes the Recurrent Imagery of Myth and Dreams* (New York: Routledge, 2012): 4.
13. Susan Greenwood "Toward an Epistemology of Imaginal Alterity: Fieldwork with the Dragon" in *The Social Life of Spirits*, Diana Espirito Santo and Ruy Llera Blanes (eds.) (Chicago: University of Chicago Press, 2014).
14. Espirito Santo and Blanes *"Spirits"*, 6–7, 12.

Introduction
Magic in Consciousness

"[S]cience is to trees as myth is to forest—they appraise different levels of analysis but are not separate from one another or necessarily contradictory."[1]

Magic is frequently defined as a convenient word for a whole collection of techniques, all of which involve the mind and its supposed effects, such as improving a relationship, curing an illness, yielding good crops, dealing with stress, or finding a better job. These techniques suggest that a focused activity or purpose is directing an altered state of consciousness, and it is this instrumental aspect of magical thought that usually gets the attention of scholars. However, the real impact of magic happens at a more fundamental level of individual awareness that includes emotions, feelings, and beliefs. Our aim is to examine the nature of what we call *magical consciousness* before the effects are judged in instrumental terms. Our understanding of magical consciousness is as an associative mode of thought. Characterised by its diffuse and holistic orientation and sense of permeability of boundaries between material and non-material perceptions of reality, magical consciousness leads to a certain "knowing with others." This orientation can be described as analogical rather than logical. Within this conception, there is no contradiction between apparently mutually incompatible and exclusive states such as "life in death" or "unity and multiplicity of being," seemingly universal features of human thought first reported by Plato and Aristotle, who probably carried on traditions originating from Parmenides, but also noted by Lucien Lévy-Bruhl in his work on mystical mentality.[2] Opening up a general sensory awareness of perceptual and emotional fluidity, analogical magical thinking exists alongside logical aspects of the mind and notions of fixed categories of phenomena. Here, it must be emphasised, we are looking at magical thought as a purified, ideal form in order to contrast it with its "analytical" counterpart, where in reality *both forms of thought occur simultaneously all the time*. Happening in varying degrees—from day-dreams, mild trance, or meditations to the most obvious expression in the mediation of practitioners of magic, such as shamans, medicine men, witches, and spirit mediums—magical thinking is often specific to a particular place and time—perhaps in relation to a divinatory question, ritual cycle or process, or a definite set of circumstances—but the associative magical thought process is similar.

Although magic is a foundational area of study in the discipline of anthropology, it is also directly linked to supposed irrational thinking, and so it meets head-on the challenges of the conceptual theoretical parameters also found in neurobiology and the natural sciences. Straightaway, "magic" is something of a commonly contested domain. Despite differences in orientation, anthropology and neuroscience are united in their common, problematic relationship with magic and human relationships with "entities of otherness," commonly understood as spirits. In neuroscience, "hearing voices" or other such "symptoms" has been evidence for psychopathology or psychosis. But a black-and-white categorization of normal and abnormal functioning is just not that easy, and experiences of other, disembodied minds has never been established as universally pathological by any field of study, though obvious extremes are easy to identify. We are not, however, concerned with the extremes, but with the more everyday experiences of the non-material minds reported in the countless mantic and magical practices reported all over the world by all peoples.

A commonality between both disciplines is that the "magical" affective aspect of cognition has been sidelined due to an emphasis on a certain understanding of rationality, a result of the academic focus on abstract and emotionally detached thought.[3] Cognitive anthropology, for example, starts from the premise that culture consists of a corpus of intergenerational and transmissible knowledge, and the objective of anthropology is to discover how that knowledge is organised. There are assumptions that cognition consists of a process of matching sensory experience to stable conceptual schemata, much of which is imposed by the mind through beliefs rather than direct experience.[4] Bourdieu, who argued that cultural knowledge is generated within contexts of people's involvement with others in *habitus*, a process of life embedded in practical contexts, challenged this view,[5] but he did not go into the interior subjective or intersubjective space of images and representations.[6] Here, both emotions and magical experience are theoretically invisible. By contrast, we engage with the issue of affective magical experience with the aim of contributing to cognitive science more generally. Cognitive science stands at the crossroads where the natural sciences and the human sciences meet; it is "Janus-faced," for it looks down both roads at once, and "[o]ne of its faces is turned toward nature and sees cognitive processes as behaviour. The other is turned toward the human world (or what phenomenologists call the "life-world") and sees cognition as experience." Our present study is a move beyond such oppositions.[7]

EXAMINING MAGICAL CONSCIOUSNESS

Magic has traditionally been examined within a rationality debate that focuses on issues of instrumentality. In his book *A Cognitive Theory of Magic*, Danish scholar of religion Jesper Sørenson holds that magical beliefs create a particular form of conceptualization whereby human reasoning depends on the ability to understand one thing in terms of another; to be able to "map inferential potential between distinct experiential and onto-logical domains." This is what Sørenson refers to as "conceptual integra-tion" gained through the use of metaphor and metonymy.[8] Sørenson defines magic as a ritual practice "aimed to produce a particular pragmatic and locally defined result by means of more or less opaque methods." In manip-ulative magic, the aim is to change schematic aspects of entities belong-ing to one domain by manipulating entities belonging to another domain. Metaphor and metonymy are used to express hard-to-grasp terms.[9] Here, magic becomes associated with rituals that create a blended space where elements from profane and sacred worlds mix; for example, the Eucha-rist creates such a combined conceptual area whereby the bread and wine, from the profane domain, come to contain the essence of Christ, from the sacred domain.[10] Sørenson's instrumental theory of magical ritual shows how people maintain magical beliefs through rituals; however, his work, while it shows certain cognitive mechanisms, does not explain how magic is experienced—what is going on when people communicate with spirits, or how they come to foretell the future or cure the sick.[11]

Magic is often seen as functioning as a form of misplaced science that people seek out in order to obtain direct results, whether these involve bring-ing rain or a new lover. And it is this functional aspect that most frequently interests scientists so that they can assess its effects, and then often compare magic unfavourably with science. This is particularly relevant to the ques-tion of how magic, as a mode of consciousness, can be examined while avoiding the common extremes of materialistic reduction and an uncritical belief in spirits. This position presents certain obstacles. Even anthropology, as a social science that is more traditionally inclined to view the spirit beliefs of other cultures with more empathy of understanding, still bases its theo-retical attitude on the scientific method, while at the same time acknowledg-ing the reality of magic in people's lives.

However, ignoring other aspects of the mind amounts to a silence regard-ing a whole dimension of human life, and so it is important to discover a dif-ferent orientation. For anthropologists, specific knowledge gained through fieldwork is understood using a detached, analytical, academic model that is often far removed from the world of lived experience, and differing types of knowledge are often not acknowledged.[12] Thus, magical thinking, while val-ued in itself as an emic "native" expression in anthropology, has been firmly located outside the habitual etic domain of anthropological enquiry and theorisation: "natives" may think what they like, but science really knows best about "reality." For some anthropologists today, there is a distinction between knowledge about magic—what people say and do about it—and knowledge actually from magical consciousness. In its most extreme form, magic is ultimately not true; knowledge that comes from it is untrustworthy and not accessible by the scientific method. Therefore, there are no means to verify its assertions. There is a curious paradox in anthropological studies of magic that abhors universal understandings, and looks at cultural specifics but, at the same time, errs towards general analyzing tendencies that bypass the process of magic as a form of affective cognition. Little attention thus far has been given to understanding magic as an aspect of consciousness. While it is acceptable, or even required, for informants to report manifestations of spirits, the anthropologist should not cross the line between scientific objectivity and his/her own subjectivity. First-person research should include experimental efforts by the anthropologist to achieve any experience necessary to understand the research situation and should be open to other similar scholarly interventions, but also empirical analysis that exposes modern cultural bias. As David J. Hufford notes:

> As was true for Copernicus and as is true for Darwinian evolution, any fair and effective inquiry begins with rigorous methods and controls for cultural bias. Science is not the problem, but the cultural bias of scientism is. In a long struggle scientism captured the flag of rationality. If we are to understand the ubiquitous experience of human spirit encounters and beliefs we need rationality back.[13]

To move beyond the cultural bias of scientism, rationality needs to be reclaimed for magical consciousness. Magic has its own form of reason, as we hope to demonstrate in Chapter 1.

In neuroscience, "hearing voices" or other such "symptoms" has been evidence for psychopathology or psychosis, but in clinical practice, there is no simple rule to determine if hearing disembodied voices represents true pathology or is merely an unusual occurrence in what would otherwise be a normal, everyday experience. Seeing and hearing dead loved ones, for example, is remarkably common during the time period right after a loved one dies. Is this "psychosis?" Religious practice often involves feeling a spiritual presence or having an inner sensation of an outside will or force. Is this "psychosis?" These are not easy questions with clear-cut answers, though the neurobiological literature sometimes is taken to have such clear-cut answers. In reality, however, the neuroscientific corpus, though it contains an unprecedented amount of detail on the inner workings of the brain, still largely consists of a body of neural correlates. This can be very useful for pharmacological or psychosurgical interventions. It does not, however, provide us with the key to deeper questions about the nature of mind and its interaction with matter. And so our approach is to examine magic head-on, not through its instrumental aspects, but as a process of associative thought. In Chapter 3, we will examine some interdisciplinary challenges that face us.

While it is perhaps evident that the aspect of consciousness that we categorise as "magical" cannot be adequately assessed by the classification and conceptualisation of the scientific method as it is currently formulated, it can be analysed as a particular mode of thought that can be understood as a form of knowledge in its own right, much as the ancient Neoplatonists might have approached it. In the West, the dichotomy of "rational" and "nonrational" approaches to knowledge has a long history, with full, thorough treatments dating back at least as far as the Neoplatonists of the late antiquity. Here, we see, for example, Plotinus,[14] arguing that the deepest truths about the nature of reality and the gods can be obtained by a purely detached and rational contemplation, whereas later students, such as Iamblichus[15] and Proclus,[16] assert strongly that true communion with Truth and the Divine cannot be completely achieved through rational contemplation alone, but must involve "theurgy" or ritual acts involving affective, associative magical thinking. These ancient authors felt there was no way to truly approach and connect with the Divine—and hence achieve the highest level of knowledge—without accessing non-verbal, physiognomic, and ecstatic/emotional modalities. This ancient approach (one among many that have cropped up at various times in history) has been more recently overshadowed by scientism, the putatively "scientific" approach that ignores such magical thinking as irrational, useless, or a distraction. The present volume seeks to rectify that unnecessary bias and think critically about magical thinking. Science and magic have too long been jammed into a false dichotomy, with science overruling magic every time, when in fact a truly scientific approach, one that goes beyond the cultural bias of scientism, would involve an attempt to see what these two approaches typically aim for, so that we might compare and contrast them fairly and then arrive at a new synthesis without reduction to either.

Studies of consciousness are the usual purview of philosophy rather than anthropology or neuroscience. Anthropologists tend to view consciousness as a social rather than a psychological or neurobiological matter, often taking it for granted, neglecting its significance, or seeking explanations in social structure or "culture."[17] A definition of "consciousness" as a "knowing system" comes from its Latin origin in *conscius*, meaning "knowing with others, participating in knowledge,"[18] or "sharing the knowledge of anything, together with another."[19] Further clarification of consciousness as "not asleep; awake; awareness of one's own existence, sensations, thoughts and environment; subjectively known; capable of complex response to the environment"[20] invites an examination of magical consciousness as a communal aspect of human cognition. The term "consciousness" has been used in the cognitive, artificial intelligence, philosophical, and other scientific traditions to refer to a "number of interrelated behaviours characteristic of complex systems that respond to their environment." Of course, there are many different kinds of consciousness. These include those that range beyond the rational and egoic forms, engaging with what is conceptualised as forms of spirit, soul, mind, self, and transcendental human capabilities, as well as relationships with other beings.

Some neuroscientists have reservations about the using the term "consciousness," seeing it as problematic to define and preferring to divide up aspects of perception to determine correlates,[21] although there are movements of making connections in terms of the common capabilities and continuity between the brains of current fish, amphibians, reptiles, mammals, and birds, in an evolutionary sense.[22] Opinions about the distribution of consciousness range from a position—influenced by theological doctrine—that holds that only human beings have consciousness to the standpoint that everything might be construed as having consciousness.[23] In this latter view, consciousness is not seen as suddenly arising at a certain evolutionary point, and the development of the mind—from unrecognizable to recognizable—occurs in all forms of matter. As psychologist Max Velmans puts it:

> In the cosmic explosion that gave birth to the universe, consciousness co-emerged with matter and co-evolves with it. As matter became more differentiated and developed in complexity consciousness became correspondingly differentiated and complex.[24]

Recently, a group of prominent neuroscientists and theoretical physicists, including Stephen Hawking, Philip Low, Jaak Panksepp, Diana Reiss, David Edelman, Bruno Van Swinderen, and Christof Koch, signed a proclamation called The Cambridge Declaration of Consciousness at the First Annual Francis Crick Memorial Conference, held at the University of Cambridge on July 2012. This declared that human beings were not unique in possessing neurological substrates that generate consciousness:

> We declare the following: The absence of a neocortex does not appear to preclude an organism from experiencing affective states. Convergent evidence indicates that non-human animals have the neuroanatomical, neurochemical, and neurophysiological substrates of conscious states along with the capacity to exhibit intentional behaviors. Consequently, the weight of evidence indicates that humans are not unique in possessing the neurological substrates that generate consciousness. Non-human animals, including all mammals and birds, and many other creatures, including octopuses, also possess these neurological substrates.

This is a significant move in a relational neurological pattern, and a start at opening up channels of communication between disciplines that challenge conventional scientific understandings. Here, we see continuity between different species in the recognition of similar neuroanatomical, neurochemical, and neurophysiological features, as well as the ability to show intention and affective states. We should note, however, that the problems and challenges of dealing with consciousness do not end here. The above-mentioned declaration assumes an equation of the mind and brain, or a dependence of the mind on the brain, that is not shared by all those who study consciousness.[25] This part of the issue—the so-called "mind-body" problem—has a centuries-long history as well, and is the elephant in the room in all these discussions (as we will discuss later in Chapter 2 of this volume).

American biologist Gerald Edelman has defined consciousness as an ecological habitat "ultimately beyond the physical"[26] in which the brain lives, develops, and constructs its experiences and values.[27] Such a relational definition of consciousness correlates with magic as a participatory, associative aspect of the human mind. Tim Ingold points out that the mind is not given in advance of the individual's entry into the social world, but is fashioned through a lifelong history of involvement in relationships with others; "it is through the activities of the embodied mind (or enminded body) that social relationships are formed and reformed," and psychological and social processes are "thus one and the same."[28] Within this habitat there are a variety of cross-cultural modalities in which people can be conscious, including "alternative" magical modes of mind. Anthropologist Charles D. Laughlin has categorised these as "polyphasic" due to their use of altered states of consciousness, such as the dreaming, contemplation, trance, and ecstatic modes of awareness, as valid forms of knowing. By contrast, "monophasic" cultures, such as those found largely in Western contexts, place more value on the so-called "normal," everyday modes of awareness.[29] Neither of these modalities should be axiomatically privileged in analysis, and either may help us to understand what is going on in the other[30]. A notion of "perceptual diversity" allows us to access knowledge through a variety of processes, including those of a "transrational" nature not considered valid by a science based primarily on reduction, quantification and the experimental method[31].

With regard to the specific modality of magical consciousness, it can be understood as a psychodynamic process that embodies a multi-way interaction of communication with a different reality of spirits, non-material entities, and other beings of an "otherworldly" nature, as is the norm in Asian societies that have sophisticated techniques for experiencing "magic" through subtle body practices. These techniques have existed for many centuries in the world and arise from a widespread way of thinking about consciousness that differs considerably from the modern (but not ancient), conventional Western ways of thought.[32] The issue is how to recognise the autonomous status of consciousness without invoking non-material concepts, or assuming the existence of a mind separate from the body. There is a need for a model that is materialist in broad sense, but also includes a wider range of phenomena that includes a non-material or spirit dimension.

A defining characteristic of magical consciousness is the engagement with an inspirited world, and a fundamental issue has been how to work with non-material, invisible domains. How do we understand and integrate perceptive and sensorial alterity, or otherness, in studies of how the intangible works within a field of consciousness with other beings material and non-material in a total field? In physiological terms, the associative awareness of magical consciousness can be said to correlate with the workings of the right hemisphere of the human brain; this has a wide take on the world, compared to the narrow focus of the left hemisphere, as developed in the work of British psychiatrist Iain McGilchrist. Both hemispheres are involved with all the brain's functions, such as emotion, reasoning, visual imagery, and mathematical thinking, but they have different orientations.[33] By engaging with the right hemisphere orientation, it is possible to understand the fullness of the mutability of magical consciousness. The two orientations arising from the two hemispheres function interchangeably and may be said to be two antithetical potentialities, the one deconstructive or perhaps reductive, and the other integrative and holistic. Although they work in differing ways, they also have complementary tendencies. A common problem results when right-brain notions, which have their own kind of validity, are treated as if they have the validity of left-brain thinking.[34] The idea behind viewing right-brain activity as separate from the workings of the left hemisphere to illustrate magical consciousness is emphatically not to create a dualism, but a distinction that illuminates significant differences in awareness that can be studied by neurobiology and anthropology.

Another important concern to keep in mind is that all of the neurobiological data we are looking at is correlative, but not necessarily causative, in these domains. When looked at naively, neuroscientific data can give the illusion that neural regions are "activated" and "create" various sorts of mental activity. This is essentially a view of mind and matter that is espoused by various kinds of philosophical materialism. Despite the fact that this assertion has yet to be proven (and in fact we know of no way in which it really "could" be proven), it continues to be commonly assumed out of hand, often without acknowledgement. Even when this difficulty is recognised, we encounter the phenomenon of what Karl Popper referred to as "promissory materialism," in which it is assumed that once we acquire a sufficient level of neuroscientific data, we will be able to explain the great mystery of how the brain "creates" consciousness—such assertions are normally followed by vague, hand-waving invocations of mid-level "emergence"—i.e., treating consciousness as an "emergent" property of a physical system. This of course rules out the possibility that the brain may not actually create consciousness/the mind, but rather exists in some other sort of relationship with the mind as explored by a variety of philosophers, physicists,[35] and psychologists.[36] Thus, the question of exactly what sort of minds magical practitioners are engaging with becomes an even deeper mystery—one that neuroscience may not be able to solve.

Moreover, the aforementioned materialistic paradigm often emphasises the "bottom-up" effects of the body on the mind (such as neurotransmitters, neural patterns, etc.) while neglecting the extremely important "top-down" effects of the mind on the brain. These top-down effects of mind over matter can be seen in studies of placebo effects,[37] neuronal plasticity,[38] and many other phenomena[39] that empirically show that knowing what the brain is doing is only half the story.

The mind associated with that brain (however one may define such a mind) must be studied from angles that may not be approachable from a purely materialistic perspective. What neuroscience "can" do, however, is teach us a great deal about how the brain and body work, as however the mind may interact with the body, we know that the body has a long evolutionary history and we are continuing to learn more about how it works, what it does, and (at least from an evolutionary perspective) why it does it. Thus, whatever the mind and consciousness are, neuroscience is teaching us a great deal about how and what the brain and body present to consciousness, and why they do so. Understanding exactly what the mind does during magical action, however, requires not only a neuroscientific perspective, but *also* a cultural, subjective, and mythological perspective, as these are all known to have top-down effects on the body itself.

With that behind us, let us look at two sorts of mental activity that will help us understand magical consciousness as compared with analytical consciousness. The following table shows the differences:

Table Intro.1 Qualities of Analytical and Magical Thinking

Formal Quality	Analytical	Magical
Time	sequential	cyclical/non-linear
Space	distinct	diffuse
Distinction	particular	holistic
Emotion	dispassionate	emotionally *rich*
Concepts	concrete	abstract/ambiguous
Symbolism	literal	metaphorical, mythological
Explanation	causal	interpretive
	mechanical	willful-intentional
	logical	analogical
Binding of perceptual elements	linear cause-effect	associative, synchronous
Neurobiological correlates	left brain	right brain
Dream-wake primary influence	wakefulness	dream
Self	distinct	"shape-shifting"

One might propose that magical consciousness taps into the "primary process," or unconscious thought processes that are characterised as metaphoric rather than the thoughts of consciousness, especially the verbalised thoughts expressed in the "secondary process." This presentation, however (derived from Freud in his classic *Interpretation of Dreams*), privileges the analytical over the magical—a temptation we are attempting to resist. Freud furthermore attached the primary process to "the unconscious" and elevated the secondary process to "consciousness." These distinctions, however, need not be kept, as associative magical thinking does not necessarily require any particular level of consciousness to function, and we suspect this differentiation may stem from Freud's own cultural context, which equated magical thinking with "primitive" peoples. However, magical thinking is pervasive cross-culturally and can be found operating normally in all sorts of everyday conscious activities, as it has done probably throughout human history and pre-history. What mantic techniques do, however, is apparently tip the scales in favour of magical thought, as much as working intently on a difficult physics problem might tip thinking modes in the other direction—each has its own ends and its own modalities and strengths. Nevertheless, despite these objections, the dichotomy as presented by Freud does approximate what we are using to differentiate types of thinking. Thus, we find it a useful distinction, while rejecting the implicit prioritization of the secondary process as superior to the primary process, as we also reject the association of the primary process with nineteenth-century notions of "primitivity," and any particular connection with a level of consciousness. Indeed, some magical practitioners report that mantic/magical consciousness can be "hyper-real," presenting enhanced kinds of awareness that one would associate not with a "dimming" of consciousness (such as is often spoken of by Jung), but with a heightening of consciousness leading to insight or wisdom.

The subject matter of primary process discourse is different from the subject matter of language and consciousness, whereby "[c]onsciousness talks about things or persons, and attaches predicates to the specific things or persons which have been mentioned. In primary process the things or persons are usually not identified, and the focus of the discourse is upon the *relationships* which are asserted to obtain between them."[40] It is the aspect of relationship that is common to the primary process and magical consciousness (further explored in Chapter 4). Magical consciousness works on many brain levels of awareness, unconscious and conscious, and can be highly trained and shaped by the will of the individual so that the contents of the unconscious filter through and relate with consciousness, as demonstrated by the thought processes of magical practitioners, such as shamans or other specialists in this form of awareness.

A DIFFERENT PROCESS OF THINKING

Labelled in numerous ways through the centuries, both positive and negative, it is true to say that the manifestation of magical thought as a process of consciousness has been neglected in academia. The historical reasons for this lack of attention are due to a widespread ambiguity in the concept of magic inherent in European cultures. A disenchanted world of modernity came into existence through the complex interplay of a number of political, religious, and ideological factors, including the Protestant Reformation, the Renaissance, colonial contact with non-Western societies, the Enlightenment, political developments in Europe and North America, and the rapid development of technology and science in the nineteenth and twentieth centuries. Much of the modern antagonism to magic was the result of struggles over cultural authority, especially between secular and religious institutions. In this process, the belief in spirits—the traditional core of religious traditions—came to be identified, at least by many intellectuals, as hostile to science.[41] In consequence, particularly due to a legacy of a peculiarly defined and increasingly positivistic "rationalism" (far removed from the rationalism of Plato) arising during the eighteenth-century Enlightenment, and the development of the scientific method, magical thinking is now generally contrasted with science. Science in the past has labelled magic as wrong; at best, it is logical thinking based on false premises, or at worst, it is mere superstition, the stuff of primitive error.

Due to this specific line of development of Western thought, the natural and social sciences have generally disregarded magical thinking as a legitimate form of knowledge;[42] this has had important theoretical implications for our study. Since its first use as a term in Greece in the fifth century BCE, magic has been considered a marker of otherness. Arising initially from Greek contact with the Persians, who were the Greeks' political enemies, it came to refer to that which was illicit, suspicious, and had to do with potentially powerful actions by others. The origin of the concept stems from the ancient Iranian *maguš*, whom the Greeks referred to as a threatening foreign culture. Herodotus referred to the *mágoi* as one of the seven Median tribes in charge of religious rites and the interpretation of dreams. The dominant Greek concept of "magic" came to be associated with charlatanism, fraud, and unsanctioned rites performed in private by ritual entrepreneurs outside institutionalised cults; notwithstanding, Plato referred to *mageía* as the "worship of the Gods" amongst the Persians, and, as we have discussed already, the Greek and Roman Neoplatonists felt strongly that true knowledge of the universe could only come through "theurgic"— that is, magical—practice. Nevertheless, in general, the Romans took up the Greeks' negative attitude towards magic as a fraudulent, ritual art.[43] However, in more recent Western history, positive attitudes towards magic were taken by Renaissance magicians influenced by the *Corpus Hermetica*, a collection of first-to-third-century Greek texts that sought to bring the individual closer to the deity; in particular, Marsilio Ficino (1433–1499), a Neoplatonist, and Giovanni Pico della Mirandola (1453–1494) regarded magic as an elementary force pervading natural processes.[44] Eventually, "magic" became an extremely versatile and ambiguous abstract category that could be associated with the art of the devil, or a path to the gods.[45] The boundary between what is considered to be magic and what is considered to be religion was, and still is, impossible to draw; any conceptual lines will inevitably always remain blurred.

Making a conceptual division between magic and science is much easier. During the seventeenth-century Scientific Revolution, the practical elements of experimental magic were taken up by some natural philosophers, such as Francis Bacon, to develop what would later become known as the scientific method. Bacon incorporated the experimental method of the magician in a reformed natural philosophy, into which the good ideas in magic were incorporated while the bad ones were labelled as magic and denounced.[46] This shift in thinking involved a change in worldview that moved from an integrated conception of the material and non-material worlds—which included many disciplines that are today seen as separate areas of study, such as music, medicine, optics, and metaphysics—to a process that is now identified as "science," a term first coined in the nineteenth century.[47] Thus, the development of science and the Enlightenment critique of natural magic, *magia naturalis*, a seventeenth-century discipline that investigated magic as a natural force, led magic to increasingly become viewed as irrational in comparison with science. In more recent times, magic has been explored by social scientists as offering an explanation for erroneous beliefs (Frazer and Tylor); in opposition to the social cohesion of religion (Durkheim and Mauss); as a cathartic release of emotional tension in the absence of reason and practical knowledge (Malinowski); as forming a logically coherent set of beliefs and practices that are nevertheless inferior to science (Evans-Pritchard); and more recently still, magic has been seen as an analytical counterpoint to modernity's rational progress (Meyer and Pels). This rather jaundiced view still prevails within historical studies and the social sciences today. For example, Wouter Hanegraaff, writing in 2012, calls the term "magic" an "important object of historical research, but definitely unsuitable as an etic instrument for doing research."[48] Psychologists Leonard Zusne and Warren H. Jones, in their *Anomalistic Psychology*, which was first published in 1982, assign magic to anomalistic phenomena, i.e., behaviours and experiences that have been explained in paranormal, supernatural, or occult terms. They argue that magical thinking "is wholly or partly at the root of any explanation of behavioural and experiential phenomena that violate some law of nature," and that the roots of magic include "the absence of information about the physical causes of the events that surround us," and further claim that reification and self-awareness are used as two compensatory strategies.[49]

More recently, in 1997, Stuart A. Vyse, author of *Believing in Magic: The Psychology of Superstitions*, found that superstitious behaviour, while not "psychopathological" or limited to traditional cultures or people with "low intelligence," arose from "accidental conditioning," which occurred due to repeated, apparently successful actions associated with waiting in high-tension moments, such as before exams, when playing sports, or when gambling.[50] Psychological research has uncovered that magic is a culturally pervasive mode of thinking in children and adults. Malinowski's observation that we are prone to magical thinking when confronted with stress and uncertainty has led to a number of empirical studies. One of these is Keinan's 1994 study of how the Israelis' beliefs in magic increased while being threatened by SCUD missiles during the 1991 Gulf War. This type of research refers mainly to the judgement of certain forms of cognitive orientation that are branded as "superstitious," and is usually characterised by negatively framed interrogations that bypass the emotions and shortcut the complexities of magical thought processing.[51] Note also how the correlation does not really address the validity of magical thinking—that people under stress resort to whatever tools they can to obtain knowledge should be no great surprise and sidesteps the issue of whether or not magical thinking results in useful knowledge. On that question, arguably a much more relevant and interesting question, such studies are silent and therefore of limited usefulness.

Certain answers are presupposed that immediately make magical thought suspect. Magical consciousness "works" through analogical rather than logical thought patterns, but it is often assumed to be a lesser form, or prior stage, of logical thinking. Consequently, it is frequently compared unfavourably with the more conventional cognitive processing, and is then shown to be incomplete or misguided. Thus, the other ways in which we perceive reality are considered less important. The study of magic by cognitive and evolutionary psychologists has not differed greatly from that of other psychologists. A 2007 study of superstitions, magic, and paranormal beliefs by Lindeman and Aarnio characterised magic as "category mistakes where the core attributes of mental, physical, and biological entities and processes are confused with each other."[52] Increasingly, psychologists assumed that all things mental could be explained from the inside out, i.e., from brain events occurring within the individual, while anthropologists took the opposite view, that the life of the mind could only be approached from the outside in, as through the social and cultural influences on the person. Two broad defensive streams of enquiry resulted: the anthropological one interpreted field observations and the narratives of informants to capture the emic view; the other, the psychological stream, isolated mental processes and studied them experimentally in the supposedly context-free setting of a laboratory.[53]

Needless to say, none of these definitions are particularly helpful in defining or examining magical consciousness and so in this sense, they offer us an opportunity to explore a field that is relatively unexamined. We will show

how magical thinking as mytho-poetic thought came to be eclipsed by the critical thinking of the scientific attitude that developed during the period of the Enlightenment. A more integrated scientific attitude that incorporates mytho-poetic and critical thinking comes within our focus. Magic generally has to do with alterity or "otherness," and magic as an aspect of consciousness in Western thought has certainly been other to science and religion; this offers us a chance to discover new ways of thinking about how we create meanings in our lives, and, more broadly and ambitiously, what it is to be human. Thus, it can be seen that what we term as magical consciousness does not correspond with analytical thought, the conceptual foundation of science, but rather is a different process of thinking altogether. Indeed, magical worldviews are frequently articulated through mythology, a form of mytho-poetic thinking that is hard to translate into the language of science due to the fact that meanings can only be fully expressed in metaphorical terms.[54] Myths form their own language, and, as Carl Kerenyi puts it in his study of the science of mythology, "The water must be fetched and drunk fresh from the spring if it is to flow through us and quicken our hidden mythological talents." Mythology is a body of material contained in tales about gods and god-like beings, and it is the movement of this material that becomes something "solid yet mobile" and "substantial and yet not static." A living mythology "expands in infinite and yet shapely multiplicity;"[55] it speaks emotionally to the individual in the creation of meanings, but also relates to a lived reality in social and practical terms, as Malinowski has pointed out long ago.[56] Our study of the mythological thinking of magic enables a deeper understanding through an anthropological and neurobiological analysis of the manner in which it helps to shape patterns of relationships between phenomena.

A felt sense of the participatory awareness of magical consciousness does not exclude a search for causality: a spell, a ritual, or a special object can carry both a sense of invisible connectedness and a causal intention or interpretation of the world. This mode of thinking can be visualised metaphorically as a web of connections, and this means that minds are not always unequivocal. They are able to give more than one explanation to the same occurrence; and they can hold naturalistic and magical interpretations that reflect the right- and left-brain orientations simultaneously. The magical explanation is often associated with an affective component, while the naturalistic one tends to be logical, meaning that magical thinking, although allowing for causal reasoning, is still processed differently. By developing a sustained anthropological and neurobiological examination of magic as an affective process of the mind, this study provides a unique account of magical consciousness as associative process correlated with right hemisphere brain activity that has wide ramifications that affect the whole organism and its environment. As we will see below, this is a complex interaction that defies any sort of biological or cultural essentialism. Furthermore, we will see that the study of magical consciousness repeatedly returns us to those thinkers who question whether or not the mind should be defined as completely within the skull. Magical consciousness is a holistic and connective sort of thinking process that is inherently non-reductive and whole-greater-than-parts in its essence, which includes mind-mind and mind-environment relations.

More akin to the Greek notion of the psyche, the "magical mind" of magical consciousness is closely aligned to an animating principle related to a non-material essence of breath, life, and soul. The magical mind thinks *with* other beings. In this sense, it is similar to the notion of the psyche articulated by Aristotle in 4 BCE. Aristotle thought the soul was equivalent to the psyche, that it was the "principle of life" that animates. Aristotle's conception of the psyche was as the form or soul of all living organisms, including plants and other animals, as well as human beings. Thus, a key issue is how to bring back the spirit and overcome *dissociation*, and here, we approach the problem of the Western understandings of the phenomenal world. In this study, we engage with the troublesome issue of "spirits," "subtle bodies," or "energies," without reducing them to individual psychology or seeing such phenomena as real in certain cultural contexts, but not real in a scientific sense. We seek to find a non-reductionist, conceptual area where there could be an intermediate level, or series of levels, between the material and non-material realities.[57]

A METHOD FOR EXPLORING THE MIND

The present study brings about a creative interchange between Greenwood's own lived experience of magical consciousness and a theoretical analysis with the aim of working toward a methodology for its examination. Having spent over twenty years as a fieldworker examining various practices of Western pagans and magicians, Greenwood has had many experiences of magic. In conventional anthropological methodology, she would be required to remain more detached, or if she did have an experience, not to include it in her research data. An objection for some anthropologists has been the issue of the ethnographer "going native," with a supposed fine line between taking the native's point of view and the anthropologist fully experiencing the affective aspects of magic, such as relating with spirit beings or other such non-material entities. In Greenwood's doctoral research,[58] she wrote that she sought to create a communication between scholarly analysis and the magical spirit panoramas of her informants; she wanted to develop the critical eye of the anthropologist, but also an empathy that was sensitive to her informants' involvement with an inspired magical otherworld. She took a deliberately participatory approach, arguing that anthropological engagement with magic was a valuable tool of research, not to be contrasted with scientific truth. Indeed, when it is cognition or the mind that is being examined, the dismissal of experience becomes untenable, even paradoxical.[59] In anthropological terms, Greenwood did become a "native," although we are all potentially natives of this mode of thought as cultures are not homogenous, and no one can be a fully native insider or outsider.[60] In this sense, Greenwood is drawing on a subjective magical orientation of consciousness that potentially we all have, while also maintaining her objective analytical orientation as an evaluating perspective. Edith Turner, who has argued that to understand spirit healing in Zambia she needed to sink herself fully within it, records, "Thus for me, 'going native' achieved a break-through to an altogether different worldview, foreign to academia, by means of which certain material was chronicled that could have been garnered in no other way."[61] This position follows what has later been called "first person" research in the tradition of William James who, in *Principles of Psychology*, first published in 1890, resisted reductionism and used his own inner workings of mental life to study some of the most extreme and challenging phenomena and what they might mean.[62] We will be examining magical consciousness from the perspective of the actual first-person experience of Greenwood as an in-depth, specific example of how magical thinking is part of a panhuman mode of thought. We develop this approach in the present work. By going deeper into the lived experience of the anthropologist's life, Greenwood demonstrates the development of the process of magical consciousness. In this regard, and in subsequent research, Greenwood has built up a considerable, largely untapped "database" of personal, magical experiences. This was considered to be invaluable primary material that needed to be brought back into the fold of academic discourse as a first person narrative of the process of magical consciousness.

STRUCTURE OF THE BOOK

The volume is divided into three parts. The four chapters in Part One are a dialogue between anthropology and neurobiology. Each engages with some of the issues and challenges that come from such an interdisciplinary study of magical thinking. Chapter 1 outlines a fundamental historical context for understanding how magic has become disregarded as a form of reason in the natural and social sciences. As far as the examination of magic is concerned, the Enlightenment was a "century of shadows" in the privileging of logical reason (logos) over analogical reason (mythos). This has led to magic, and its "mystical," mytho-poetic form of thinking, being viewed as "irrational" and not valued as a legitimate form of knowledge. Logical, analytical, and analogical magical modalities frame the universe in different ways and regard minds and spirits from different perspectives, and Chapter 2 examines some of the main challenges faced in the search for the integration of the two orientations. Biogenetic structuralism and placebo effects are considered from a neurological point of view with the aim of clarifying differences and similarities. Chapter 3 highlights a "dense interactivity" between anthropology and psychology to reveal a more complete interdisciplinary understanding of the notion of "psychic unity." Magic has largely been examined in terms of logical (as opposed to analogical) rationality and instrumentality, but we seek to illuminate a prior process of the relationship of the individual within his/her social environment. Without resorting to either cultural or biological determinism, we examine how the constants of the individual psyche may contribute to ideas about magic coming from archetypes, the collective unconscious, and metaphors. Chapter 4 engages in a search for a theoretical framework that enables a comprehensive examination of the experience of magical consciousness as a living, breathing "unity in multiplicity." Drawing particularly on the work of Gregory Bateson, we seek to provide a language, a metaphorical vocabulary, of the relationships between different types of knowledge. By breaking down the dichotomies of mind/body and mind/nature, we look to an intercommunication of disciplines in the connection of ecosystems as "minds in nature." A "metaphorical language" is sought to bring different types of knowledge together by the process of "abduction," the intuitive reasoning that comes from analogical thinking in metaphors.

In Part Two of this volume, Chapters 5 to 15, Greenwood shows how magical awareness happens at the most fundamental level, prior to any instrumental shaping through rituals or spell-making. Evolving from her doctoral fieldwork on British practitioners of magic—where she searched for communication between worlds of magic as they are experienced, and an academic language for their examination—these chapters reveal the anthropologist's research on her experiential ethnography of the mind. Immersing herself into the process of magical consciousness, she experiences "the dragon" as metaphorical thread-like patterns of connectedness gained through memories, particular relationships, dreams, poems, and stories. The experience of the anthropologist, through the act of creating a first person research narrative, intertwines personal, physical, social, and spiritual aspects of magical consciousness in a synchronistic web of connections. Part Three, Chapter 16, analyses Greenwood's narrative and offers an analytical response to the preceding experiential section of the volume. The aspects covered include an examination of the neurobiological correlates of "the self," an analysis of "the dragon," and the anthropologist's research from this perspective. Our aim is to reach a creative place of being able to recognise both analytical and magical orientation parameters in a way that is complementary rather than in opposition.

NOTES

1. Erik D. Goodwyn *The Neurobiology of the Gods: How Brain Physiology Shapes the Recurrent Imagery of Myth and Dreams* (New York: Routledge, 2012): 87.

2. *The Notebooks on Primitive Mentality of Lucien Lévy-Bruhl*, Peter Riviere (trans.) (Oxford: Basil Blackwell, 1975); Bradd Shore *Culture in Mind: Cognition, Culture and the Problem of Meaning* (Oxford: Oxford University Press, 1998): 27, 313–314; Susan E.J. Greenwood *The Anthropology of Magic* (Oxford: Berg, 2009): 30–43.

3. Christina Toren 'The Child in Mind' in Harvey Whitehouse (ed.) *The Debated Mind: Evolutionary Psychology Versus Ethnography* (Oxford: Berg, 2001): 155.

4. Tim Ingold *The Perception of the Environment* (London: Routledge, 2000): 161–162.

5. Pierre Bourdieu *The Logic of Practice* (Oxford: Polity Press, 1990): 52–65, quoted in Ingold *The Perception of the Environment*, 161–62.

6. Ingold *Perception*, 162.

7. Francisco J. Varela, Evan Thompson, and Eleanor Rosch *The Embodied Mind* (Cambridge, Massachusetts: The MIT Press, 1992): 13.

8. Jesper Sørenson *A Cognitive Theory of Magic* (Lanham, Maryland: Rowman & Littlefield, 2007); 'Magic Reconsidered: Towards a Scientifically Valid Concept of Magic' in *Defining Magic: A Reader*, Bernd-Christian Otto and Michael Strausberg eds.) (Sheffield: Equinox, 2013): 233.

9. Sørenson "Magic Reconsidered," 234.

10. Sørenson *Cognitive Theory*, 232–234.

11. Edward Bever 'Current Trends in the Application of Cognitive Science to Magic' *Magic, Ritual and Witchcraft*, University of Pennsylvania Press (Summer 2012): 10.

12. Gregory Bateson *Naven: A Survey of the Problems Suggested by a Composite Picture of the Culture of a New Guinea Tribe from Three Points of View* (Cambridge, UK: Cambridge University Press, 1936): 1–2.

13. D. J. Hufford 'Evaluating Complementary and Alternative Medicine: The Limits of Science and of Scientists' *Journal of Law, Medicine & Ethics*,31(2) (2003): 198–212; D. J. Hufford *The Terror That Comes in the Night: An Experience-Centered Study of Supernatural Assault Traditions* (Philadelphia: University of Pennsylvania Press, 1982).

14. Stephen MacKenna and B.S. Page (trans.). *The Six Enneads of Plotinus* (New York: Forgotten Books, 1917).

15. Emma C. Clarke, John M. Dillon, and Jackson P. Hershbell (trans.) *Iamblichus: On the Mysteries* (Georgia: Society of Biblical Literature, 2003).

16. E.R. Dodds *Proclus: The Elements of Theology* (Oxford: Clarendon Press, 2004).

17. Anthony P. Cohen and Nigel Rapport 'Introduction' to *Questions of Consciousness* (ASA Monographs 33) Anthony P. Cohen and Nigel Rapport (eds.) (London: Routledge, 1995): 1–2.

18. W. Morris (ed.) *The American Heritage Dictionary of the English Language* (Boston: Houghton Mifflin, 1981): 283, quoted in Michael Winkelman *Shamanism: A Biopsychosocial Paradigm of Consciousness and Healing*, 2nd ed. (Santa Barbara, Calif.: Praeger, 2010): 92.

19. *Oxford English Dictionary*, 1989: 756, quoted in Winkelman *Shamanism*, 92.

20. Morris (ed.) *Dictionary*, 283, quoted in Winkelman *Shamanism*, 92.

21. David Edelman 'Interviews on Consciousness' on *Cephalove* http://cephalove.southernfriedscience.com 22nd October 2010, accessed March 5, 2013.

22. R. Rial, M. Nicolau, A. Gamundi, M. Akarrir, C. Gurau, and S. Esteban 'The Evolution of Consciousness in Animals' in *Consciousness Transitions: Phylogenic, Ontogenetic and Physiological Aspects* H. Liljenstrom and P. Arhem (eds.) (Amsterdam: Elsevier, 2008): 56.

23. Max Velmans 'Sentient Matter' in *The Handbook of Contemporary Animism* G. Harvey (ed.) (Durham, UK: Acumen, 2013): 363.
24. Velmans "Sentient," 371.
25. Robert C. Koons and George Bealer (eds.) *The Waning of Materialism* (Oxford: Oxford, 2010).
26. Gerald Edelman *Bright Air, Brilliant Fire. On the Matter of the Mind* (Harmondsworth: Penguin, 1992): 170–175.
27. Anthony P. Cohen and Nigel Rapport 'Introduction' to *"Questions,"* 6.
28. Ingold *Perception,* 171.
29. Charles D. Laughlin 'Consciousness in Biogenetic Structural Theory' *Anthropology of Consciousness* 3(1–2): 17–22.
30. Cohen and Rapport 'Introduction' to *Questions,* 13.
31. Tara Waters Lumpkin 'Perceptual Diversity: Is Polyphasic Consciousness Necessary for Global Survival' *Anthropology of Consciousness* 12(1) (March/June 2001): 2.
32. Geoffrey Samuel and Jay Johnston 'Foreword' in *Religion and the Subtle Body in Asia and the West: Between Mind and Body* Geoffrey Samuel and Jay Johnston (eds.) (Oxford: Routledge, 2013): xiii.
33. Iain McGilchrist 'Paying Attention to the Bipartite Brain' *The Lancet* 377 (9771) (March 26, 2011): 1068–1069; Iain McGilchrist *The Master and His Emissary: The Divided Brain and the Making of the Western World* (New Haven, CT: Yale, 2009).
34. Gregory Bateson and Mary Catherine Bateson *Angels Fear: Towards an Epistemology of the Sacred* (Chicago: University of Chicago Press, 1988): 58.
35. Henry Stapp *Mind, Matter and Quantum Mechanics,* 2nd ed. (New York: Springer, 2004).
36. Kelly et al. *Irreducible, passim.*
37. Fabrizio Benedetti *Placebo Effects* (Oxford: Oxford University Press, 2009).
38. Jeffrey M. Schwarz and Sharon Begley *The Mind and the Brain: Neuroplasticity and the Power of Mental Force* (New York: HarperCollins, 2003).
39. Kelly et al. *Irreducible,* 117–236.
40. Gregory Bateson *Further Steps to an Ecology of Mind* (Chicago: University of Chicago Press, [1972] 2000): 139.
41. David Hufford 'Modernity's Defences' (paper given at a private seminar at *The Center for Theory and Research*, Esalen, California, October 2013): 47.
42. Susan Greenwood 'Magical Consciousness: A Legitimate Form of Knowledge' in *Defining Magic: A Reader* Bernd-Christian Otto and Michael Stausberg (eds.) (Sheffield: Equinox, 2013): 197–210.
43. Otto and Stausberg *Defining,* 17.
44. Francis Yates *Giordano Bruno and the Hermetic Tradition* (Chicago: University of Chicago Press, [1964] 1991).
45. Otto and Stausberg *Defining,* 16–17.
46. John Henry *Knowledge Is Power: How Magic, The Government, and an Apocalyptic Vision Inspired Francis Bacon to Create Modern Science* (Cambridge: Icon Books, 2002): 5, 64, 79.
47. John Henry *The Scientific Revolution and the Origins of Modern Science* (Basingstoke: Macmillan, 1997): 172, cited in Susan E.J. Greenwood *The Anthropology of Magic* (Oxford: Berg, 2009): 134–135.
48. Wouter Hanegraaff *Esotericism and the Academy: Rejected Knowledge in Western Culture* (Cambridge: Cambridge University Press, 2012): 168, cited in Otto and Stausberg *Defining,* 196.
49. *Anomalistic Psychology* (1982, 1989): 2, 13, 31, cited in Otto and Stausberg *Defining,* 3, 196.

50. *The Psychology of Superstitions* (Oxford: Oxford University press, 1997) cited in Otto and Stausberg *Defining*, 196.
51. For example, Lysann Damisch, Barbara Stoberock, and Thomas Mussweiler 'Keep Your Fingers Crossed! How Superstition Improves Performance' *Psychological Science* 21(7) (2010): 1014–1020.
52. M. Lindeman and K. Aarnio 'Superstitious, Magical, and Paranormal Beliefs: An Integrative Model' *Journal of Research in Personality* 41 (2007): 734, cited in Otto and Stausberg *Defining*, 196.
53. Jerome Bruner 'Foreword' in *Culture in Mind: Cognition, Culture and the Problem of Meaning* Bradd Shore (eds.) (Oxford: Oxford University Press, 1998): xiii–xiv.
54. Greenwood *Anthropology of Magic*, 74–91.
55. Carl Kerenyi 'Prolegomena' in *The Science of Mythology* Carl G. Jung and Carl Kerenyi (eds.) (London: Routledge, 2002): 1, 31.
56. Bronislaw Malinowski *Myth in Primitive Psychology* (London: Kegan Paul, 1926).
57. Geoffrey Samuel and Jay Johnston (eds.) *Religion and the Subtle Body in Asia and the West: Between Mind and Body* (Oxford: Routledge, 2013): xv.
58. Greenwood *Magic, Witchcraft and the Otherworld* (Oxford: Berg, 2000).
59. Varela et al. *Embodied*, 13.
60. Kirin Narayan 'How Native Is a 'Native Anthropologist?' *American Anthropologist* (New Series) 95(3) (September 1993): 671, 682.
61. Edith Turner 'The Reality of Spirits: A Tabooed or Permitted Field of Study' *ReVision* 15 (1992): 28–32.
62. Kelly 'Introduction' to *Irreducible*, xvii.

Part One

A Dialogue Between Anthropology and Neurobiology

1 The Analogical Reasoning of Magic

More than 20,000 years ago, prehistoric humans in southern Africa painted lines on cave walls, bringing them to life with images of humans and animals. Neuropsychological studies of altered states of consciousness suggest that these marks might be indications or recordings of certain kinds of brain activity,[1] but when asked for an explanation, some contemporary Kalahari San people explain them as "threads of light" from the sky to take shamans (n/omkxaosi) climbing or gliding upwards while in trance to visit god and his vast herd of animals.[2] One explanation of the cave art is based on materialistic neurobiology, whereas the other relies on indigenous "magical" meanings, such as those studied by anthropologists.[3] If each explanation for the prehistoric painted lines is seen as plausible, then we need some form of incorporating these very different interpretations. The issue is to find a basis for a common ground. The nineteenth-century German ethnologist Adolf Bastian first coined the term "psychic unity" to express the conviction that all human beings shared the same basic mental framework; this indicated a species-wide similarity in mental reasoning capabilities.[4] Indeed, mitochondrial DNA evidence suggests that for 200,000 years, all humans have essentially shared the same bloodline, and many scholars are "beginning to concede the existence of a core human psyche,"[5] so this perspective seems valid. However, the thorny issue of psychic unity confronts us. An emphasis on one particular type of reason has sidelined "the reasoning of magic." Too long viewed as irrational, magic in the form of an aspect of consciousness needs to be brought back into focus to show the character of analogical thinking and its foundation as a mode of human thought. A study of the concept of psychic unity will reveal some of the historical and deeply rooted challenges that we face in our interdisciplinary study of magical consciousness.

This chapter will outline the contours of the problem of psychic unity in anthropology and its consequences for a study of magic. Here, we criticise the particular brand of "reason" espoused by eighteenth-century Enlightenment thinkers, which was irrational because it was incomplete and too narrowly focused, but not "reason" in principle. The ancients felt it was entirely rational to follow the advice of a god experienced in a dream because they knew magical consciousness was a valid kind of experience that contained real-world applicable and useful information. To criticise magical thinking because it has diffuse categories and looks for correspondences rather than causality, etc., is just as unreasonable as critcising analytical thinking because it is overly reductive. Both are rational and reasonable, in their own ways. We argue for a balance between holism and reductionism, between shape-shifting boundaries and clear, sharp categories of magical and analytical thinking. In Chapter 4, we will examine the analogical process of reasoning through metaphors in the work of Gregory Bateson, but for the present, we need to understand the historical background to the valorisation of analytical reasoning and its influence on science. Rather than an Enlightenment belief in a psychic unity based on human analytical reasoning as something separate from or superior to nature, the issue would be one of "perceptual diversity" encompassing psychic unity within diversity, one that included the reasoning of mystical mentality. Perceptual diversity is a complex, synergistic system that evolves and changes, and is created by an interaction of human biology, physical environment, individual development, and culture.[6]

THE VALORISATION OF ANALYTICAL REASON

The current dominant scientific notions of psychic unity are founded on logical, analytical reasoning, rather than the analogical and intuitive thought of magical consciousness. The origins of the valorisation of analytical reasoning as a mode of thought lie in the Enlightenment. When philosopher René Descartes associated the mind with individual human reasoning in the seventeenth century, this form of reason became the basis of the analytical knowledge of the Enlightenment. Truth in the Cartesian sense was derived from rational reflection rather than from the untrustworthy senses of a body that was associated with an animal-like, mechanical instinct.[7] Descartes's work contributed to a mechanical philosophy that not only marked a definite break with the past, but also set the seal upon how science would come to be seen. God was seen as having created the world as a perfect, rational machine. Humans could become part of that rationality through the knowledge of the self-perfection of God's design; if God's laws of nature were rational, then it was through reason that people could discover them. The Enlightenment derived its concrete, self-evident proof from scientific thinking and the analytical spirit, as philosopher Ernst Cassirer puts it, "In the progress of natural science. . . the philosophy of the Enlightenment believes it . . . can follow step by step the triumphant march of the modern analytical spirit."[8] This analytical spirit conquered all reality; it reduced natural phenomena to a single universal rule, a cosmological formula not found by accident, nor a result of sporadic experimentation, but the rigorous application of the scientific method.[9]

As the term suggests, during this period, an attempt was made to shed greater light on the conduct of human affairs: the perceived dark mysteries of the traditional attitudes in religion and political life were pushed back, and in their place, a new outlook informed by reason and the power of scientific research and discovery arose.[10] The Enlightenment would come to shape the rationalistic foundations of what came to be seen as "science" in the nineteenth century,[11] as well as the benchmark for how anthropology and other social sciences would conduct fieldwork and produce theoretical analyses based on ethnographies of different and very varied cultures around the world. Of course, analytical reasoning is valuable and essential for the gathering of objective information, but it still forms the basis of the current scientific enterprise and tends to exclude other forms of knowledge, specifically magic. The problem concerns the manner in which the focus on one type of reason has influenced the development of the scientific method, and the way that this has become an ideological, theoretical benchmark in the natural and social sciences. To understand exactly why the pull of this form of reason was so strong in Western cultures, making the experience of magic at worst an unbelievable superstition, or at best, misguided and non-scientific, it is important to see its context within Enlightenment culture and thinking.

Comprising a "loose, informal, wholly unorganised coalition of cultural critics, religious sceptics, and political reformers from Edinburgh to Naples, Paris to Berlin, Boston to Philadelphia," the Enlightenment made up a "clamorous chorus" that was, nevertheless, united on a programme of secularism, humanity, cosmopolitanism, and freedom from arbitrary power, freedom of speech, and of "moral man to make his own way in the world;" it was a momentous event in the history of the Western mind[12] and it was formed on the basis of analytical reason. Influenced by Greek rationalist thinking and making a decisive mark on the history of Western thought in the eighteenth century, the Enlightenment developed into an age of intellectual exploration and the expansion of objective reality. As Ernst Cassirer notes, for this age, knowledge of its own activity, intellectual self-examination, and foresight were the "proper function and essential task of thought" that led to the knowledge of objective reality:

> Thought not only seeks new, hitherto unknown goals but it wants to know where it is going and to determine for itself the direction of its journey . . . Yet its thirst for knowledge and intellectual curiosity are directed not only toward the external world; the thought of this age is even more passionately impelled by that other question of the nature and potentiality of thought itself. Time and again thought returns to its point of departure from its various journeys of exploration intended to broaden the horizon of objective reality.[13]

All the diversity, breadth, and various energies of the mind were held together in a common centre of force, an essentially homogeneous, formative power.[14] Consequently, the period of the Enlightenment came to be "completely permeated by the idea of intellectual progress," and this conception of reason became the unifying and central point of the century: "all thinking subjects from all nations, all epochs, and all cultures" were freed from the "changeability of religious creeds, of moral maxims and convictions, of theoretical opinions and judgements."[15] There was a steady vanquishing of magical worldviews by critical thinking and the development of a particular view of science that came to dominate understandings of psychic unity.

As it stands, the biological answer to the psychic unity problem will necessarily be different from the anthropological and cognitive answers because all three have varying assumptions regarding how the issue is to be handled,[16] each coming with its own associated subsequent problems. The biological and some proposed cognitive solutions typically involve a variant of materialism, a very prominent and normally (but not always) unspoken framework, in the neurosciences in particular. Materialist "solutions" to the psychic unity problem come with the subsequent additional problem of explaining exactly how brains "create" the mind. Philosopher David Chalmers labelled this issue the "hard problem of consciousness."[17] This problem dates back to the earliest materialist explanations of mind, going as far back as Anaxagoras, the fifth-century BCE Greek Pre-Socratic philosopher, and no solution is anywhere in sight—it appears that we do not even know how to approach this problem. This is because of a number of philosophical issues—stemming from Cartesianist mind-body dualism and developed during the Enlightenment valorisation of analytical reason—are embedded in the central concern of the psychic unity problem, as we will discuss in the next chapter. For the present, it is to anthropology that we turn to see the biggest separation between the brain/mind and culture.

ANTHROPOLOGY'S OLDEST AND MOST VEXING QUESTION

While Enlightenment notions of a psychic unity of humankind are the theoretical bedrock of modern anthropology, rather paradoxically, an entrenched debate on a unity/diversity dichotomy between the natural and social sciences has prevailed. As the example of the prehistoric cave markings at the beginning of this chapter suggests, the natural sciences approach magic as "altered states of consciousness," a by-product of brain activity and couch explanations in Western discourse, whereas anthropologists more usually offer cross-cultural explanations that emphasise meaning. However, it can be suggested also that anthropologists find themselves in a tricky position between the magical and analytical modalities of thought. Coming from an objectively based discipline, they also paradoxically support the notion of a psychic unity based on universal, analytical reasoning. This has resulted in "a wedge being driven between ideas about culture and mind,"[1] and has led to a hiatus between disciplines. By linking psychic unity with cultural heterogeneity, cultural differences can only be linked superficially with the mind; however, the notion of psychic unity tended to remain an unexamined "doctrine of faith."[1] Thus, the notion of psychic unity has proved to be contradictory and theoretically troublesome within anthropology, due to a deeply held emphasis on cultural diversity.[18] Whereas the belief in psychic unity expresses an anti-racist ideal, that all human beings share the same mental capabilities for reason, it does not account for the psychic differences embodied in cultural variation, the traditional anthropological field of study. A general effect of the psychic unity debate in anthropology has thus been twofold: firstly, it has created something of a culture/mind dualism, making a dialogue between, for example, anthropology and neuroscience more difficult; and secondly, its focus on analytical reason as the basis for psychic unity has excluded magical thinking, thus branding it irrational, despite the fact that there is essentially no basis for this judgement.

The potentially rather contradictory position of holding to cultural differences and at the same time asserting a universal psychic unity founded on analytical reason has led to what Bradd Shore, in his book *Culture in Mind*, has called "anthropology's oldest and most vexing question."[19] The dualism between a multivocality of cultures and the universal conception of the mind has arisen due to anthropologists having a penchant for particularistic rather than all-embracing accounts of human experience, resulting in a "wedge being driven between ideas of culture and mind." Variety and diversity are the bread and butter of ethnographic research and cultural differences define the very discipline of social anthropology itself, and so this concept is where the false dichotomy has arisen between psychic unity and psychic diversity or cultural differences. The result of this dichotomy is that the "psychic unity muddle" in anthropology creates contradictions that are problematic. This legacy marginalises anthropology from the "deepest currents of the cognitive revolution."[20] To overcome this dualism, Shore suggests that:

> If the mind exists at the intersection of brain and extrinsic models, we need to model brain-culture interactions so that they reveal at one and the same time the general cognitive processes of information processing and meaning construction as well as the culturally diverse manifestations of those processes in action. Neither dimension is more basic or more important than the other.[21]

There is, however, another aspect of the psychic unity problem, and that is the aforementioned valorisation of analytical reasoning over the reasoning of magic.

In anthropology, this effect can be seen in the Durkheimian influence that took a strong commitment to a psychic unity whereby the properties of the mind, while being socially derived, were formed through the processes of logical classification. For Durkheim, the philosophical notion of "participation" represented a logical core of scientific thought whereby primitive and modern thought were two stages in a single evolutionary process,[22] a notion later taken up by Claude Lévi-Strauss, most obviously in *Mythologiques*, his enormous corpus of work on mythologies. Here, Lévi-Strauss sought to show myth as the evolutionary precursor to science in a study of how logical, rather than analogical, unconscious processes were formed; and also how they could be analysed for complex symmetry and universal mental structures. Myths might differ from culture to culture, but there was a logical psychic unity in the manner that the human mind addressed them.[23]

The interwoven issues surrounding the mind and culture with an emphasis on the universality of analytical reasoning are obvious to the counter notions that so-called primitive peoples have less reasoning abilities than the supposedly "civilised" cultures, but an exclusive focus on logic has made magic as an analogical aspect of human thinking largely invisible, despite its ubiquity. The Eugenics social movement saw "race improvement" and selective breeding as a way of dealing with all social ills. The human subject was thought, in this conception, to be determined by hereditary factors, and there were dangerous and reactionary social implications; most anthropologists were keen to distance themselves from this position. Franz Boas, in *The Mind of Primitive Man* (1911), for example, focusing on the different mentalities of the Eskimos in Baffinland, northern Canada, argued that culture was essentially a mental phenomenon to be understood by anthropological and historical analysis. In consequence, Boas became increasingly committed to an extreme cultural deterministic theory and postulated an unbridgeable gap between culture and biology.

In his theoretical critiques of racism and the biological theories of culture, Boas suggested that there was a dichotomy between nature as biology and culture as understood by anthropology and history. In so doing, he underestimated the importance of biology and thus impeded the emergence of a scientifically adequate anthropological paradigm that recognised the importance of the interaction between biological and cultural processes. In this way, the study of culture could be divorced from the study of the mind. Although Boas did not see the individual as wholly determined by culture, nor did he deny that some aspects of human behaviour were organically determined, he did see both cultural and biological determining factors as mediated by the active psychological interaction of the human subject.[24]

The psychic unity dilemma in anthropology can be seen most clearly in the work of Clifford Geertz. In his influential paper "The impact of the concept of culture on the concept of man" (1966), Geertz considered cultures not as behavioural patterns, but as a set of control mechanisms of plans and rules for the governing of behaviour that were removed from the minds of individuals and re-inscribed on the collective level. The domain of cultural symbols was social rather than psychological, public rather than private, and placed in an inter-subjective space of social interaction where they imposed meaning on experience. Culture was a social symbolic system not found in the interiority of the individual mind.[25] Geertz thought that culturally orchestrated landscapes were found inscribed in the brain, that *"the human brain is thoroughly dependent upon cultural resources for its very operation*; and those resources are, consequently, not adjunct to, but constituents of, mental activity."[26] Through "interpretive" or "symbolic" anthropology, Geertz sought to create a distinctive mode of cultural analysis with the view that culture was a semiotic system of "structures of signification."

However, the spectre of psychic unity could not disappear from his analysis. Geertz's early work had looked at the implications of hominid evolution providing a biological basis for the importance of culture in human life. At this time, he saw culture as an ensemble of structures of signification whereby symbolically mediated adaptations exerted selective pressures on evolving hominid lines, making culture an intrinsic, selective factor in evolution.[27] "Geertz's insight was that in view of the plasticity and social dependence of the human sensorium, human variation must be viewed as a constituting feature of the human rather than a superficial addition to it."[28] Geertz's view of the mind was as a relationship between the nervous system and its extrinsic sources of activation; however, this view was to change when later he came to endorse the notion of psychic unity. A denial of psychic unity, Shore argues, would appear to imply an evolutionary hierarchy of mentalities. Geertz, in order to avoid being accused of any form of racism, wavers between two incompatible models of mind: one is organic and fixed in psychic unity; while the other is emergent, contingent, and culturally diverse.[29]

Thus, Geertz seeks to dispel the Enlightenment view that underlies the universalistic notion of psychic unity by arguing that the human sensorium has a plasticity and social dependence—human variation must be viewed as a constituting feature rather than a superficial addition: "time and space, history and culture are as central to the definition of the human as the stuff of genetics."[30] Still, though, he also holds on resolutely to psychic unity. As well as not appearing to advocate an evolutionary hierarchy of mentalities, it might be, as Shore suggests, that Geertz's resistance to psychologising was a reaction to the cognitive science being conducted in his time: ideas about the mind as a computational "sorting device" for a taxonomic order, showing a limited range of cultural variability and limiting it to abstract classification divorced from action were in vogue.[31] Notwithstanding, there was a reluctance to abandon the notion of psychic unity, resulting in the awkward relationship between a fixed psychic unity and an emergent, contingent, and more ecological perception of human mental processes. Anthropologists insisted on foregrounding cultural diversity while "clinging to an unrefined notion of psychic unity."[32]

LÉVY-BRUHL AND THE MYTHO-POETIC MIND

Ironically, opportunities for the foundations of a cognitively grounded conception of culture and an intellectually rigorous vision of a psychic diversity of humanity were laid by Lévy-Bruhl with his studies of mystical mentality, but his critics never permitted this to happen.[33] If Lévy-Bruhl had indeed laid such a foundation, what would this have looked like? Lévy-Bruhl asked what it was that caused the so-called primitive mentality to show such indifference to the discursive operations of reasoning and reflection. Repeatedly arguing that this lack of interest was not due to incapacity or inaptitude, and constantly affirming that these minds were capable of scientific thought—that is, analytical reason. He noted from the reports of missionaries and travellers that they generally showed themselves to be observant, wise, skilful, clever and subtle; they just disliked the logical process.[34] In this, they were not alone. The roots of Lévy-Bruhl's view of mystical mentality lay in the mytho-poetic mentality of ancient civilisations, as well as in native thought, the direct focus of his work. What the aforementioned Enlightenment project has thus far lacked, however, is justification for dismissing such a mode of mentation as invalid, in error, or superstitious folly beyond an obvious cultural bias. This has undermined the very foundation of what should have been a more "rational" exploration of magical consciousness.

Mytho-poetic modes of mind existed largely unexamined in the history of Western thought until the early twentieth century, when Lévy-Bruhl started formulating his philosophical studies of mystical mentality. In his revisitation of the ancient Greek philosophical distinctions between mytho-poetic and critical thinking, he attempted to draw out the differences between what he came to describe as "pre-logical" primitive thought or "mystical mentality" and "logical" civilised thought. Even though it was socially derived, mystical mentality was universal to all human beings; it was not just non-Western peoples who thought mystically, but so-called civilised Westerners thought this way too, under certain conditions.[35] Lévy-Bruhl's notion of mystical participation captured the essence of the workings of this magical mode and its differentiation from the Western focus on reason. He pointed out that the "mystic mind" sees objects and entities involved in a system of participations and exclusions that constitute its cohesion and order. In other words, this is analogical rather than logical reasoning.

Lévy-Bruhl based his study of mystical mentality on the notion of "participation," the view that certain social formations, rather than mental capabilities, shaped the perception of powerful affective identifications between disparate phenomena. Unlike Durkheim's use of the term as the basis for all logical, classificatory thought, he used the philosophical notion to try and understand mystical mentality (an issue to which we return later). These participatory identifications for Lévy-Bruhl violated Aristotle's principle of "noncontradiction," the existence of apparent mutually exclusive states, such as "life in death" and the "unity and multiplicity of being."[36]

Participation is, in essence, a concept that sums up a mytho-poetic attitude of mind; it is a form of mental processing that occurs through the making of psychological associations and connections. It occurs through the creation of relationships with different things that might seem discrete in logical thought. In relation to magical consciousness, participation is a concept that describes how shamans could consider themselves to be human as well as any one of a multiplicity of different spirit helpers they might have, at the same time.

Participation describes a process of an analogical relationship, rather than mutually exclusive states; these relationships can occur on many levels, from the seemingly ordinary and mundane to the profound experience that radically changes a person's life. An example of the latter is a typical shamanic initiation whereby a shaman undergoes some form of crisis and psychological dismemberment, or a similar ordeal, to forge a link with his or her spirit guides. Participation is an orientation to the world that can be expressed through mythologies and stories; it uses a language of holism in a metaphorical mode and often engages with an inspirited worldview.[37] The discussion of mystical participation is central to our examination of magic. Participation becomes more deeply meaningful when we make the transition from individual, discrete ideas to patterns of ideas. These patterns form their own (ana)logic. Rather than the constant questions about why so-called primitive peoples were not like Westerners, or defining their mental activity as a rudimentary form of Western pre-scientific, childish, or pathological thinking, Lévy-Bruhl studied the manner in which natives thought through mystical mentality:

> Instead of imagining the primitive whom we are studying to be like ourselves and making them think as we should do in their places—a proceeding which can only lead to hypotheses, at most merely probable, and nearly always false—let us on the contrary endeavour to guard against our own mental habits, and try to discover, by analysing their collective representations and the connections between these, what the primitives' way of thinking would be.[38]

The philosopher was inviting his readers to think outside their own disciplines and their analytically focused cultures to see mystical thought as normal, complex, and developed. Thus, this orientation is analogical rather than logical; it has its own form of reason through analogy, an association or correspondence between phenomena. Although the way that Lévy-Bruhl presented mystical mentality was new, and the contexts and time during which he presented his ideas was counter to the prevailing zeitgeist, his thought had echoes in classical antiquity. Mystical mentality was in reality mytho-poetic thinking in another guise and this was not at all new.

Ironically, a great discovery of Enlightenment historiography was that, generally speaking, they adopted the ancient Greek distinction between mytho-poetic and critical thinking.[39] This process of understanding came about, according to American philosopher Peter Gay, through a fascination with classical antiquity. The Enlightenment philosophes "confronted the ancients with [the] self-confidence of men who had become their own masters,"[40] and came to see mytho-poetic, or mythical, thinking as true thinking—it reduced the world to order—but its categories were unsettled and alive, they shifted under "the potent pressure of immediate experience or become rigid under the equally overwhelming weight of tradition."[41] The mytho-poetic mind was hard for the scientific mind to grasp, for "in the mythmaking mind, state and universe, king and god, man and nature, stood for and melted into each other." Ancient peoples did not think that their king resembled divinity: he *was* divine—he was a god in human form. Likewise, rituals did not recall a miraculous event; they were that event. A warrior who made a little doll of an enemy and then pierced it with a dagger to harm the enemy was not merely uttering a wish to harm that enemy: the doll *was* the enemy; the damage to the doll was identical with the damage done in combat—"indeed, in a sense hard for the scientific mind to grasp, it *was* that combat."[42] In essence, proof and disproof was alien to the mytho-poetic mind, and it is the lack of critical analysis that is challenging for the modern scientific manner of thinking to comprehend.

Mythical thinking, as Lévy-Bruhl knew well, is an associative rather than an analytical mode of thought. For example, the Egyptians, who understood the principle of causality and whose advanced ancient civilisations were "overlaid by touches of rationality," persisted in mythical thinking, "and the sky might be thought of as a material vault above earth, or as a cow; or as a female. A tree might be a tree or the female who was the tree-goddess. Truth might be treated as an abstract concept or as a goddess, or as a divine hero who once lived on earth. A god might be depicted as a man, or as a falcon, or as a falcon-headed man. In one context the king is described as the sun, a star, a bull, a crocodile, a lion, a falcon, a jackal, and the two tutelary gods of Egypt—not so much in simile as in vital essence."[43] The ancient Egyptian was not a stranger to the simile, but the prevailing mode of thinking was linked to the directly experienced belief in the co-existence and identity of things that critical thinking would separate.[44] The Egyptians, along with other ancient cultures, such as the Babylonians and the Chaldeans, were civilised but nevertheless superstitious; they were capable of some scientific thought, but their occasional attempts at rational thinking "never tore the web of myth—it was sporadic and fitful rather than organized, cumulative, and self-critical." In addition, Gay observes, the rational skill needed to build the pyramids was never utilised to build a rational regime or religion.[45]

THE CONVERSION OF MYTHOS TO LOGOS

In comparison to the Egyptians, the ancient Greeks converted what they saw and heard of such mytho-poetic cultures during a long and laborious conquest of myth by rationality and reason—*mythos* was overcome by *logos*. In the sixth century BCE, the shift in Greek rationalist thinking had already started to happen in Miletus, on the coast of Asia Minor. Thales, Anaximander, and Anaximenes made assumptions that an underlying rational unity and order existed within the flux and variety of the world; they sought to establish a simple fundamental principle that governed nature and composed its basic substance. "In so doing, they began to complement their traditional mythological understanding with more impersonal and conceptual explanations based on their observations of natural phenomena." In this period, there was an overlap of what we would understand today as mythical and scientific modes.[46] These earliest Greek thinkers, amongst them Pythagoras, Heraclitus, and Xenophanes, were termed Pre-Socratics, due to the fact that they attempted to define the constitution of the world, unlike Socrates and later philosophers who concentrated on ethical questions. The Pre-Socratics abandoned mythological language, but were nevertheless influenced by Egyptian mythology. Thales, for example, declared that all things came from water, and this was probably an expression of the Egyptian myth of Nun, a goddess of primeval waters from which the world had arisen. There was also a central presupposition amongst Pre-Socratics that the world was a unity, despite the diversity of appearances.[47] It was this aspect of Greek thinking that so impressed the Enlightenment thinkers. As already noted, the term "magic" in fifth-century BCE Greece was considered a "marker of alterity," or otherness, referring to the illicit and suspicious, and logos came to take dominance over the more magical mytho-poetic thought. Eventually, Greek intellect came to look outward toward nature and objective universal law, a scientific view, and inward to self-knowledge and inner clarity, formalised as morality.[48]

This emphasis on logos created the intellectual environment within which Lèvy-Bruhl discussed mystical mentality. To make mystical mentality clear, Lévy-Bruhl created too much of a dualism between Western scientific thought and native mystical mentality.[49] In a dialogue with Lévy-Bruhl, Evans-Pritchard argued that natives make very acute analyses of situations that supplemented ideas about magic, often in the form of witchcraft in African and other contexts, with notions of natural causation.[50] Evans-Pritchard wrote that it was "not so much a question of primitive versus civilized mentality as the relation of two types of thought to each other in any society, whether primitive or civilized, a problem of levels of thought and experience."[51] This was a view that Lévy-Bruhl himself came to agree with after discussions with Evans-Pritchard.[52]

Whereas Lévy-Bruhl emphasised differences between so-called primitive and civilised societies, he also sought to delve into the very character of mystical thinking on its own terms. An unfortunate misconception developed within the discipline of anthropology regarding Lévy-Bruhl's use of the term "pre-logical" to describe mystical mentality, and this came to taint all of the philosopher's work for many anthropologists. The misunderstanding centred on the belief that Lévy-Bruhl came to see the error of his ideas about "primitive thinking," and that he had recanted his views after engaging in debate with anthropologists. However, while agreeing that the term pre-logical was unhelpful, rather than renouncing his former position, the philosopher devoted the rest of his life to the further study of mystical mentality, particularly the notion of participation. Lévy-Bruhl did not claim that mystical mentality was irrational, or that it was the exclusive thinking of one sort of primitive human being; neither did he use the term in an evolutionary fashion, implying that "primitives" were at an earlier developmental stage than "civilised" Western peoples.

In his *Theories of Primitive Religion*, first published in 1965, Evans-Pritchard reflected on the impact of Lévy-Bruhl's work on anthropology. He wrote that the criticism that the philosopher did not perceive how very like so-called primitives we are in many respects lost much of its force once it was recognised that his intention was to stress differences. By so doing, Evans-Pritchard said that Lévy-Bruhl spotlighted differences and left the similarities in shadow. Knowing that he was making a distortion, or an ideal construct, the philosopher never pretended to be doing anything else, and Evans-Pritchard considered Lévy-Bruhl's procedure "methodologically justifiable." In relation to Lévy-Bruhl's work, particularly in *La mentalité primitive*, Evans-Pritchard pointed out that Lévy-Bruhl had observed that in Europe we have many centuries of rigorous intellectual speculation and analysis; consequentially, we are logically orientated. Westerners seek the cause of phenomena in natural processes, i.e., not through mystical mentality, but through science. Even when we cannot account for it scientifically, we say that our knowledge is as yet insufficient.[53] By contrast, primitive thought is orientated toward the supernatural, as Lévy-Bruhl puts it: "The attitude of the mind of the primitive is very different. . . objects and beings are all involved in a network of mystical participations and exclusions. It is these which constitute its texture and order. . . if a phenomenon interests him, if he is not content to perceive it, so to speak, passively and without reaction, he will think at once, as by a sort of mental reflex, of an occult and invisible power of which the phenomenon is a manifestation."[54]

Evans-Pritchard considered that Lévy-Bruhl's magico-religious thought was incompatible with a critical and scientific view. It was not that so-called primitives were incapable of thinking critically and scientifically, but that they reasoned in different categories than Westerners. Even so, he considered the philosopher's discussion of mystical participation as "perhaps the most valuable" and original part of his thesis, noting that ideas that seem so strange to Westerners, when considered as isolated facts, become meaningful when seen as parts of patterns of ideas and behaviours. These values form systems as coherent as the logical constructions of intellect, and there is logic of sentiments as well as of reason, though it is based on a different principle. In short, Lévy-Bruhl, according to Evans-Pritchard, made too strong a contrast between the primitive and the civilised; he did not distinguish between different social and occupational strata of Western society, nor between different periods of history: "In his sense of the word, did the philosophers of the Sorbonne and the Breton peasantry, or the fishermen of Normandy, have the same mentality?" As the anthropologist pointed out, mystical notions exist alongside a body of empirical knowledge to guide them, and Lévy-Bruhl was nevertheless wrong in supposing that there is necessarily a contradiction between an objective causal explanation and a mystical one. The two kinds of explanations can be held together, the one relating to and supplementing the other,[55] as we will argue throughout this present volume in relation to analytical and magical thought.

THE PRE-LOGICAL "RED HERRING"

Notwithstanding the cogent points on Lévy-Bruhl's work made by Evans-Pritchard, many anthropologists reacted against what they saw as a challenge to the Enlightenment ideal of psychic unity based on analytical and critical reasoning and logical thought. In fact, the whole debate that ensued over the last hundred years about the rationality of so-called primitive thought was largely a reaction to Lévy-Bruhl's work. The use of the term "pre-logical" became as a "red rag to a bull" and released much anthropological ire, so much so that many of Lévy-Bruhl's important insights into different human mentalities based on analogical and mytho-poetic thinking and a different form of reasoning became lost to modern anthropology in the twentieth century.[56] Shore notes that "[i]n recognising that "mentality" lay at the intersection of a common human sensorium and a variable set of cultural representations (models), Lévy-Bruhl might well have laid the foundation for a cognitively grounded conception of culture and an intellectually rigorous vision of the psychic diversity of humanity, but his critics never permitted this to happen."[57]

Lévi-Strauss, for instance, wrote his classic works *The Savage Mind* and *Totemism* in opposition to Lévy-Bruhl's "false antinomy" between logical and pre-logical mentality. Lévi-Strauss sought to explore forms of rationality to define common human mental capacities in a "lifelong struggle against irrationality."[58] Robin Horton was another anthropologist who, in "Lévy-Bruhl, Durkheim and the Scientific Revolution,"[59] discredited Lévy-Bruhl's notion of participation in an unfavourable comparison with Durkheim's *The Elementary Forms of the Religious Life*, where he argued that traditional native thought is scientific rather mystical (see Chapter 3, this volume).[60]

The analytical, critical, and logical impulse that had caused so much antipathy to Lévy-Bruhl's work appears to be less about the differences between anthropological and philosophical or psychological approaches and more about the issues that mystical mentality, or magic in another guise, presents to anthropology as a social scientific discipline.[61] The Enlightenment vision of psychic unity, with its focus on logical reason and the dichotomous separation of the mind from culture, holds sway over a more mytho-poetic analogical and integrated view of the unity of the psyche that has its own form of reason. Notwithstanding, the works of Margaret Mead, Gregory Bateson, Ruth Benedict, Victor Turner, and Gananath Obeyesekere, among others, contrasted the Enlightenment's uniform vision of a rationalised and reasoned human nature with an analysis of different cultures. In particular, the work of Gregory Bateson will be explored later, but there were other voices of opposition too.

After the supposed Age of Reason came the so-called Age of the Irrational, a "reaction against the logical consequences of too much logic," according to historian James Webb.[62] This view is reflected in Richard Shweder's work, for example. Shweder outlined a cognitively orientated "ethnography of mind," a view of the mind that was characterised not by rationality and analytical reason, but by non-rationality and arbitrariness: "The concept of nonrationality, the idea of the "arbitrary" frees some portions of man's mind from the universal dictates of logic and science, permitting diversity whole leaving man free to choose among irreconcilable presuppositions, schemes of classifications, and ideas of worth."[63] The aim of this standpoint was to "defend the coequality of fundamentally different "frames" of understanding."[64] Problematically though, Shweder's "retreat into nonrationality" seems to emphasise the Enlightenment's valorisation of analytical reasoning by further reinforcing a dichotomy of thought based on the attribution, or lack of attribution, of one conception of rationality. In addition, Shweder subscribes to another very common, false dichotomy in anthropology: if cultural practices or beliefs are not fully determined or universally shared, then they must be arbitrary and thus, infinitely variable. Shweder assumes that arbitrariness is the only alternative to reductive and deterministic understandings of cultural practices.[65] However, as we shall demonstrate in later chapters, magical consciousness is not arbitrary. An analogical "different frame of understanding," a characteristic of magical consciousness, is not arbitrary or infinitely variable in practice, as will become clear later in this present study.

Bradd Shore has advocated a rethinking of the psychic unity muddle. The human nervous system, he argues, is a biological basis of adaptive intelligence; it is flexible and "the choice between characterizing humankind in terms of psychic unity or psychic diversity is based on a false dichotomy, and an overly essentialistic biology." Developments in cognitive psychology, evolutionary biology, and neuroscience all support the idea that human beings possess an "eco-logical brain" designed for cognitive adaptation to diverse and changeable environments. "Properly understood, the common architecture of the human nervous system accounts for important local differences in cognition, just as it accounts for universals of human cognition. Psychic unity and psychic diversity turn out to be two sides of a common coin."[66] The biological and evolutionary basis of cognition does not support the idea of a psychic unity based on Enlightenment ideals of rationality formed solely through analytical reason. The human brain is flexible, and evolves within its particular environment as a totality. The issue is one of the psychic unity of consciousness within all of nature, not *necessarily* a psychic unity based on a conception of human reason as something separate from or superior to nature.

Shore illustrates a more encompassing version of psychic unity through a poem called "Thirteen Ways of Looking at a Blackbird," by American poet Wallace Stevens (1879–1955). The poem echoes Lévy-Bruhl's notion of participation by inviting the reader—through the metaphor of blackbirds as linking threads—into varying and divergent participatory perspectives of the mind. The psychic unity expressed by Wallace Stevens forms a multiplicity that incorporates different minds, "like a tree in which there were three blackbirds." The blackbirds lead the reader, through the metaphorical world of imagination, into an expansive awareness that is characteristic of magical consciousness. In this sense, the blackbirds are guides into areas of the mind unreachable by analytical reason, logical discourse, or verbal analysis. By participating in this psychic unity, the mind leaves the safe confines of its own parameters and enters into other perspectives with their attendant emotional states. To take this further into a more defined magical consciousness requires leaving the experience of the individual body and participating in the experience of other "bodies," as in shamanic shape-shifting, for example. In relation to Stevens's poem, this opens up the possibility of imagining the world as a blackbird. Attempting to formulate a scientific explanation for understanding such an integrated world that incorporates these different types of knowledge is the challenge; it is one that we seek to address in this work.

To disregard a large part of human development by ignoring the workings of what James Webb calls "the occult mind" in relation to magical thinking does not make sense; indeed, one might say to ignore it *is* irrational! To pay no attention to the other aspects of the mind not associated with reductive analytical discourse makes the century of the Enlightenment also a "century of shadows."[67] This led to a privileging of critical over mytho-poetic thought in general. Notwithstanding, there have been attempts to integrate elements of magical thinking—in terms of imagination, intuition, and a sense of spirit—into a different conception of science. Influenced by the Pre-Socratic philosophers, the eighteenth-century *Naturphilosophen*, or philosophers of nature, attempted to reunite God, man, and the universe. For the Pre-Socratic Pythagoreans, Heraclitus, and Empedocles, the soul served as a physical link between man and the outside world; this was a reinterpretation of the idea that the soul was related to *aither*, a material of pure upper air and of the stars.[68] The Naturphilosophen adopted an intuitive approach that was reliant on analogy and paradox in their imaginative quest to attain the secrets of this universe. It was the investigative spirit of the Naturphilosophen that led Henri Bortoft, a contemporary philosopher of science, to explore an alternative imaginative and intuitive approach to science. Influenced by the German poet and scientist Johann Wolfgang von Goethe (1749–1832), an opponent of the rationalism of the Enlightenment,

Bortoft was also a student of twentieth-century American physicist David Bohm (1917–1992), a physicist who combined the Indian mystical philosophy of Jiddu Krishnamurti (1895–1986) with his own ideas about quantum mechanics.[69] The nineteenth-century psychical researcher Frederic W.H. Myers, as we will see in the next chapter, sought to examine a continuous universe with the methods of science, as did neuroscientists Francisco Varela, Evan Thompson, and Eleanor Rosch in their more recent study of Buddhist meditation, to which we will turn in Chapter 4. But before we can explore how a more integrated approach might incorporate magical consciousness, we need to examine the magical mind-body problem in more detail, and this is the subject of the next chapter.

NOTES

1. J.D. Lewis-Williams 'South African Rock Art and Beyond: A Personal Perspective' *Time and Mind: The Journal of Archaeology, Consciousness and Culture* 6(1) (March 2013): 46.
2. Lewis-Williams "Rock Art," 45.
3. Richard Katz *Boiling Energy: Community Healing among the Kalahari Kung.* (Cambridge, Massachusetts: Harvard University Press): 1982.
4. James Silverberg 'Discourse and Inference' in *Cognitive Anthropology* Marvin D. Loflin and James Silverberg (eds.) (The Hague: Mouton, 1978): 283.
5. Jaak Panksepp, 'Emotional Endophenotypes in Evolutionary Psychiatry' *Progress in Neuropsychopharmacology and Biological Psychiatry* 30(5) (2006): 790, cited in Erik D. Goodwyn *The Neurobiology of the Gods* (Hove, UK: Routledge, 2012): 13.
6. Tara Waters Lumpkin 'Perceptual Diversity: Is Polyphasic Consciousness Necessary for Global Survival' *Anthropology of Consciousness* 12(1) (March/June 2001): 4.
7. Brian Morris *Western Conceptions of the Individual* (Oxford: Berg, 1991): 6–14.
8. Ernst Cassirer *The Philosophy of the Enlightenment* (Princeton: Princeton University Press, 1951): 9.
9. Cassirer *Enlightenment*, 9.
10. John Henry *The Scientific Revolution and the Origins of Modern Science* (Basingstoke: Macmillan, 1997): 42, 19–20.
11. Henry *Scientific Revolution*, 172.
12. Peter Gay *The Enlightenment: The Rise of Modern Paganism* (New York: Norton, [1966] 1995): 3–4.
13. Cassirer *Enlightenment*, 4–5.
14. Ibid., 5.
15. Ibid., 5–6.
16. Robert C. Koons and George Bealer (eds.) *The Waning of Materialism* (Oxford: Oxford University Press, 2010).
17. David J. Chalmers *The Conscious Mind: In Search of a Fundamental Theory* (New York: Oxford University Press, 1996).
18. Bradd Shore, *Culture in Mind: Cognition, Culture, and the Problem of Meaning* (Oxford: Oxford University Press, 1998): 16.
19. Ibid., 15.
20. Ibid., 17.

21. Ibid., 39–40.
22. Robin Horton 'Lévy-Bruhl, Durkheim and the Scientific Revolution' in Robin Horton and Ruth Finnegan (eds.) *Modes of Thought* (London: Faber & Faber, 1973): 268; Greenwood *The Anthropology of Magic* (Oxford: Berg, 2009):152–155.
23. Greenwood *Anthropology of Magic*, 77–78.
24. Morris *Western Conceptions*, 167–170.
25. Tim Ingold *The Perception of the Environment* (London: Routledge, 2000): 157–160.
26. Clifford Geertz *The Interpretation of Cultures* (New York: Basic Books 1973): 76 (original emphasis); Shore, *Culture in Mind*, 5–8.
27. Geertz *The Interpretation of Culture*, 9.
28. Shore *Culture in Mind* 33.
29. Ibid., 33–35.
30. Ibid., 33.
31. Ibid., 35.
32. Ibid., 28.
33. Ibid.
34. Lucien Lévy-Bruhl *Primitive Mentality* Lilian A Clare (trans.) (London: George Allen and Unwin, 1923): 29–30.
35. Greenwood *Anthropology of Magic*, 9.
36. Shore *Culture in Mind*, 27, 313–314; Greenwood *Anthropology of Magic*, 30–43.
37. Greenwood *Anthropology of Magic*, 29–31.
38. Lévy-Bruhl *Primitive Mentality*, 32.
39. Gay *Enlightenment*, 89.
40. Ibid., 78–80, 31.
41. Ibid., 89–90.
42. Ibid., 90.
43. John A. Wilson "Egypt" in *The Intellectual Adventure of Ancient Man*, eds. Henri Frankfort, John A. Wilson, Thorkild Jacobsen, and William A. Irwin (Chicago: Chicago University Press, 1946): 62, cited in Gay *Enlightenment*, 91.
44. Gay *Enlightenment*, 91.
45. Ibid., 80.
46. Richard Tarnas *The Passion of the Western Mind: Understanding the Ideas That Have Shaped Our World View* (London: Pimlico, 2000): 19.
47. Roland Hall 'Pre-Socratics' in *The Concise Encyclopedia of Western Philosophy and Philosophers* J.O. Urmson and Jonathan Rée (eds.) (London: Routledge, 1991): 257–259.
48. Gay *Enlightenment*, 81.
49. Greenwood *Anthropology of Magic*, 23–26.
50. Edward Evans-Pritchard *Theories of Primitive Religion* (Oxford: Oxford University Press, [1965] 1990): 90.
51. Evans-Pritchard *Theories*, 91.
52. Greenwood *Anthropology of Magic*, 24.
53. Evans-Pritchard *Theories*, 80.
54. Lévy-Bruhl *Primitive Mentality*, 17–18.
55. Evans-Pritchard *Theories*, 86–89.
56. Shore *Culture in Mind*, 28; Greenwood *Anthropology of Magic*, 10.
57. Shore *Culture in Mind*, 28.
58. Ibid., 29–30.
59. Robin Horton and Ruth Finnegan (eds.) *Modes of Thought* (London: Faber & Faber, 1973): 268.
60. Greenwood *Anthropology of Magic*, 152–155.
61. Greenwood *Anthropology of Magic*, 26.

62. James Webb *The Occult Underground* (La Salle, Illinois: Open Court Publishing, 1974): 1–2.
63. Richard Shweder 'Anthropology's Romantic Rebellion against the Enlightenment, or There's More to Thinking than Reason and Evidence' in *Culture Theory: Essays on Mind, Self, and Emotion* Richard Shweder and Robert LeVine (eds.) (Cambridge: Cambridge University Press, 1984): 48, cited in Shore *Culture in Mind*, 37.
64. Shweder "Romantic Rebellion," 48.
65. Shore *Culture in Mind*, 37.
66. Ibid., 312.
67. James Webb *The Occult Underground* (La Salle, Illinois: Open Court Publishing, 1974): 6.
68. Hall "Pre-Socratics," 259.
69. Henri Bortoft *The Wholeness of Nature: Goethe's Way Toward a Science of Conscious Participation in Nature* (Lindisfarne: Lindisfarne Books, 1996).

2 The Magical Mind-Body Problem

If you'd look at nature truly
One as all examine duly!
No thing's inside, outside neither:
In is out and both are either.
Grasp it quick, let nought confound you,
Sacred secret all around you.
—Goethe Epirrhema (1819)

A magical orientation of the mind makes analogical connections (rather than logical separations), and so any dualisms of the mind and body or the mind and culture are irrelevant in this perspective. In this chapter, we look primarily from the neurological perspective at magical thought in order to examine how the individual relates to the wider whole without engaging with such dualisms of mind/body or mind/culture. The practical application of analogical reason (as opposed to logical reason) is inherent within the notion of participating in an interrelated, inspired world best described as "animistic." Animism is a relational psychic ontology found cross-culturally. Magical thinking is predominantly animistic; indeed, magical consciousness could be said to be animist thinking in action. On a vernacular or everyday level, many societies can be said to operate within a generalised animist perspective, one that views positive and destructive powers pervading the universe, particularly focussed on specific places and things.[1] Animist perspectives most likely co-exist with the major religious traditions of Hinduism, Buddhism, Judaism, Christianity, and Islam—particularly in non-Western locations. Such animist worldviews rely on a relational magical ontology that denies categorising "the inner" (what we might call the psychological) and "the outer" (a social or cultural context) in any dualistic fashion. Animism is also gaining popularity as an advocacy for a certain relational, ecological worldview involving some action or activity to live in a certain manner within a diverse community of living persons.[2] Any differences in defining "animism" more generally are largely due to emphasis, or amount to semantics in theoretical and practical application. In all conceptions of the term, "the environment" is seen as a total behavioural field that may include spirit beings.³ When experiencing the world in this modality, these spirits—which can be perceived as "minds"—pervade everything.

Thus, in magical thought, we begin with the non-material domain of spirits and/or minds, and matter becomes the odd thing that needs explanation! In an animistic perspective, spirits do not require understanding in terms of physical facts, and they are not felt to "derive" from physical, "naturalistic" (which usually means mechanical) laws. On the contrary, within an animistic worldview, the exact opposite is true: the physical world is derived from the action of non-physical, consciously experiencing spirit beings; the world is full of spirits or minds pervading everything. Causality itself is different: things do not cause other things, but within an animistic orientation, spirits or minds cause things to happen through their intent. In more formal Aristotelian terms, causality under animistic thought is seen in terms of final, rather efficient causes. Since final causes are self-derived, entities in the environment (when viewed from a magical perspective) are seen as reacting and responding to internal dynamics and causing things to happen in a self-ordered, internal fashion, rather than simply behaving due to external efficient causes. The universe is a place full of intentions, feelings, desires, and thoughts, and these make things happen. In this chapter, we focus on the individual and relationships with the wider whole, largely from a neurological perspective on the mind-body problem. But first, we look at how this problem is a "non-problem" from a magical perspective.

THE MIND-BODY PROBLEM FROM THE PERSPECTIVE OF MAGICAL THOUGHT

We have seen how magical thinking is essentially animistic. This is in stark contrast to the analytical mode. To be explicit, analytical thinking seeks explanations in terms of mechanical, linear, *efficient* causes. Within this framework, final causes look "spooky" and are highly suspect if not outright denied, as seen in the various materialistic theories of consciousness wherein mental causation (which is final causation) is flat out denied, despite the apparently self-evident truth that we each have free will and act according to internally derived and final causation. The analytical mode seeks to break systems down into interacting components—simplicity, isolation, and explicit characterisation. By contrast, magical thought seeks explanations in animistic terms. It asks not what caused what, but *who* caused what. There is a subtle way in which even the concept of causation is different in magical thought than in analytical thought. This will become apparent as we progress. The reason this is important to think about is that the analytical and magical modalities of thought frame the universe in different ways and regard minds, or spirits, from drastically different perspectives. We are treading on rarely explored ground in this analysis (indeed, this is an analytical approach to magical consciousness—a magical approach to analytical thought would be quite different!), so we must paint in broad strokes. With this in mind, some important generalisations can be made.

First, when thinking *purely* analytically, we should point out that minds become very puzzling and enigmatic when it comes to explaining events, hence eliminativist theories that hold that some common sense notions, such as the animist beliefs in spirits, do not exist in cognitive processes. On one hand, many models that purport to "explain" consciousness simply deny its existence at all, claiming that the mind is "nothing more" than some combination of various psychological and biological processes involving X dynamics and Y structure. From these hyper-analytical modes we find that minds become explained out of existence completely, and the notion of spirits does not even come into the equation. Less reductive models, however, take conscious qualia, *mental causation* and subjective experiences seriously, and actually bridge from analytical thinking to animistic (that is, magical) thought, to varying degrees.

In philosopher David Chalmers's[4] remarkable (and highly analytical), non-reductive exploration of the mind-body problem, we can see how a non-reductive, analytical mode of thinking deals with minds. In defending his essentially dualistic, anti-materialist theory of the mind, Chalmers spends a great deal of time explaining how conscious experience (which is the most irreducible form of the mind in this model) is not logically supervenient upon the material universe and is thus a different sort of thing from the physical. The sheer level of effort required to make this conclusion within the analytical mindset is impressive. This level of effort is required, however, because of the constraints of the analytical mode: in the Western version of "naturalism," the universe is taken to be a set of physical entities interacting due to a small number of simple physical laws. Minds are a mystery in this mode because minds are not simple objects interacting with other objects. Minds are not a matter of complex structures and dynamics—no, there are certain irreducible qualities of minds that cannot be easily explained when tackled head on analytically and non-reductively. These include subjectivity itself, phenomenal qualia, and the coherent sense of self, and *mental causation*, just to name a few. In the analytical mode, conscious experience—and to a lesser extent, "minds"—requires some kind of explanation. That there is no explanation and logically cannot be any physical explanation of consciousness is entirely Chalmers's point, and he makes it very well. This leaves his famous "hard problem" of neuroscience: how can we account for the qualia of experience, or the more subjective aspects of conscious, in terms of physical laws? Put another way: how does the mind "arise" out of matter? He argues that we cannot, even in principle, explain how conscious experience arises from any known physical laws. This leaves consciousness in an odd place, causally speaking—is the mind causally irrelevant to the grinding of mechanical natural laws?

Perhaps here we reach the limit of what the analytical mode of explanation and understanding can really provide for us as we try to comprehend lived experience. The very simple, but unexplainable, fact that we have a mind, which we know because we experience it directly, proves that the mind exists. And yet, we cannot analytically explain it without simply denying it (as eliminativists do). Chalmers makes an admirable attempt at putting together some psychophysical laws, but ultimately concludes that a set of correlations between minds and matter are the best we can do. The mind itself must be simply part of the fabric of the universe; he ends up advocating for a dual aspect theory that is not too distant from panpsychism, a position he is not terribly thrilled about but nonetheless feels compelled to take seriously:

> Personally, I am much more confident of naturalistic dualism than I am of panpsychism. The latter issue seems to be very much open. But I hope to have said enough to show that we ought to take the possibility of some sort of panpsychism seriously: there seem to be no knockdown arguments against the view, and there are various positive reasons why one might embrace it.[5]

At the end of Chalmers's exploration of the mind-body problem, he is left with the dilemma of what to do with our minds. He winds up considering the possibility that the universe may simply have some kind of consciousness imbedded in its very fabric. This is but one example of a highly analytical examination of this issue. What about a *magical* exploration of the mind-body problem? Admittedly, there are far fewer approaches to the mind-body problem from the magical mode that are treated with such scholarly rigor in existence. There is no Chalmers-ian equivalent of an exploration of the mind-body problem from the magical perspective. But, in the spirit of pioneering exploration, perhaps here we can sketch an outline of what one might look like.

MAGICAL MINDS PERVADE EVERYTHING

As mentioned previously, magical thinking is predominantly animistic. The view that all of life is infused with spirit, soul, and consciousness was common in the ancient world, prior to the dawning development of the rationalising scientific worldview; indeed, Plotinus argued that the universe should be considered a god itself. Eighteenth-century poet and artist William Blake tried to re-invoke this mode of thinking after it had shifted toward a more detached mechanistic outlook. Blake envisioned a world in which every creature was an inspirited person living within the total freedom of its Imagination[6] (as we will explore in Chapter 9 of this volume). This conception of the mind stands in contrast to the dissociated Cartesianist notion of psyche that equated the soul and mind with a thinking substance separate from the body and all other matter. Such an encompassing psychic worldview is often expressed as a form of animism.

Chalmers's famous "hard problem" of neuroscience asks: how can we account for the qualia of conscious experience in terms of physical laws? He argues that we cannot, even in principle, explain how conscious experience arises from any known physical laws.

In comes the animistic point of view: from an animistic perspective, minds do not require explanation in terms of physical facts, and minds are not felt to "derive" from physical, "naturalistic" (which usually means mechanical) laws. On the contrary, under an animistic worldview, the exact opposite is true: the physical world is derived from the action of non-physical, consciously experiencing minds, and the world is full of minds pervading everything. To illustrate, consider the following thought experiment. My friend Bozo the clown throws a pie at me and hits me in the face. There are two methods of explanation for why I was struck by Bozo's pie. The first involves the typically Western *materialistic* approach: first, we consider that the pie moves according to the laws of projectile motion. Proceeding backwards, I can explain the motion of the pie in terms of the mechanical force exerted on the pie by Bozo's arm and hand, which is explained by firing of the muscles in Bozo's arm and hand, which is explained by the neural activity of Bozo's brain, which was before that stimulated by Bozo's psychological and cognitive mechanisms involving memory, motivation, etc. As Chalmers would point out, nothing in this account of behaviour requires that Bozo have any conscious qualia about pies, or me, or anything else. But there is another explanation for why Bozo hit me with a pie: Bozo wanted to. That is, I can explain the behaviour of the physical world of airborne pies in terms of the mind(s) that are felt to be "responsible" for this observed behaviour. Here, Bozo's conscious mind is the ultimate causal agent and the physical facts are only minor details.

This essentially animistic worldview looks at the minds responsible for the physical world, not only those minds mysteriously associated with other humans and animals, but the minds behind other chaotic, self-motivated, and typically unpredictable phenomena, including the day-to-day events in one's life and the very motions of the universe itself. For animism, the world is full of non-physical minds that act according not to the mechanical laws of physical causation, but by the mental laws of motivation, intention, desire, and emotion. Such things are felt to be part of everything. Thus, we see that animistic explanations are an example of magical thinking in action, rather than analytical thinking. Magical thinking, at its heart, however, is rooted in the simple "belief" in the existence of non-physical minds as explainers of phenomena—that is, animism explains events in terms of final causation.

Responding to the hard problem of consciousness, the animist and magical thinker would say there is no hard problem, because minds are not created by matter. Rather, minds are primary and explain the phenomena of the physical world, perhaps creating matter itself during the act(s) of creation. To exclude the mind from the explanation because of an adherence to such axioms as the causal closure of the physical world (a popular axiom in physical science and philosophy that posits only efficient causation and denies final causation) is therefore to eliminate the mind from the equation as "causally irrelevant" (this is something Chalmers goes to great lengths to avoid doing, despite the fact that his approach strongly suggests such an epiphenomenalist viewpoint). The magical thinker, however, does not view minds as causally irrelevant, but asks, "Who intended for this to happen?" The classic example of this dichotomy is in Evans-Pritchard's description of the Zande rationale for the granary collapse: the Zande knew full well that the granary collapse was "caused" by termites eroding the foundational structures. This physical explanation was, however (in converse to the Western philosophical viewpoint), "causally irrelevant" to their inquiry, which was, "[W]hich mind intended for the granary to collapse at just this moment?" Note how the key difference between these two types of explanations is *the presence* and *absence of context*: the physicalist explanation involves local, isolated, abstract causes of granary collapses in general, irrespective of context. It is just a few steps away from saying the cause of the granary collapse is "gravity." The animist explanation involves the entire environment, and happens at a specific place and time, involving specific people—i.e., it has a very rich context. It is the specific context that interests the Zande, for it is in this condition (that is, of rich interconnection) where minds are most important as explanatory elements. The physicalist explanation, for the Zande, is generally true, but for the most part irrelevant. In other words, for the animist, it is not conscious experience that is causally irrelevant to the physical world, but rather the physical world is causally irrelevant to the world of conscious experience.

COMMUNICATION BETWEEN TWO MODALITIES OF THOUGHT

Though these views appear to be mutually exclusive, we take the position that they are simply a result of two modalities of thought—whereas the analytical mode results in physical, mechanical kinds of causal explanations that leave conscious experience and intent as mysterious, causally irrelevant "epiphenomena," the magical mode results in explanations involving intent and mental "causation" of a different kind, in its extreme formulation making physical events causally irrelevant (perhaps they might be called "epiphysica"). Neither do we give primary ontological privilege, though it is interesting to leave this subject with the following observation: we know everyone experiences his/her own mind as a fundamental fact (with the exception of radical eliminativists, who argue their own minds out of existence and can therefore be disregarded in this context). This cannot be said about the physical world, which must be experienced through the filter of a conscious mind. Thus, we see that magical thought includes an important mode of thinking that infuses everything with minds and intentions and places them firmly in the dense interweaving of a large-scale holistic context that connects everything to everything else.

When viewing the world in this modality, spirits and or minds permeate everything. But unlike Chalmers's analysis, it is assumed at the outset that the universe is full of minds and spirits—it is not concluded at the end of the analysis, conceded as a begrudged possibility.

As we discussed in the previous chapter in relation to the dialogue between Lèvy-Bruhl and Evans-Pritchard on mystical mentality, analytical and magical perspectives appear to be mutually exclusive, but are common to all human thinking, whether "native" or "civilised." We take the position that they are simply the results of two modalities of thought—whereas the analytical mode results in physical, mechanical kinds of causal explanations that leave conscious experience and intent as mysterious, causally irrelevant "epiphenomena," the magical mode results in explanations involving intent and mental "causation" of a different kind, in its extreme formulation making physical events causally irrelevant (perhaps they might be called "epiphysica"). In other words, I do not care about projectile physics; I want to know why the hell Bozo is throwing pies at me. Similarly, the Zande might not care about universal gravitation or termite biology, they want to know who made the granary collapse at just the moment a friend was under it. In any case, to neither modality of thought do we give primary ontological privilege. It is interesting to point out that just as at the end of Chalmers's reasoning he had to concede the possibility of panpsychism, at the end of the Zande analysis, termites and gravity had to be conceded as causal factors that did *not* involve minds, and so it had to be conceded that there were aspects of experience that were non-mental and non-psychic. Thus the yin-yang of the two approaches eventually led to the other. The difference, perhaps, is the starting point.

MAGICAL MINDS AND THE ISSUE OF "THE SELF"

Many scholars have sought to avoid any orientation of discomfort arising from the two modalities of magical and analytical thought by adopting a "methodological parallelism" between psychological mental phenomena and physiology. William James, for example, argued for methodological parallelism in *The Principles of Psychology* (1890). The brain and the mind were mixed and unfathomable;[7] there were two parallel and closed, but yet somehow correlated, causal chains, whereby the relationship between the two chains was metaphysical rather than a scientific problem. This allowed psychologists the "luxury of ontological agnosticism while they got on with their work."[8] In trying to overcome such parallelism, Emily Williams Kelly returns to some fundamental questions of empirical psychology advocated by nineteenth-century British classicist and psychical researcher Frederic W.H. Myers, (1843–1901), who was one of few scholars who attempted to go beyond determinism in *Human Personality and Its Survival of Bodily Death* (1903). Myers had a belief in the scientific method, and in the continuity of the universe; he saw all phenomena, mental and physical, as continuous, coherent, and amenable to the rational and empirical methods of science. Indeed, scientists must address all phenomena, particularly those that did not fit into current views. He saw a central problem in a psychophysiological correlation: the mind-matter problem at the heart of psychology.[9]

For Myers, there were centres of consciousness that had many complex automatic actions and perceptions, outside the awareness of primary consciousness. These were to be regarded as personalities or selves—such as intelligent sources of thoughts, feelings, and actions, but not necessarily alternative states—that could operate concurrently with a supraliminal self and with each other. Secondary or subliminal conscious centres could sometimes display awareness of each other, of the thoughts and actions of primary or supraliminal consciousness and the environment. In formation, those produced by the communicating consciousness were sometimes veridical and could not be accounted for in terms of the knowledge gained through sense experience or "normal" means. Above both the supraliminal and subliminal selves there was an "I," or a Superliminal Self that not only embraced both the supra and subliminal selves, but also was aware of all activity that occurred in each. It had its roots in a transcendental environment, and it provided an overarching unity of the psyche. Most importantly, it survived the shock of physical death.[10] Here, then, was a model for overcoming the mind-body problem.[11]

However, Myers's work was never taken up seriously by psychologists, so much so that the historian of religion Jeffrey J. Kripal could note that over twenty-five years of studying comparative mystical literature professionally, he could see that most scholars would be familiar with William James' writing, but not Myer's.[12] Although Myers was deeply influenced by the history of Western mysticism, particularly in its Platonic and Neoplatonic origins, his work is best located in its method and thought, as in this example from his treatment of a famous miracle at Lourdes in *Human Personality*:

> It is **not** true, a thousand times it is not true, that a bottle of water from a spring near which a girl saw a hallucinatory figure will by miraculous virtue heal a Turk in Constantinople; but it is true that on some influx from the unseen world,—an influence dimly adumbrated in that virgin figure and that sanctified spring,—depends the life and energy of this world every day.[13]

Myers looked for a comparative model of the human psyche that could make sense of specific occurrences under whatever cultural and historical guise they were expressed: beyond A and B, there is an X^{14} (an issue to which we will return in the next chapter in relation to Jung's archetypes).

Anthropologist Geoffrey Samuel suggests that conscious awareness of the external world is mediated by interpretation from the senses as a complex interaction of biological processes—affected by hormonal flows and neural structures—and the cultural influences through which we perceive the world, including spoken and written language as well as visual media. Our perception of emotions in relation to experience includes the ways in which culture and language help the structure or awareness of such sensations that is built up through our interactivity in relation to our environments. Samuel has further developed these ideas in his book *Mind, Body and Culture* (1990), in which he suggests how cultural and biological understandings of the human organism can be integrated in a single model that does not privilege either.[15]

Samuel's later co-edited book with Jay Johnston, *Religion and the Subtle Body in Asia and the West: Between Mind and Body* (2013), focuses on "subtle body" concepts and practices. These, they claim, are often seen as intermediate between the "mind" as spirit and/or consciousness, and "matter," and they treat mind and matter as continuous: consciousness has a material aspect, but it is less solidly material than ordinary physical matter.[16] Covering Indo-Tibetan, Chinese, Neoplatonism, New Age, Sufism, yogic practices, and also shamanic and magical practices,[17] these all assume a common basis or substance for both mind and body, and mind and matter. If we take an enactive and holistic rather than a monadic view of the human psyche, we can gain another perspective on the magical mind-body problem that takes us beyond an implacable dichotomy between naturalistic and supernaturalistic ideas about the mind (we will return to this aspect in later chapters in this volume). What is the relationship between the self and local and global levels? Francisco Varela, Evan Thompson, and Eleanor Rosch see "the self" as a cognising subject that is fundamentally fragmented, non-unified, or divided.[18] As an alternative to cognitivism, whereby human cognition is seen as a representational manipulation of symbols after the fashion of a digital computer, they prefer a view shaped by the concepts of "emergence" or "connectionism," by looking at systems or networks of components before arriving at a standpoint of being "enactive" —seeing the mind as the mirror of nature, addressed from science.[19]

A MORE INCLUSIVE APPROACH

Another way of looking at the mind/culture issue in relation to the issue of magical consciousness is through notions of multiple centres of consciousness. This might be liberating in terms of studying a total field of relations as might be experienced in a magical frame of mind. According to Myers, certain forms of knowledge, such as mathematical, geometric, and poetic knowledge, pre-existed their human discovery and could be accessed through "particularly gifted individuals." Myers applied a scientific method to religion in order to find a comparative model of the human psyche that could make sense of mystical events under whatever cultural or historical guise in which they were expressed.[20] Here, Myers follows a Neoplatonic rather than an evolutionary perspective stating that, contra Darwin, the psyche is inherent and revealed.[21] The mind evolves to receive powers enfolded in a universe; drawing as it ultimately does on Plato, for whom there was a separation between an inferior realm of Becoming and a superior realm of Being, united through a notion of participation.[22] Myers's work is useful in the generation of ideas because it goes beyond a materialistic determinism in its extension of psychology's empirical base to apprehend continuity in the universe. In Myers's view, all phenomena, mental and material, are continuous, coherent, and amenable to rational, empirical methods of understanding, particularly those that do not fit into current views and can be studied by scientific method.[23] Myers's aim was to reconcile the conflict between science and religion, and naturalism and supernaturalism. The biological organism, instead of producing consciousness, is the adaptive mechanism that limits and shapes ordinary waking consciousness out of a larger, mostly latent, self. This presents an expanded view of consciousness: out of innumerable potential or psychological processes, only the most useful for survival have emerged, and these are determined by natural selection.[24] The human individuality, says Myers, is like a "practically infinite reservoir of personal states, as a kaleidoscope which may be shaken into a thousand patterns, yet so that no pattern can employ all pieces contained in the tube."[25]

This corresponds with accounts of shamanistic magical experiences of consciousness as a multiplicity of alternative modes of mind coming from various spirit beings, all of which can be felt at the same time, to greater or lesser degrees. For instance, during a shamanic healing, a shaman might drum himself, as well as a client, into a trance, as well as feeling what might be going on for the client, picking up sensory perceptions of other spirit beings, and going deeper through time, as well as possibly through different lifetimes, and so on. If we understand that the beings so encountered form part of a spirit dimension that has a different order of existence than the material dimension of reality, then it is possible to take the view that they possess a mind that can "inhabit" a physical being, and that this is a part of a wider consciousness.[26] It is interesting to note that the information produced by such communication is sometimes veridical and cannot be accounted for solely in terms of the knowledge gained through sense experience and "normal" means. This is particularly useful when discussing spirit possession or "co-consciousness" (rather than pathology or psychosis). Here, meaning is crucial.

Meaning is central to a magical perspective. For example, Greenwood walking on the grounds of Glyndebourne, an open-air opera house nestled in the English South Downs, she recalled how she had stopped to look at a reflection of a beautiful sweet chestnut tree in a lake. The water of the lake seemed to hold memories of other worlds and as she looked deep into its depths, she felt that she was experiencing the Norse mythological cosmic tree Yggdrasil. The reflections on the water encompassed the magic of the tree with the weaving of different realities of the surface and depths of the water. It seemed as though the multiple worlds were communicating with her as they surfaced from deep channels under the water's surface, and from somewhere inexpressible by words. The experience took her back to the time when she was working on her doctoral thesis on Western magicians. As part of her research, she had studied the Kabbalistic Tree of Life as an apprentice ceremonial magician and learned that the first lesson in working magic was to "Know thyself," after the Delphic oracle. The Kabbalah is a sacred Jewish mystical glyph of esoteric knowledge arranged around ten symbolic spheres, each one having intrinsic qualities. The student of Kabbalah meditates on each of these spheres in turn and on the connecting pathways between the spheres to deepen his/her awareness of him/herself and his/her connection with God, with the aim of increasing his/her spirituality. All the spheres are interconnected, and while they each have their own attributes, they are also related one to another, and to the inner self of the practitioner, as well as the whole cosmos. Together they represent the creation of existence and all reality, both material and spiritual.[27] Learning to live her life through understanding what the Kabbalistic spheres meant to her personally and universally, Greenwood came to interlink the mythical geography of the Tree of Life with day-to-day experience. Rather than seeing it as an abstract, "out there" cosmological tree, she incorporated it into her own life to make it meaningful, and trees as a connector point linked the Kabbalistic tree with the Nordic cosmic tree Yggdrassil, as she recounts:

> Remembering the Tree of Life, my mind started opening to the landscape of the mythological imagination, associating one thing with another. As I stood and stared at the landscape before me at Glyndebourne, these worlds came to mind in the language of poetry, a language of magical consciousness:

Lily pads floating on the lake,
gleaming.
Sweet chestnut tree, majestic, towers over,
reflected darkly in the water,
glistening.
Into the ripple-depths,
clouds float among the branches.
Rising to the surface
there to be glimpsed,
fleetingly.

The sweet chestnut tree mirrored in the water seemed to encapsulate all of life in that moment—the lily pads on the surface of the lake, the sky floating among the branches, and a hint of the ripple depths, the dark mysteries beneath. It was here, below, that she sensed the dragon was lurking in her subconscious. She needed to try and go deeper.

As she looked deep into the water's depths, she felt that she was experiencing the mythological cosmic tree Yggdrasil in her imagination. The reflections on the water encompassed the imagination of the tree with the weaving of different realities of the surface and depths of the water. It seemed as though the multiple worlds were communicating as they surfaced from deep channels under the water's surface, and from somewhere partly inexpressible through words. A more in-depth example of this process forms the second section of this volume.

CHALLENGES FROM AN ANALYTICAL PERSPECTIVE

The challenges to a more inclusive approach to mind-body unity are particularly clearly seen in the view within cognitive science that likens the brain to computer hardware and the mind to a computer programme. Here, there is a search for the human universals of cognition attributed to innate structures and acquired schemata, or programmes that differ by culture. In this view, humans come universally equipped to enable different cultural schemata or programmes. Cognitive anthropology examines the diversity of cultural content in the programmes, and cognitive psychology focuses on the structure and functioning of the devices.[28] The mind works as a large number of small, simple processors, massively interconnected and operating in parallel, countless pathways; knowledge is acquired through the establishment of particular patterns of connection. The body in such views is nothing more than an input device to receive information to be "processed" by the mind, rather than playing a part in cognition leading to a "disembodied problem solving."[29] An example of this is cognitive anthropologist Dan Sperber's claim that the diversity of cultures depends on the universalism of cognitive science. Sperber argues that "the greater the diversity of the culture that humans are capable of acquiring, the greater the complexity of the innate learning abilities involved."[30] Sperber's assumptions about cultural diversity rest on beliefs, "representations acquired through social communication and accepted on the ground of social affiliation,"[31] but according to Ingold, most cultural learning takes place through trial and error practice, albeit in social, structural situations.[32]

The problem of psychic unity, as discussed in the previous chapter, for example, is commonly shelved using a number of explanations, ranging from simply equating the mind and brain, to making promissory materialist references to "emergence." Other times, the problem is simply ignored or explained by treating the mind as a meaningless epiphenomena of matter or a purely illusory phenomena. Neuroscientists Humberto Maturana and Francisco Varela's work in *Autopoiesis and Cognition* offers an emergent picture of the mind as derivative from but—in some respects at least—autonomous of the material level.[33] Here, the self is emergent, deriving from its material basis of a neural/bodily complex; it develops through individual growth and maturation by a process of self-construction termed "autopoiesis." Neural components and circuits act as local agents that emergently give rise to the self on a global level.[34] A collective element becomes a part of each person, the individual, and the social, interacting between the analytical, linear, causal thinking and magical, non-linear, intentionality based thinking. Later work by Francisco Varela, with Natalie Depraz, makes a link between neurophysiology and imagination as a process of "upward causation" balanced by "downward causation" on a physiological level mediated by the specific social and physical environment of the growing organism, whereby the emergent self can learn "languages" to represent and grasp its own internal processes.[35] However, the idea of emergence does not necessarily solve all of the concerns raised by the vexing problems that arise when comparing biology to psychology and anthropology.

None of these standpoints make sense within the context of magical thinking, as magical thinking sees non-material minds in everything and acting everywhere, containing unity-in-multiplicity and interconnecting minds. For the magical thinker, the universe is full of minds and the Mind, and it pervades absolutely every part of the universe. From a magical perspective, the materialist explanations of the mind are simply incompatible, which may explain why a long history of materialist dominance has dismissed, derided, or ignored magical thinking because it is inherently anti-materialistic.

THE INTERACTION PROBLEM

Dualist explanations (Cartesian and otherwise), which treat the mind as a separate, non-material entity that is ontologically distinct and (usually) on equal footing with matter, however, has their own problem: the interaction problem. This problem is, simply as follows: if the mind and matter are separate "substances" (for lack of a better term), how do they interact with one another? One solution is dual-aspect monism:[36] that is, that the mind and matter are both properties of a single monistic substance that is not directly observable; when viewed under "objective" circumstances it looks like the brain, and when viewed "subjectively," it looks like the mind. From this view, the mind is not seen as deriving from matter, but is rather proposed to be another property of matter (or vice versa). Truly dualist solutions to the problem of psychic unity, however, have not been taken very seriously since Descartes. It should be mentioned, however, that Descartes's solution to the interaction problem was notoriously problematic: he felt that they interacted minimally somehow "in" the pineal gland. Thus, though Descartes granted the mind full ontological, and even divine, status that is fully compatible with the principles underlying magical thinking, the interaction was so bare that it radically dissociated mind from body. This *dissociation* is frequently misidentified as one of the harmful after-effects of Descartes's "dualism," when it is really the minimal interactionism that is to be criticised, rather than the dualism per se. Dualistic models that are more compatible with magical thinking require a tertium quid more substantial than the one Descartes provided in order to allow for the fully connective aspect of magical consciousness. This is not to say, however, that such theories are nowhere to be found. Dualistic theories are much more prominent in anthropology than they are in neuroscience (though they are rarely explicitly worked through with rigor), but often the second entity is not the "mind" but "culture," with varying levels of equation and/or dissociation between the two; sometimes the "mind" is the tertium quid between the body and culture.

Treatments of the interaction problem also date back to antiquity; a remarkably prescient and thorough account of the interaction problem can be found in the fifth century CE writings of Plotinus, an important figure in Neoplatonic philosophy. As the Neoplatonists valued magical thought highly and did not think of it as the enemy of rational analysis but rather a complement to it, such writings have regained a certain degree of relevance in light of all we have been discussing. We are unable to review Plotinus in full here, but it is interesting to note that his approach to the mind-body problem (especially in light of the "theurgic" ideas of his followers Iamblichus, Proclus, and Ficino) presages some of the important points we are trying to make. Plotinus's treatment of the interaction problem was to propose a tertium quid he labeled "the Couplement," which bridged pure mind and matter, and came complete with its own unique properties, essence, and nature that allows for a much greater richness, interconnection, and diversity of interaction than Descartes's nearly schizoid perspective. Roughly speaking, rather than the mind and matter barely touching at a single point in the pineal gland, the mind is seen as deeply intertwined with the body on every level. Plotinus famously (and beautifully) proposed that the mind "illuminates" the body, just as light illuminates the air. Though light comes from a source external to matter (hence the dualism), it nevertheless permeates the manifold parts of the body through and through, everywhere present in every part, a unity-in-multiplicity, but transcendent in origin, the penumbra even extending beyond the body and mingling with other illuminated fields. Plotinus's treatment, though not without its problems, thus avoids the concerns that emerge from collapsing the mind into matter (as occurs in various forms of materialism), which often eradicates the possibility of magical consciousness and other important things, like free will and human dignity. This Neoplatonic and frankly dualist perspective finds its descendants in some distantly similar treatments of the psychic unity problem coming, curiously enough, from quantum physics, as seen in the work of Henry Stapp,[37] Stuart Hameroff, and Roger Penrose.[38]

BIOGENETIC STRUCTURALISM: INTEGRATING NEUROBIOLOGY WITH PSYCHOLOGY AND ANTHROPOLOGY

The field of biogenetic structuralism is a synthesis of neurobiological, anthropological, and phenomenological approaches to human nature that presages and overlaps with our approach here. Walter Freeman, biogenetic structuralist, and anthropologist Charles D. Laughlin point out that neurobiologically, the mind does not passively record the world as it is, but anticipates certain kinds of sensory information that it selectively seeks out to help structure its "cognized world," or world of mentally structured phenomenal experience, and this very fact blurs the boundary between mind/body, culture/nature, and, we add, self/other. As we will see, magical modes of thinking emphasise this blurred quality through several distinct mechanisms, making things "blurrier" and therefore enhancing the feeling of connectedness that often accompanies it, though the things connected can vary greatly. Laughlin explains that:

> The human nervous system did not evolve as an empirical tabula rasa which passively records objective and veridical information about the operational environment, but rather as a community of cells that actively organizes itself into adaptively functioning models of the world.[39]

Biogenetic structuralists therefore argue that the brain plays a fundamental part in magical experience through its capacity to *co-create* a *cognised* and *highly symbolic* world—that is, one in which the mind participates through its various biological mechanisms. In ritual, this cognised world is different from the everyday world, since it is

> thoroughly symbolic in nature. The symbolic function amounts to the relationship between a sensory object and neurocognitive, neuroendocrinal, neuroimmunological, or other somatic processes intent upon this object. . .[it] is the means by which the whole network of models mediating the meaning of an object is neuro-dynamically associated with that object.[40]

It appears that the magical frame of mind that accompanies intense rituals involves not merely abstract ideas floating in space, but flesh-and-bones neurobiology and physiological "top-down" effects. Psychoneuroimmunologists, for example, suggest that concentration on certain kinds of vivid imagery (used often in ritual performance) may produce enhanced immunological activity at specific body regions,[41] encourage the elimination of pain and anxiety, or balance the autonomic nervous system functions in various ways, as can dancing, drumming, chanting, using entheogens, fasting, sleep deprivation, or physical ordeals.

Laughlin argues that symbolically rich rituals (which is most of them) may furthermore intensify right-brain processing. "The alternative reality depicted in ritual performance may thus come alive in individual experience and in an intuitive grasp of cosmic and psychic relations."[42] This "alternative reality" corresponds closely with the overall perspective fostered by magical thinking in (near) isolation; i.e., the way the world appears when thinking magically. By comparison, when we adopt the typical Western approach and selectively "turn off" magical thinking processes, the universe appears disproportionately mechanical, arbitrary, and devoid of purpose. The advantage is that it is more easily analyzed and predicted. As the typical Western approach takes this as the "correct" position, it is not surprising that such a position appears to be the only one available; as we will see later, selectively ignoring magical thinking leads to a number of absurdities and other problems that have been identified by a number of thinkers.

For now, note that Laughlin also observes that magical thinking (in ritual) uses myths—sacred narratives—in a specific way, by providing a way for ritual performers to *participate* in the myth as a lived experience through metaphor. A function of myth, according to Laughlin, is to provide an explanation for the origin of the cosmos and for society, to explain life and death, and to answer the "why" questions. Note that these explanations are *magical* explanations rather than *analytical* explanations. They involve "why" questions as well as "who" questions. They are not linear cause-effect explanations, but instead involve meaning, significance, purpose, and intentionality—all hallmarks of magical thinking. Myth provides a cosmology that helps to interpret experience—this is crucial for human functioning, as interpretation imparts meaning to the events of life, and without it, we are left without any meaning, as we saw earlier in this chapter.

PLACEBO EFFECTS: ALTERING BIOLOGY AND PHYSIOLOGY WITH MINDS ENGAGED IN MAGICAL THOUGHT

Meaning is perhaps the most crucial element of what is known as the placebo effect—the effect in which our physiology is shaped by medical interventions that do not have anything to do with biochemistry or other linear mechanisms of healing known to medical science. The most relevant data available to understand how such thinking can affect physiology, hinted at by Laughlin, are therefore in the growing field of placebo studies. The placebo effect is a long-known, "top-down" effect in medical science, where the patient responds to treatment that does not have a specifically identified biochemical or surgical, analytical mechanism. In other words, a person who responds to back pain by the administration of a sugar pill is experiencing the placebo effect. Often dismissed as a nuisance phenomenon, an example of "quackery" or a confounder of research trials, the placebo response is actually highly relevant to the questions posed by the present work because placebo studies examine exactly the kinds of physiological responses to actions that are known not to have any directly measurable biochemical or surgical cause. The effect is therefore related to social variables, mental images, cultural beliefs, magical thought, and so forth. Thus, to understand the wider question of how a magic ritual, such as a Western pagan witchcraft sabbat, or moon ritual, to a divinatory ritual among the Azande, might affect biology, it is worth going into placebo responses in greater detail.

We are only now beginning to understand what factors go into placebo responses; however, the efficacy of many healing rituals has been touted throughout the ages, and it is likely that ancient humans have used the placebo response to maximal effect simply through generations of trial and error. Placebo researchers Shapiro and Shapiro even go so far as to say, "The history of medical treatment is essentially the history of the placebo effect."[43]

Physician, psychoanalyst, and placebo researcher Richard Kradin observes that placebo responses are universal, and that "[d]espite long-standing beliefs to the contrary, no specific personality traits distinguished placebo responders from nonresponders; rather, what was important was the context created by the caregivers."[44] The placebo effect has emerged in some literature as a legitimate subject of study in itself, and as will be seen, placebo effect studies provide us with many examples of ways in which symbolic experiences can affect the physiology of the brain and body, and in some cases, there are solid clues as to the precise mechanism of how this works.

WHAT SYSTEMS CAN BE INFLUENCED BY PLACEBO EFFECTS?

Anthropologists Thomson et al.[45] argue that "direct embodied experience" may be the most important part of placebo responses, and they argue that the placebo response may be an evolutionarily adaptive trait. Kradin agrees: "It is likely the placebo response was selected for its adaptive effects."[46]. According to placebo researcher and neurobiologist Fabrizio Benedetti, "The placebo effect is a real psychobiological phenomenon whereby the brain is actively involved and anticipates a clinical benefit. . . the psychosocial context can produce therapeutic effects in a variety of ways, regardless of the administration of a placebo."[47] Koshi and Short continue by arguing that the placebo is a highly significant kind of psychosocial interaction between patient and physician (two socially constructed roles), and does not equal "quackery:" "Studies mentioned here showed that meaning can have considerable physiologic action. . . . Therefore, placebo is not the equivalent of "no therapy.""[48]

Placebo effects, to date, have been observed in a variety of mental and physical disorders, including irritable bowel syndrome,[49] depression,[50] pain,[51] Parkinson's disease,[52] cough and asthma (Benedetti 2009: 188–189), dyspepsia, ulcerative colitis, Chron's disease,[53] multiple sclerosis, epilepsy, dementia,[54] arthritis, ulcers, hypertension, warts, and cancer.[55] One famous study showed that for chronic knee pain, a "sham" procedure was effective and showed a persistent alleviation of symptoms; it was equal in effectiveness to a common knee surgery.[56] In a large meta-analysis of depression therapies, Sapirstein and Kirsch[57] concluded that 73% of therapeutic responses to antidepressant medication were due to psychological factors surrounding the administration of antidepressant medication and other nonspecific factors, as opposed to 27% that were due to the drug itself. For Goodwyn, as a psychiatrist, this means that he has to treat nine patients successfully with antidepressant medication before he can be reasonably certain that at least one of them improved due to the drug itself and not placebo effects. Placebo interventions have been shown to cause measurable change in brain physiology in brain imaging studies[58] that are distinct from those associated with medication.[59] The placebo response to depression has also been shown[60] to be long lasting rather than temporary, as is the common misconception.

Medical anthropologist Daniel Moerman points out that sham medical procedures for chest pain, lumbar disc herniation, knee surgery, and Ménière's disease often show similar responses to actual procedures.[61] In some cases, these sham procedures produce improvements in symptoms that last for years. Other studies have shown placebo effects to be highly significant and inducible via *symbolically meaningful* visual, auditory, and olfactory stimuli, as well as *ritually*. All had conscious as well as unconscious effects.[62] These, as we will see, are correlated with psychologically resonant principles (the cognitive branch) and agree with many of the observations of anthropologists (the cultural branch). Interestingly, the placebo effect is not unique to humans—it has been observed in other animals.[63]

Most ailments can improve with placebo—or "nonspecific"—interventions, and these appear to depend greatly on the subject's state of mind. Shapiro and Shapiro[64] suggest that modern treatments—in first world nations, that is—do not maximise the potential placebo enhancement of treatment, and furthermore, the placebo response appears to be state related rather than trait related.[65] Other factors include the subject's state of suggestibility and expectation of a cure,[66] the number of visits made during a treatment course,[67] and the perceived *meaning* of the symptoms.[68] More frequent administration of a medication, larger pills, newer pills, and even the *colour* of a pill can enhance or diminish placebo responses, as does the physician's optimism/pessimism, reputation, and personality, and what the patient is told about the treatment and by whom.[69] One dramatic case observed a euglycemic patient with multiple personalities in which one of the alter egos was an insulin-dependent diabetic.[70] This case provides fascinating evidence of how the mind can profoundly affect the brain and body. Medical anthropologist Moerman[71] argues that the placebo response should be re-conceptualised as a "meaning response," citing a large array of studies.

Mind/body researcher Richard Kradin observes that many aspects of the doctor-patient relationship can promote well being, including "touch, gaze attunement, imagery and meaning."[72] Kradin argues that placebo and nocebo response are types of Jungian complexes,[73] recalling that Jung[74] suggested complexes were *mediated by internal images*:

> Might mental images mediate placebo responses? The idea at first sounds odd, but the fact is that images are linked to most responses by the nervous system.[75]

Kradin has thus already connected the biological and depth psychological aspects of such responses. Elsewhere, he observes that the data on the placebo response argues for a comprehensive, self-regulatory system, which of course was presaged by Jung in a "crude but characteristically prescient manner"[76] in his theoretical construct of the Self,[77] which is a kind of homeostatic aspect of the mind that works toward the healing of psychological trauma and greater functioning in life and society. Finally, Kradin's research points to a system that has both innate factors and factors acquired early on in development, is nonlinear in response, is strongly correlated with unconscious mind-body physiology, and can be invoked in therapy:

> Rather than as a mechanistically ineffective treatment or as a confounder of clinical trials, [the placebo] may soon be accepted as a scientifically objective endogenous mode of healing rooted in nonlinear mind-body physiology.[78]

PLACEBO MECHANISMS: THE MIND AFFECTING THE BODY

The mechanism of the placebo effect is currently under investigation, but so far has been shown to be related to not only to universal human brain systems,[79] but also those brain systems interacting in *socially significant* settings. How does this happen? We are only beginning to understand the answer to that question; however, medical science now has established firm links between the brain (and hence, via correlation, the mind) and the immune system, the cardiovascular system, the respiratory system, the gastrointestinal system, and the skin.[80] In the immune system, for example, the brain[81] has specific receptors for the molecular signals known as cytokines that are produced by the immune cells. In other words, when an infection is occurring, the immune cells release a variety of cytokines, and the brain senses what is going on. "The brain "listens" continuously to the molecular chatter generated by ongoing immune and inflammatory responses. . . the brain "knows" when an immune reaction is taking place."[82] Researchers explain further:

> The brain continuously receives, integrates, and interprets many streams of information. As the information and its subjective "meaning" are neurally represented, dedicated neuronal circuits respond to perceived

risks and opportunities by altering internal physiology . . . The clinical effects of mental processes on physiology are profound.[83]

All of this discussion brings us to a fundamental issue in neuroscience: the mind-body problem (or, perhaps the mind-brain problem): how does a hunk of cerebral matter "give rise to" something so ephemeral and phenomenally rich in qualia as lived, subjective experience? Western thought on this issue has been intense and active for a long time, but, as we have alluded to already, it has largely been approached from the perspective of analytical thinking. When this is done, a certain number of well-known problems emerge. As we explore magical consciousness in this book, of course, once we introduce neuroscience, we cannot escape the mind-body problem, as it underscores the entire analysis. But, as we have emphasised here, the mind-body problem actually changes its complexion when we look at it from a magical perspective as opposed to an analytical perspective. In the next chapter, we explore this issue further.

NOTES

1. Geoffrey Samuel 'Panentheism and the Longevity Practices of Tibetan Buddhism' draft chapter for *The Idea of the Divine: The Panentheist Model: The Divine as Both Immanent and Transcendent* Loriliai Bernaclei and Philip Clayton (eds.) (Leiden: Brill, 2013): 91–92.
2. Graham Harvey (ed.) *The Handbook of Contemporary Animism* (Durham, UK: Acumen, 2013).
3. Irving Hallowell *Culture and Experience* (Long Grove, IL: Waveland Press, [1955] 1988): 87; Graham Harvey (ed.) *The Handbook of Contemporary Animism* (Durham, UK: Acumen, 2013).
4. David Chalmers *The Conscious Mind: In Search of a Fundamental Theory* (New York: Oxford University Press): 1996.
5. David Chalmers *The Conscious Mind*, 299.
6. Kathleen Raine *Golgonooza: City of Imagination* (Ipswich, Suffolk: Golgonooza Press, 1991): 11–12.
7. Emily Williams Kelly 'F.W.H. Myers and the Empirical Study of the Mind-Body Problem' in *Irreducible Mind: Toward a Psychology for the 21st Century* Edward F. Kelly, Emily Williams Kelly, Adam Crabtree, Alan Gauld, Michael Grosso and Bruce Greyson (eds.) (New York: Rowman and Littlefield, 2010): 58.
8. R.M. Young *Mind, Brain, and Adaption in the Nineteenth Century: Cerebral Localization and Its Biological Context from Gall to Ferrier* (Oxford: Clarendon, 1970): 233; Kelly, 'F.W.H. Myers and the Empirical Study of the Mind-Body Problem' in *Irreducible*, 57.
9. Williams Kelly 'F.W.H. Myers' in *Irreducible*, 60–66.
10. Adam Crabtree 'Automatism and Secondary Centers of Consciousness' in *Irreducible*, 363–364; Williams Kelly 'F.W.H. Myers' in *Irreducible*, 332–334.
11. Edward F. Kelly 'A View from the Mainstream: Contemporary Cognitive Neuroscience and the Consciousness Debates' in *Irreducible*, 46.
12. Jeffrey J. Kripal *Authors of the Impossible: The Paranormal and the Sacred*, (Chicago: University of Chicago Press, 2011): 6.

13. F.W.H. Meyers *Human Potential* 1: 215, quoted in Kripal *Authors*, 42–43.
14. Kripal *Authors*, 43.
15. Geoffrey Samuel *Mind, Body and Culture: Anthropology and the Biological Interface* (Cambridge: Cambridge University Press, 1990).
16. Geoffrey Samuel 'Subtle-body Processes' in *Religion and the Subtle Body in Asia and the West: Between Mind and Body* Geoffrey Samuel and Jay Johnston (eds.) (Oxford: Routledge, 2013): 261; Greenwood *The Anthropology of Magic* (Oxford: Berg, 2009): 146–149.
17. Samuel and Johnston *Subtle Body*, 1; Greenwood 'On Becoming an Owl: Magical Consciousness' in Samuel and Johnston *Subtle Body*, 211–223.
18. Francisco J. Varela, Evan Thompson, and Eleanor Rosch *The Embodied Mind: Cognitive Science and Human Experience* (Cambridge, Massachusetts: The MIT Press, 1992): xvii.
19. Varela, "Embodied", 7–9.
20. Kripal *Authors* 38–43.
21. Kripal *Authors*, 69–72.
22. Greenwood *Anthropology of Magic*, 40–41.
23. Williams Kelly 'F.W.H. Myers' in *Irreducible*, 63.
24. Ibid., 73–79.
25. Frederic W. H. Myers 'The Subliminal Consciousness' *Proceedings of the Society for Psychical Research* 8 (1892): 363.
26. Greenwood *The Nature of Magic* (Oxford: Berg, 2005): 97.
27. Greenwood *Magic, Witchcraft and the Otherworld* (Oxford: Berg, 2000): 49–82.
28. Ingold *Perception*, 163.
29. Ibid., 165.
30. Dan Sperber *On Anthropological Knowledge* (Cambridge: Cambridge University Press, 1985): 43.
31. Sperber *Anthropological Knowledge*, 59.
32. Ingold *Perception*, 164.
33. H.R. Maturana and F.J. Varela *Autopoiesis and Cognition: The Realization of the Living* (Dordrecht: Eidel, 1980) quoted in Geoffrey Samuel *Subtle-Body Processes: Towards a Non-Reductionist Understanding* in Samuel and Johnston *Subtle Body*, 259.
34. Samuel *Subtle Body*, 259.
35. Francisco Varela and Natalie Depraz "Imagining: Embodiment, Phenomenology, and Transformation" in *Buddhism and Science: Breaking New Ground* B.A. Wallace (ed.) (New York: Columbia University Press, 2003): 195–230, cited in Geoffrey Samuel 'Autism and Meditation: Some Reflections' *Journal of Religion, Disability and Health* 13 (2009): 89–90.
36. For an explanation of dual-aspect theory in relation to neuroscience and psychoanalysis, see Mark Solms and Oliver Turnbull *The Brain and the Inner World* (New York: Other Press, 2002).
37. Henry Stapp *Mind, Matter and Quantum Mechanics*, 2nd ed. (New York: Springer, 2004).
38. Stuart Hameroff and Roger Penrose 'Consciousness in the Universe: A Review of the "Orch OR" theory' *Physics of Life reviews* (2013). http://dx.doi.org/10.1016/j.plrev.2013.08.002.
39. Charles Laughlin 'Ritual and the Symbolic Function: A Summary of Biogenetic Structural Theory' *Journal of Ritual Studies* 4 (1990): 15–39.
40. Ibid., 20.
41. Robert Ader (ed.) *Psychoneuroimmunology*. (New York: New York Academic Press, 1980); W. F. Ganong 'The Neuroendoctrine System' in *Neuroregulation of Autonomic, Endocrine and Immune Systems* R.C.A. Frederickson (ed.) (New York: Martinus Nijhoff, 1986); Laughlin "Ritual," 30.

42. Laughlin "Ritual," 30–1.
43. A.K. Shapiro and E Shapiro 'The Placebo: Is It Much Ado About Nothing?' in *The Placebo Effect: An Interdisciplinary Exploration* Harrington (ed.) (Harvard: Harvard University Press, 1999): 13.
44. Richard Kradin *The Placebo Response and the Power of Unconscious Healing* (New York: Routledge, 2006): 85.
45. J.J. Thompson et al. 'Reconsidering the Placebo Response from a Broad Anthropological Perspective' *Cultural Medical Psychiatry* 33(2009): 112–152.
46. Kradin *Placebo*, 117.
47. Fabrizio Benedetti *Placebo Effects* (London: Oxford University Press, 2009): viii.
48. E.B. Koshi and C A. Short 'Placebo Theory and Its Implications for Research and Clinical Practice: A Review of the Recent Literature' *Pain Practice* 7(1) (2007): 13.
49. L. Vase et al. 'Increased Placebo Analgesia Over Time in Irritable Bowel Syndrome (IBS) Patients Is Associated with Desire and Expectation But Not Endogenous Opiod Mechanisms' *Pain* 115 (2005): 338–347.
50. A. Khan et al. 'The Persistence of the Placebo Response in Antidepressant Clinical Trials" *Journal of Psychiatric Research* 42(2007): 791–796; A.F. Leuchter et al. 'Changes in Brain Function of Depressed Subjects During Treatment with Placebo' *American Journal of Psychiatry* 159 (2002): 122–129; A.K. Vallance 'A Systematic Review Comparing the Functional Neuroanatomy of Patients with Depression Who Respond to Placebo to Those Who Recover Spontaneously: Is There a Biological Basis for the Placebo Effect in Depression? *Journal of Affective Disorders* 98 (2007): 177–185.
51. L. Colloca and F. Benedetti 'Placebos and Painkillers: Is Mind as Real as Matter?' *Neuroscience* 6 (2005): 545–552.
52. L. Colloca et al. 'Overt Versus Covert Treatment for Pain, Anxiety, and Parkinson's Disease' *Lancet Neurology* 3 (2004): 679–684; McRae et al. 'Effects of Perceived Treatment on Quality of Life and Medical Outcomes in a Double-blind Placebo Surgery Trial' *Archives of General Psychiatry* 61(4) (2004): 412–420; B. S. Oken Placebo Effects: Clinical Aspects and Neurobiology' *Brain* 131 (2008); 2812–2823.
53. Benedetti *Placebo*, 195.
54. Oken "Placebo Effects," 2812–2823.
55. Kradin *Placebo, passim.*
56. J.B. Moseley et al. "A Controlled Trial of Arthroscopic Surgery for Osteoarthritis of the Knee' *New England Journal of Medicine* 347 (2002): 81–88.
57. G. Sapirstien and I. Kirsch 'Listening to Prozac But Hearing Placebo? A Meta-Analysis of the Placebo Effect of Antidepressant Medication' *Prevention and Treatment* 1 (1996): 3–11.
58. Vallance "A Systematic Review," 177–185.
59. Leuchter et al. "Changes in Brain Function," 122–129.
60. Khan et al. "The Persistence," 791–796.
61. D. Moerman *Meaning, Medicine and the 'Placebo Effect'* (New York: Cambridge University Press): 2002.
62. Koshi and Short "Placebo theory," 13.
63. R. Ader and N. Cohen 'Behaviorally Conditioned Immunosuppression and Murine Systemic Lupus Erythematosus' *Science* 215 (1982): 1534–1536.
64. A.K. Shapiro and E. Shapiro *The Powerful Placebo: From Ancient Priest to Modern Physician* (Baltimore: Johns Hopkins University Press): 1997.
65. The opposite of the placebo, or "nocebo" effect has also been demonstrated in a variety of settings; Furthermore there does not appear to be a single placebo effect but many.

66. A. Bandura *Self-efficacy: The Exercise of Control* (New York: Cambridge University Press): 1997; V. De Pascalis et al. 'The Contribution of Suggestibility and Expectation to Placebo Analgesia Phenomenon in an Experimental Setting' *Pain* 96 (2002): 393–402; D.D. Price et al. 'An Analysis of Factors That Contribute to the Magnitude of Placebo Analgesia in an Experimental Paradigm' *Pain* 83 (1999): 147–156.
67. K.B. Thomas 'Medical Consultations: Is There Any Point in Being Positive?' *British Medical Journal* 133 (1987): 455–463.
68. H.B. Brody and D. Brody 'Placebo and Health—II. Three Perspectives on the Placebo Response: Expectancy, Conditioning, and Meaning' *Advances in Mind-Body Medicine* 16 (2000): 216–232.
69. Moerman "Meaning," *passim*.
70. E. Rossi *Mind Body Therapy: Methods of Ideodynamic Healing in Hypnotherapy* (New York: Norton, 1992).
71. Moerman "Meaning," *passim*.
72. Kradin *Placebo*, 147; see also Colloca et al. "Overt vs. Covert," 679–684; Oken, "Placebo Effects," 2812–2823.
73. Richard Kradin "The Placebo Response Complex" *Journal of Analytical Psychology* 49 (2004): 617–634.
74. Carl Jung 'The Structure and Dynamics of the Psyche' in trans. *The Collected Works of C.G. Jung*, Vol. 8 H. Read, M. Fordham, G. Adler and W. McGuire (eds.) R.F.C. Hull (trans.) (New York: Routledge and Kegan Paul, 1919).
75. Kradin *Placebo*, 186.
76. Kradin *Placebo*, 190.
77. Carl Jung 'Aion: Researches into the Phenomenology of the Self' in *The Collected Works of C.G. Jung*, Vol. 9ii H. Read, M. Fordham, G. Adler and W. McGuire (eds.) R.F.C. Hull (trans.) (New York: Routledge and Kegan Paul, 1959a).
78. Kradin *Placebo*, 197.
79. Kradin *Placebo*, *passim*; F. Benedetti et al. 'Neurobiological Mechanisms of the Placebo Effect' *Journal of Neuroscience* 25 (45) (2005): 10390–10402; S.C. Lidstone and A.J. Stoessl 'Understanding the Placebo Effect: Contributions from Neuroimaging' *Molecular Imaging and Biology* 9 (2007): 176–185; H.S. Meyberg et al. 'The Functional Neuroanatomy of the Placebo Effect' *American Journal of Psychiatry* 159 (2002): 728–737; Oken "Placebo Effects," 2812–2823.
80. G.I. Viamontes and C.B. Nemeroff 'The Physiological Effect of Mental Processes on Major Body Systems' *Psychiatric Annals* 40(8) (2010): 367–379.
81. Ibid., 367–379.
82. Ibid., 371.
83. Ibid., 379.

3 Dense Interactivity
Interdisciplinary Challenges

In this chapter, we outline the challenges involved in a study of magical consciousness between the "dense interactivity" between psychology and anthropology. We seek to show a process of thinking that occurs prior to the more usual focus on magical instrumentality, such as the attempt to harm an enemy by manipulating a doll, or endeavouring to attract rain by sprinkling water in the air.[1] Our investigation of magical consciousness using interdisciplinary methods seeks to achieve a more complete description and understanding of the psychic unity of the individual *in context* with his or her social environment, allowing for a fuller description of each individual, as well as each culture. It requires a model for how the individual psyche influences and contributes to the formation of recurrent psychocultural religious/magical forms, and vice versa. That is, depth psychologists searching for a field in which to explore the rationale and details behind comparing individual dream content and ubiquitous mythic motifs will be able to find it in such a model, since its recurrence is suggestive of a constant intrapsychic and psychocultural dynamic for an individual in his or her cultural context. And anthropologists, seeking to explore precisely how the constants of the human individual psyche may contribute to a magical idea, or how a particular structure interacts with each individual psyche (reflecting the approaches of both Jung and Lévy-Bruhl, respectively), will be better equipped to do so, and in a manner which avoids false dichotomies of mind and culture, or resorting to reductive or causal explanations, or biological or cultural determinism. This approach of what we call "dense interactivity" between psychology and anthropology is well suited to the study of magical consciousness because of the simultaneously private and public nature of such thinking.

THE PROBLEM OF DIFFERENT APPROACHES

Psychology (with its offspring, neuroscience) and anthropology are both about human behaviour, but their approaches have traditionally been very different. In psychology, for example, traditionally, the data gathered was from the members of the scientist's own culture, on an individual basis, and the investigator was often a physician, like Freud or Jung. By contrast, in the past, anthropology has gone beyond the parent culture to study a completely different culture. The boundaries between anthropology and psychology have been erected because the different perspectives they offer speak in divergent ways to the psyches of the individuals who identify themselves as one or the other discipline. Perhaps because of these different approaches, psychology and anthropology have diverged from one another since the earliest days of their inception. Despite this, or even because of it, it is therefore all the more striking when both psychologists and anthropologists come to similar (though not identical) observations. Take, for example, the observations of the theoretical ancestor of sociologist Émile Durkheim and psychologist Carl Jung concerning the unconscious influences on human behaviour:

> Inside each one of us, in varying proportions there exists part of yesterday's man; it is yesterday's man who inevitably predominates in us, since the present amounts to little as compared with the long past. . . . But we do not sense this man from the past, since he is so much a part of us; he is the unconscious part of ourselves. Consequently, we do not take him into account, any more than we take account of his legitimate requirements. On the contrary, we are very much aware of the most recent acquisitions of civilization since, being recent, they have not yet had time to settle into our unconscious.[2]—Émile Durkheim
>
> The conscious mind thinks as a rule without regard to ancestral preconditions and without taking into account the influence this a priori factor has on the shaping of the individual's fate. Whereas we think in periods of years, the unconscious thinks and lives in terms of millennia. . . We are still living in a wonderful new world where man thinks himself astonishingly new and "modern." This is unmistakable proof of the youthfulness of human consciousness, which has not yet grown aware of its historical antecedents.[3]—Carl Jung

Since the days of the early anthropologists—influenced by their sociologist-founding theorist Durkheim—and psychoanalysts, individual and cultural systems have been largely viewed in isolation with vague, incomplete, or sometimes simply inaccurate references to the other. This tendency has persisted to varying degrees. When psychoanalysts reference anthropological data, if they reference it at all, it is often distorted, dismissed, misused, or incomplete.[4] At the same time, when anthropologists refer to psychological principles, it is often vague, cursory, or oversimplified.[5] This is unfortunate since both subjects so obviously influence one another, with neither deserving of causal primacy. In depth psychology, the individual's internal dynamics are the primary focus of attention in interpretive efforts, whereas in anthropology, the individual's place in a particular cultural context forms the basis of analysis. In a theory of psychocultural interaction, both must be kept in place, with the interaction between the individual and cultural context itself as the primary focus. We believe that it is important to recognise that the boundary between the individual and the collective is, at best, blurry and permeable, and at worst, an artificial boundary that has introduced the artefact of divergent disciplines of study and all the difficulties such an introduction has generated. This is especially important in a study of magical consciousness. A "Western"-style analytical frame of mind threatens to reduce godlike psychic forces, or the spirit belief of others, to biological, psychological, and cultural abstractions, and this reduction and mechanical explanation is the great strength and power of the analytical mentality.

Nevertheless, it is the primary purpose of this volume to suggest that this is but one of two equally potent ways of understanding the world that are complemented (not opposed by) the magical mode of thinking. At all points we resist setting up a hierarchy of knowledge that poises one epistemology over the other; both are available to *homo sapiens* (and possibly other animals) and we leave it as an unmoved mover of experience that can appear two different ways, depending on one's particular frame of mind. This is a fairly unusual way of looking at things from the point of Western thought, but we have found it to be a natural consequence of a deeper exploration and a non-dismissive, non-reductive understanding that is approached by both psychology and anthropology along independent lines. Thus, our view is that neither individual psychology nor cultural forms and structures are solely responsible for one another. Nor can they lay claim to the status of a first principle; rather, both interact with each other.

The results of intentional states are always multifactorial, with biological, cognitive, depth psychological, and cultural variables feeding into a continual dialogue of response, internal/external stimuli, re-orienting, learning, and responding.[6] By suggesting that all aspects should be examined through the individual psyche and its dynamics in combination with a continual feedback with the individual's cultural environment, we seek to avoid strictly reductive and causal explanations, biological determinism, or cultural determinism. Several suggestions are in order to examine dense interactivity: Firstly, all aspects of a particular endeavour should be examined with a "binocular vision," which includes the individual psyche and its dynamics in combination with that individual's continual feedback with his/her surrounding culture and its symbolic forms. Secondly, strictly reductive and causal explanations, such as behavioural stimulus-response circuits, biological determinism, or cultural determinism, should be considered partial and incomplete. As the results of intentional states are always multifactorial, with biological, cognitive, depth psychological, and cultural variables feeding into a continual dialogue of response, internal/external stimuli, re-orienting, learning, and responding,[7] intentional states and meaning interpretation are more useful than mechanistic models. Thirdly, in depth psychology, the individual's internal dynamics are the primary focus of attention in interpretive efforts.

In anthropology, the individual's place in a particular cultural context has generally been the main focus of attention. In a theory of psychocultural interaction, both must be kept in place, with the interaction between the individual *and* the cultural context itself as the primary focus. Fourthly, it is important to recognise that the boundary between the individual and the collective is, at best, blurry and permeable, and at worst, an artificial boundary that has introduced the artefact of divergent disciplines of study and all the difficulties such an introduction has generated. This is *especially* important in a study of magical consciousness. Both fields have partially recognised this fact at various times: Geertz with the suggestion that all thinking is actually public in nature, and Jung with the recognition that intrapsychic dynamics of a shared nature—his archetypal images—can play out in public arenas. A full integration of these caveats, however, has not been forwarded thus far.

THE COLLECTIVE ELEMENT

With the recognition that what goes on in an individual psyche is a complex interplay of cultural symbols and imagery, combined with innate organizing processes that guide and direct learning and conceptualisation, it is clear that—just as Jung and Durkheim proposed, albeit in different terms—there is a "transpersonal" or collective element within each individual psyche that orders the life experience of a person that nevertheless feeds into this same collective element. As we discussed in Chapter 1 in relation to psychic unity, developments in cognitive psychology, evolutionary biology, and neuroscience support the notion of an "eco-logical brain" that adapts to diverse and changeable environments. Thus, neither culture nor the individual psyche can be seen as being dependent upon the other in any simple way, and the collective element—whether one calls it the collective unconscious, the *conscience collective*, or from a magical perspective, seen variously as an inspirited universe, and/or the realm of the gods—is a critical element of the behaviour of both individuals and cultures. This is particularly true of magical consciousness, as we will see in the following chapters. To exemplify this dense interactivity, we propose a new way of looking at the mind and culture as a combined entity: mind-culture, which contains both the individual sense of interiority and identity along with the collective element, both of which emerge in a person's lifetime and play a part in the whole of a person's subjective experience. The collective element has a long history because it contains both generational cultural elements as well as (and in combination with) various biological constants that are universal to all humans that have combined with those cultural elements. This gives us a picture of the psyche as both individual and collective, but free of false dichotomies.

Neither the cultural expression nor the innate conceptual tendencies can fully account for the collective element in a particular culture or person, just as water cannot be accounted for solely by knowing the properties of hydrogen or oxygen, so it is understood to be an inextricable blend of rich local variations of universal themes and structures. The collective element acts on individuals early in development and affects individuals and cultures through its mythic narrative power during times of strife and revolution as a biocultural, behavioural motivator.[8] Individuals will react to this with varying levels of insight as to its influence on them. In the above example, the collective element would be composed of the human "primary processes," or biological-emotional internal conflicts that strive for the self, as well as other primary drives that strive for acceptance within a group (Freud's id-superego conflict, or Jung's analysis of the various complexes that vie for conscious control—both theories have been expanded and modified by more recent depth psychologists) combined with a collection of vivid symbols (themselves highly recurrent throughout history and across cultures) known to everyone, absorbed at an early age, and capable of profound interactions with those primary processes.

The potency of the collective element is partly due to both its depth psychological and sociological unconscious origin. In this perspective, Jung's collective unconscious and Durkheim's *conscience collective*, preferring neither, are combined into "the collective element." Blending them in this manner resolves the false nature-nurture dichotomy that has plagued both disciplines for so long. This collective element moves us like gods (and in fact will be experienced by the personal element often in godlike imagery, particularly in a magical state of mind). We should note here that we are describing the collective element while firmly in a Western-style analytical frame of mind, which threatens to reduce such godlike psychic forces to biological, psychological, and cultural abstractions. This is to be expected because of the mental frame in which we are analysing such things. In other words, this is no surprise, because reduction and a mechanical explanation are the great strengths and powers of the analytical mentality.

Nevertheless, it is the primary purpose of this book to point out that this is but one of two equally potent ways of understanding the world that are complemented (not opposed by) the magical mode of thinking. Thinking magically, such a reduction does not occur because the very structure of the universe changes its timbre and constitution when we adopt this naturally recurring, inherited mode of thought—this will become apparent as we progress. In any case, viewing the collective element magically is to see it in its magical light: that is, not as a collection of isolated, highly distinct mechanical interactions of varying types, but as a living, breathing unity-in-multiplicity of eternal divine powers and/or inspirited beings. How this living, breathing unity-in-multiplicity is conceptualised and experienced is one of the wonders of the study of magico-religious thinking. At all points we refuse to set up a hierarchy of knowledge, which poises one epistemology over the other. We are left with the brute fact that both are available to *homo sapiens* (and possibly other animals) and we leave it as an unmoved mover of experience that can appear two different ways, depending on one's particular frame of mind. This is naturally a fairly unusual way of looking at things from the point of Western thought, but it is a natural consequence of a deeper exploration and non-dismissive, non-reductive understanding that is approached by both psychology and anthropology along independent lines.

DEEPENING THE ROOTS WITH BIOLOGY AND COGNITIVE SCIENCE

In order to integrate the foregoing model of psychology and anthropology with the biological and cognitive sciences, we have to recognise that the simple models of linear causality are not appropriate. In other words, as anthropologist Clifford Geertz has observed, we cannot simply assume a layered approach in which biology "causes" psychological functions, which in turn cause anthropological structures/functions. A more realistic approach that recognises the inherent dynamic complexity of all of these disciplines is to adopt a "circular causality" approach, as discussed by theoretical neuroscientist and philosopher Walter J. Freeman.[9] Freeman incorporates neuroscience in a manner that connects the normally reductive and linear observations of biology and cognitive neuroscience with concepts much more germane to both depth psychology and anthropology—these are intentionality and will. Without going into too much detail, for the present work, it is recognised that in discussing the human mental state in magical thought, numerous factors interact with one another in a dynamic fashion, rather than in the linear fashion challenged by Geertz. In Freeman's model, basic neurobiological responses from the brain constantly interact with environment: "Circular causality expresses the interrelations between levels in a hierarchy: a top-down macroscopic state simultaneously influences microscopic particles that bottom-up create and sustain the macroscopic state."[10]

This basic model provides the primary structure for an interdisciplinary analysis of magical consciousness: biological tendencies will interact and incorporate environmental states such as cultural expressions, symbols, norms, as well as the history of prior states in a continual process of feedback adjustment. As Freeman observes, the maintenance of this outlook is crucial to understanding the social sciences (among other sciences): "These exceedingly complex relations, involving faith and meaning among family and friends, may be seriously violated by reduction to unidirectional causes."[11] This formulation highlights a point Freeman discusses at length: that as the self develops, the dichotomy between subjective and objective becomes blurry and less useful for analysis. As the collective element becomes a part of each person, these two elements interact in complex ways. Here, we are witnessing perhaps the boundary between analytical, linear, causal thinking and magical, non-linear, intentionality-based thinking, as we discussed in Chapter 2.

THE NEED FOR A COHERENT MODEL

The question is how can anthropological, neurobiological, and psychological ideas be compared in a way that eliminates the misrepresentations that have plagued depth psychology, neuroscience, and anthropology in relation to each other?

In his influential *The Interpretation of Cultures*, Geertz analyses the relationship between biology, psychology, and sociology, and clarifies what is now widely accepted within anthropology, that the debates about whether biology determines culture or vice versa were poorly conceived in principle. Minds and cultures do not predict each other, but continually interact with each other and influence each other. He showed this by calling into question the usual assumption regarding the study of behaviour:

> As one analyzes man, one peels off layer after layer, each such layer being complete and irreducible in itself, revealing another, quite different sort of layer underneath. Strip off the motley forms of culture and one finds the structural and functional regularities of social organization. Peel off these in turn and one finds the underlying psychological factors. . . . Peel off psychological factors and one is left with the biological foundations—anatomical, physiological, neurological—of the whole edifice of human life. . .[however] Despite first appearances, there is no serious attempt here to apply the concepts and theories of biology, psychology, or even sociology to the analysis of culture . . . but merely a placing of supposed facts from the cultural and subcultural levels side by side. . . .There is no theoretical integration here at all but mere correlation, and that intuitive, of separate findings.[12]

Many previous theories of culture implicitly assumed that there was some kind of foundational "human nature" upon which an external culture operated, and the interaction of the two produced the varieties of human behaviour, thus implicitly assuming a too-rigid dissociation of nature and nurture that has been difficult to extract. Freud and Jung both fall into this category, as did several of the early anthropologists; later psychologists rarely refer to anthropology at all. But Geertz highlights the problems with any model that views biology, psychology, and culture as distinct "layers:" such a model glosses over the dense interaction between them and does not fully account for the particulars of the interactions in any case. Geertz argued that such facts make any discussion of a culture-independent human nature very problematic, and took this as evidence that the continued search for cultural universals—a subject that occupied Freud and even more so Jung, not to mention early anthropologists—was ill advised. Geertz's influential ideas encouraged anthropologists toward a near-complete disinterest in universals,[13] as we saw in "the psychic unity problem" in Chapter 1. We will return to the subject of universals a little later.

There are blinders on all sides. Anthropologist Roy Rappaport,[14] for example, in his discussion of ritual as self-communication, refers frequently to psychology when he argues that "given the extent to which in solitary rituals various parts of the psyche ordinarily inaccessible to each other may be brought into touch, and given the extent to which the emotions of participants may respond to the stimuli of their own ritual acts, it is reasonable to take ritual to be auto-communicative."[15] Similarly, his discussion of the non-discursive aspects of ritual and the emotional and physiological systems it engages, the psychological balancing effect of ritual, the internal conflict brought on by excessive alternatives, the effects of altered conscious states, the proposed physiological effects of ritual belief, the concept of the *numinous* which occupied Jung especially in his writings, and the dissociation of the psyche describes phenomena in a comparatively cursory manner that would benefit from the insight of a neurobiologically informed depth psychology.[16]

Another example is Geertz's discussion of the emotional effect of one's "explanatory apparatus" in ascribing meaning to life's experiences.[17] Here, a failure to explain life's vicissitudes leads to a "deep disquiet," but this would benefit from the discussion of case material in which such disquiet could be analytically described. This would not only confirm or modify Geertz's hypothesis, but also enrich it. Furthermore, his exploration of the emotional effects and praxis of more basic instincts in the Rangda and Barong ritual or in Balinese cockfighting depend upon Freudian concepts of eros versus thanatos, and id versus superego, respectively, thus calling for a more intensive examination of these interpretations in light of the more recent depth psychological thought. Geertz is sensitive enough to recognise this difficulty, and even outlines the psychological lacunae in his own theorizing when he states, "There is a good deal of talk about emotions "finding a symbolic outlet" or "becoming attached to appropriate symbols"—but very little idea of how the trick is really done."[18] The present volume attempts to look at such "tricks" and offers some proposed models for how they are done. Elsewhere, Geertz recognises the individual psychology that is implicit in much anthropological thinking: "Anthropology is only apparently the study of customs, beliefs, or institutions. Fundamentally it is the study of thought."[19] Lévi-Strauss is another example of an anthropologist who leaned heavily in the direction of psychology to explain his theory of myth, though he was highly critical (and off the mark) of Jung, and to a lesser extent, Freud.

UNIVERSALS

We have seen how anthropology can benefit from depth psychology. Now we shall explore how depth psychology can gain from anthropological inquiry. This is because psychology has traditionally used the data from cross-cultural similarities to bolster its statements about how human nature and individual minds work. The hunt for universals was an occupation of early anthropologists, but as we have discussed in previous chapters, in the middle of the 20th century, it fell out of favour. Geertz's influence was strongly felt here, in his criticism of the overemphasis on universals at the expense of the particulars needed to generate a thick description of human culture. But universals have experienced a resurgence of interest, particularly in light of the investigations of evolutionary psychologists[20] and cognitive anthropologists.[21] A revisiting and perhaps reworking of Jung's theory of the collective unconscious and the "archetypes," in particular, due to its "midway" status between individual and social psychology, is a fertile area to mine.

With respect to universals, anthropologist Donald Brown[22] points out that anthropology has traditionally fallen victim to three main assumptions that have precluded the study of universals. Firstly, by showing its Durkheimian legacy, that culture is a distinct phenomenon that cannot be reduced to psychology or biology; Secondly, that culture is the primary determinant of human behaviour; and thirdly, that culture is largely arbitrary. These assumptions, taken at face value, would seem to preclude any integration with psychology whatsoever, in that it rigidly and excessively reduces psychology to anthropology. These assumptions furthermore may have developed from Geertz's analysis (along with several widely cited ethnographies of Margaret Mead),[23] but are clearly counter to his original formulation. Ironically, it was the *lack* of fully contextualised (i.e., thickly described) information later gleaned by subsequent ethnography on the peoples originally studied by Mead that overturned the assumptions her analysis fostered. To cite another example, Brown shows how Malinowski's claim that Freud's concept of the Oedipus complex was not universal has been seriously challenged by later analysis.[24] But despite these challenges to the above three assumptions, and despite the obvious applicability of depth psychology to anthropology, and vice versa, Brown observes that "[a] great many other anthropologists will not be. . . convinced because they are sceptical or hostile toward psychology in general."[25] We suggest, however, that this situation need not continue.

CULTURAL UNIVERSALS AND "ARCHETYPES"

Universals were especially important for Jung, as his theory of "archetypes" depended heavily upon his observations of the widespread distribution of various recurrent religious motifs. Jung linked his theorizing on archetypes to recurrent motifs:

> The material brought forward—folkloristic, mythological, or historical—serves in the first place to demonstrate the uniformity of psychic events in time and space.[26]

To explain this uniformity, he posited that the unconscious mind contained instinctual processes that did not contain innate stories so much as nudge the psyche to create stories with similar themes and structures in the presence of typical life situations:

> Archetypes, so far as we can observe and experience them at all, manifest themselves only through their ability to *organize* images and ideas, and this is always an unconscious process which cannot be detected until afterwards.[27]

Jung theorised that archetypes work by "activating" in the presence of appropriate stimuli. He furthermore argued that archetypes are context-sensitive, requiring the proper environmental stimulation before "activating:"

> We experience archetypal situations, that is, situations that humankind has experienced from time immemorial. These situations that always repeat themselves, in various forms. We experience them as we have experienced them at all times.[28]

Thus, we see even here that a closer reading of Jung reveals a more subtle integration of individual and cultural contents, as opposed to a simple dichotomy of distinct minds and cultures distantly interacting. Unfortunately, Jung was not systematic enough to emphasise this point throughout his writings. In anthropology, even Geertz, whose approach appears to have unintentionally (and inaccurately) championed the kind of extreme relativism Brown warns against, acknowledges the important caveat that:

> [M]an's nervous system does not merely enable him to acquire culture, it positively demands that he do so if it is going to function at all. Rather than culture acting only to supplement, develop, and extend organically based capacities logically and genetically prior to it, it would seem to be ingredient to those capacities themselves.[29]

This kind of interactionism is strongly supported by much of the recent work in evolutionary psychology. The study of universals in anthropology, however, does not necessitate a return to a dualistic model of a culture-free "human nature" upon which an arbitrary culture is superimposed. It does not require a reduction of culture to psychology or biology, either. What it does, in the context of a densely interactive and overlapping model of "depth sociology," is in effect rework the concept of human nature itself, as a capacity that includes and operates *within, through, and from* culture, which is not separate from biology and psychology, but tightly interwoven within it. Thus, universals are in fact universals in human nature that include a dense interaction between culture, psychology, and biology. These are the universals of *experience*, which includes magical thinking as well as analytical thinking.

Brown defines several types of universals: *Absolute* universals are experiences that are present in all societies yet are characterised, without exception. Examples of these include the concepts of luck and precedent, body adornment, division of labour, romantic love, enthnocentrism, emotion-specific facial expressions, fear of snakes, and specific kinds of tools, such as cutters, pounders, piercers, and containers. *Near* universals are those that appear with very few exceptions—fire use, domestic dog keeping, and the use of the colours red, white, and black in rituals are examples. *Conditional* universals include if-then statements such as, if a society expresses a preference for handedness, it will always be the right hand. *Statistical* universals are ones that are not universal but appear so often in unrelated societies that they far exceed chance, such as, in a large number of unrelated languages, the term representing the pupil of the eye is a word meaning "little person."[30] Brown writes:

> Anthropological study of universals has been spotty at best, unified neither by theory nor by sustained inquiry. . ..In contrast to anthropologists, psychologists have been much more open to the discovery of presumably universal features of the human mind. But only rarely have psychologists conducted their research outside the modernized Western world, so the cross-cultural validity of the numerous mental processes and traits they have identified has often been in doubt.[31]

Brown identifies three causes for universals: First, the diffusion of ancient cultural traits, examples of which include the use of fire and tools. These were developed at a very early time in human history due to their utility and were passed on to all cultures. Note that even diffusion, however, must align well with universal human tendencies in order to survive countless generational transmissions, as it is itself not a neutral process.

The second cause is cultural reflection, which likely indicates universal experiences such as the differentiation of kin terminology. The third cause, for Brown, stems from "those universals whose causes lie more or less directly in the nature of the human mind, or that are features of the human mind."[32] Of the latter, Brown comments:

> Recalling what was said earlier about disciplinary differences, it should be noted that those sociocultural anthropologists who are most qualified to document universals are *not as a rule well qualified to explain them, [since they] are neither psychologists [nor] biologists.* . . . Anthropologists usually define culture in terms that distinguish it from nature. . . . Other definitions of culture correctly acknowledge a continuous intermixing *with* nature.[33]

The present work seeks to assist in this explanation, at least in regard to the subject of magical and analytical thinking. Compare this newer anthropological data with Jung's early speculations on human nature; building on the known universals in his time, of which many more now are known, Jung described his "collective unconscious" and its "archetypes:"

> [T]he instincts are not vague and indefinite by nature, but are specifically formed motive forces which, long before there is any consciousness, and in spite of any degree of consciousness later on, pursue their inherent goals. Consequently they form very close analogies to the archetypes, so close, in fact, that there is good reason for supposing that the archetypes are the unconscious images of the instincts themselves, in other words, that they are *patterns of instinctual behaviour.* The hypothesis of the collective unconscious is, therefore, no more daring than to assume there are instincts. . .[archetypes] are not in the form of images filled with content, but at first only as *forms without content*, representing merely the possibility of a certain type of perception and action.[34]

This basic definition of the archetype has undergone near-endless elaboration and mystification, some of which was done by Jung himself, but if we eschew such excesses and return to the kernel of Jung's idea here, and acknowledge the dense interactivity of individual minds and cultures, we can see a new concept emerging that incorporates the mind and culture simultaneously.

The aforementioned tendencies are obviously not merely due to individual universal psychological factors, but those factors *in the full context of* a surrounding culture that has built itself upon countless generations of continual feedback. Out of this interaction, it makes sense that certain forms would recur regardless of particular cultural lineage, to produce statistical, conditional, near, or absolute universals, depending on the intensity of *both* the individual tendencies in question, *and* the regularity of the cultural stimuli in question. This includes regularities of magical thought as well as analytical thought.

With this model, we achieve a new level of clarity, insofar as we cannot simply document the occurrence of countless universals, but also begin to account for their biology and their psychology—that is, we can begin to see what contributes to their formation. To understand these *recurrent psychocultural forms*, then, is to understand not only the recurrent cultural problems dealt with by all peoples—hence the psychic unity—but to provide an independent measure of the intensity of the tendencies responsible for the form in question, as the varying degrees of universality ranging from the statistical to the absolute give us a partial measure of their instinctual insistence. Each culture known becomes, then, a "natural experiment" in which such individual human tendencies do not *cause* such-and-such a form, but contribute, at varying levels of urgency, to the dense vortex of the continual interaction of the individual with his/her environment and culture.

APPLICATIONS IN MAGICAL CONSCIOUSNESS

Any consideration of human neurobiology, psychology, or culture in the study of magical consciousness needs to be seen, therefore, in a fully inter-active light, neither reducible to the other at any level, but tightly interact-ing at all levels simultaneously. Out of this complex interplay of biology, psychology, and culture emerge recurrent psychocultural forms of varying degrees of universality and specificity. Such universals are not the final word in cultural or individual characterisation—both require a "thick descrip-tion" for a complete understanding of their context. But knowledge of uni-versals highlights that what is constant in the human mind is relevant in varying degrees to *all* cultures, and what is constant in all cultures will be relevant to each human mind. Whether one chooses to view variably uni-versal psychocultural religious forms, as Jung did, as a host of "archetypes," all waiting with varying degrees of potential energy to spring spontaneously into any mind at any time, or simply as a description of the attractor points that often emerge in many people's biological, psychological, and cultural religious narratives regardless of origin, may not be so much an empirical matter as it is an interpretive matter, and dependent upon one's choice of thick description. The experiential section of the present book will illustrate this later when Greenwood explores "the dragon" in a magical frame of mind; the dragon can be viewed as such an attractor point.

THE COLLECTIVE UNCONSCIOUS

The notion of archetypes as enduring patterns or principles that are "inher-ently ambiguous and multivalent, dynamic, malleable, and subject to diverse cultural and individual inflections, yet that possess a distinct under-lying formal coherence and universality,"[35] is salient for our examination of magical thought. The archetype has undergone several treatments since Jung's essentially psychological definition of the term. For Jung, the arche-type represented the subjective side of an unspecified number of universal themes that existed "in the unconscious". Universal patterns of thought and narrative were, for Jung, the result of a layer of the mind he proposed as the "collective unconscious." The collective unconscious contains inherited dis-positions toward certain kinds of thought, image, and narrative that guide magical as well as analytical thinking, though the emphasis is normally placed on their influence on magical thought in the form of stories about gods or heroes in recurrent mythic stories, ancient and modern. Whether or not archetypes are derived from biology is actually an open question,[36] as they have also been seen as possibly deriving from universal complex princi-ples of organisation that themselves transcend biological principles.[37] Either way, the archetype represents a link between the universal and the particu-lar, as they are universal tendencies that guide the imagination in particular ways that nevertheless use local data, life experiences, and cultural images as building materials with which to build upon a universal framework.

Thus far, we have argued that the individual mind and its surrounding culture cannot be seen as distinct, distantly interacting entities that can easily be analysed in a "pure" sense, devoid of any influence. Instead, we have argued that both the individual mind and its surrounding culture must be viewed as densely interacting at all levels of analysis, such that we end up with an individual mind as it relates to a collective element. This collective element is akin to Jung's collective unconscious, but it is more, as we are incorporating the insights of cultural analyses Jung did not have access to. It exists not only in every psyche, but it exists as a more or less unified entity influencing culture itself, as it contains all conceptual and perceptual tendencies that are universal in human minds. Among these include tendencies to:[38]

- divide things into "inner" and "outer" divisions
- classify things as metaphorically "masculine" or "feminine"
- think in terms of "light" and "dark," with light representing knowledge and dark with unconsciousness or fertile chaos
- equate the vertical spatial dimension with the positive or "transcendent"
- attend to nuances of symmetry and equate symmetricality with ideas of "balance" or favourable status
- attend to ideas of "purity" and "impurity," with the former as preferable
- to think of things as having an irreducible "essence"
- be aware of, nonverbally express, and colour experience in terms of universal emotions such as rage, lust, fear, love, playfulness, grief
- personify the environment

These universal tendencies do not exist in isolation, of course, nor can they be considered to be entirely innate *unless* we allow for a somewhat expanded definition of innateness (adopted by nativist psychologists), that simply regards anything innate as spontaneously and reliably emerging in an organism regardless of its psychological environment. These tendencies to divide objects into "animate/inanimate," the ability to draw pictures of one's dreams, the tendency to personify, the tendency to express pride and shame in identical ways, just to give a few examples, even develop in the congenitally blind.[39] Thus, even though each of us develops in the context of a surrounding culture, there appear to be a number of universal conceptual and perceptual tendencies that emerge spontaneously despite wide variation in the surrounding context. Accordingly, however, these same innate, universal tendencies of the mind continue to interact with the surrounding culture to generate forms that become progressively more idiosyncratic to that culture, even though at their origin, they spring from a common universal and identical source. The roots, therefore, do not vary; it is the foliage that varies.

Nevertheless, those same fertile roots continue to exist in every individual mind and as such, connect all human beings at the deepest level; here, we can see how the unity-in-multiplicity applies to humans in different cultures, which perhaps gives us a clue as to how the psychic unity problem may be addressed. Whereas, for example, one culture may view the sun as a goddess (as in Norse and Japanese mythology, for example), another culture may view the sun as a god (as in many Mediterranean mythologies). The common root, however, is to see the sun as somehow representing "the Divine."

The collection of innate tendencies therefore can be seen as the collective element of every mind, and in every person will be the same at the root, but different in the precise details, depending upon the modulations on the universal framework that occur in the precise culture. Upon these modifications, still more modifications will occur within a person's sub-culture (branches, perhaps), followed by his/her own individual experience (leaves). In any case, the tree metaphor reaches its limit when we realise just how reactive and creative the collective element can be. From clinical practice in the mental health professions, we know that in response to new life experiences and challenges, the collective element can spontaneously generate new mental images, emotions, and even physical symptoms that manifest in dreams, fantasies, and disturbances of mood or perception, particularly when an individual is in a receptive state such as sleep or trance state—states which appear to encourage magical processing. These spontaneous expressions of the collective element often come in the form of symbols or metaphors.

METAPHOR

Jung noticed early on that dream thought is largely metaphorical thought; such is the case in magical thought from the analytical perspective. From the magical perspective, metaphors and symbols are often taken at face value as expressions with a greater degree of reality than "mere" metaphor. Generally speaking, the recent cognitive linguistic work on metaphor[40] classifies the metaphor as a conceptual "link" between something known to something relatively unknown. For example, "love is like a journey" takes something rather intangible and difficult to pin down conceptually, and presents it as "like" something that is easy to conceptualise (i.e., objects moving in space). Much of human thought is metaphorical in nature, and in fact metaphors cannot be completely described except in terms of other metaphors. In the final analysis, love is indeed "like" a journey, but this conceptualisation in itself defies an easy linguistic reduction.

Furthermore, metaphors are inherently whole-making, taking diverse, interrelated phenomena and roping them together under a single visuospatial or otherwise concrete sensual imagery that appears as a coherent, irreducible expression of meaning that contains much that is non-verbal and emotional. Dreams often make plays on words, but in a dream we don't think in words but in pictures, so what is really a metaphorical idea becomes a pictorial representation. If we feel we are at "a crossroads in life" and contemplating a difficult choice, we may dream about actually standing at a crossroad somewhere.

Such metaphorical symbols, therefore, while they can be analysed, can only be verbally explained up to a point. The reason for the limit is that they are non-verbal images and emotion-laden symbols. There is something primary about the raw image that cannot be fully reduced to a verbal formula, because imagery and pre-verbal communication are older and more basic than linguistic thought and capture the whole-greater-than-parts, subjective quality of the image. There is truth to the story of the dancer Isadora Duncan who, when asked the meaning of her routine replied, "[I]f I could tell you that, I would not have needed to dance it." Dreams and other spontaneous expressions of the collective element often contain this feature—they contain musical, visual, and somatic communications that cannot be fully expressed in words without losing meaning.

Thus, each individual can be seen as being in close "contact" with the collective element, from which s/he emerged through his/her continual interaction with the surrounding culture throughout life, that is not identical with him/her, but is not entirely separate from him/her either. This collective element contains powerful universal emotional, conceptual, and perceptual tendencies that, by the time they may be reflected upon consciously, have already been heavily modified (but not created) by the surrounding cultural images, stories, and metaphorical expressions. The expressions of this collective element is most commonly encountered during times of relaxed attentional focus, such as in a dream, reverie, or trance state—states that favour magical perspective. Under the analytical mode, such expressions would be seen as the mechanistic responses of the mind. Under the magical mode, it is the unified-but-multiple expression of the spirit world, the gods, or, as we will see later, "the dragon," and it is proper in this modality to think of it as having a final causation, intentionality, and mentality of its own. In the next chapter, we will explore a theoretical framework that enables the comprehensive examination of magical consciousness as a living, breathing unity-in-multiplicity. A "metaphorical language" is sought to bring different types of knowledge together by the process of "abduction," the intuitive reasoning that comes from thinking in metaphors.

NOTES

1. Jesper Sørenson 'Magic Reconsidered: Towards a Scientifically Valid Concept of Magic' in *Defining Magic: A Reader* Bernd-Christian Otto and Michael Strausberg (eds.) (Sheffield: Equinox Publishing, 2013): 230.
2. Durkheim *L'evolution pedagogique en France* (Paris: Alcan, 1938): 16.
3. Carl Jung, 'The Archetypes and the Collective Unconscious' in *The Collected Works of C.G. Jung, Vol 9i* H. Read, M. Fordham, G. Adler and W. McGuire,

(eds.) R.F.C. Hull (trans.) (New York: Routledge and Kegan Paul, [1959] 2006): para 499.

4. A. Orlandini 'The Transforming Power of Ritual' *Journal of the American Academy of Psychoanalysis and Dynamic Psychiatry* 37(3) (2009): 439–456. Staude "from depth psychology," *passim.*

5. Brown "Universals, Nature and Culture," *passim*; Gras "Myth and Reconciliation," *passim*; Haule "Jung in 21st Century," *passim.*

6. Water J. Freeman 'Consciousness, Intentionality, and Causality' *Journal of Consciousness Studies* 6 (1999): 143–172.

7. Freeman 'Consciousness,' *passim.*

8. Erik Goodwyn 'Depth Psychology and Symbolic Anthropology: Toward a Depth Sociology of Psychocultural Interaction' *The International Journal for the Psychology of Religion* 24 (2014): 1–17.

9. Freeman 'Consciousness,' *passim.*

10. Ibid., 146.

11. Ibid., 168.

12. Geertz "Interpretation," 37–43.

13. Brown "Universals," *passim.*

14. Rappaport "Ritual," *passim.*

15. Ibid., 51.

16. such as J. Brüne (Ed.), *The Textbook of Evolutionary Psychiatry* (New York: Oxford, 2008); Goodwyn "Neurobiology," *passim*; Patrick McNamara *The Neuroscience of Religious Experience* (New York: Cambridge University Press, 2009); Jaak Panksepp (Ed.), *The Textbook of Biological Psychiatry* (New York: Wiley-Liss, 2004); Mark Solms and Oliver Turnbull *The Brain and the Inner World* (New York: Other Press, 2002); D. J. S. Stein (Ed.), *Cognitive Science and the Unconscious* (Virginia: American Psychiatric Press, 1997); Van der Hart O et al., *The Haunted Self* (New York: W. W. Norton and Co, 2006).

17. Geertz "Interpretation," 100.

18. Ibid., 207.

19. Geertz criticising Lévi-Strauss, "Interpretation," 352.

20. cf. Brüne "Evolutionary Psychiatry," *passim.*

21. Robert N. McCauley and E. Thomas Lawson *Bringing Ritual to Mind* (New York: Cambridge, 2002); Pyysiäinen "Supernatural," *passim*; Whitehouse and Laidlaw "Religion," *passim.*

22. Brown "Universals," 6.

23. Ibid.

24. Margaret Mead *Coming of Age in Samoa* (New York: Morrow, 1928); Margaret Mead *Sex and Temperament in Three Primitive Societies* (New York: Morrow, 1935).

25. M. Spiro *Oedipus in the Trobriands* (Chicago: University of Chicago Press, 1982).

26. Brown "Universals," 38.

27. Carl Jung 'The Structure and Dynamics of the Psyche' in *The Collected Works of C.G. Jung, vol 8* H. Read, M. Fordham, G. Adler and W. McGuire, (eds.) R.F.C. Hull (trans.) (New York: Routledge and Kegan Paul, 1919): para 436.

28. Ibid., para 440.

29. L. Jung and M. Meyer-Grass M (Eds.) *Children's Dreams* (Boston: Princeton University Press, 2008): 162.

30. Brown "Universals," 68.

31. Ibid., *passim*; Donald Brown, "Human Nature and History" *History and Theory* 38(4) (1999): 138–157; Donald Brown 'Human Universals, Human Nature and Human Culture' *Dædalus Fall* (2004): 47–54.

32. Brown "Universals, Nature and Culture," 50.
33. Ibid.
34. Ibid., 51–52, emphasis added.
35. Jung "Archetypes," para 91–99, emphasis original.
36. Tarnas *Passion*, 406.
37. Erik Goodwyn *The Neurobiology of the Gods* (Princeton: Routledge, 2012).
38. Erik Goodwyn 'Recurrent Motifs as Resonant Attractor States in the Narrative Field: A Testable Model of Archetype' *The Journal of Analytical Psychology* 58 (2013): 387–408.
39. Goodwyn "Neurobiology," 183–189.
40. Erik Goodwyn 'Approaching Archetypes: Reconsidering Innateness' *Journal of Analytical Psychology* 55(4) (2010): 502–521.
41. George Lakoff and Mark Johnson *Philosophy in the Flesh* (New York: Basic Books, 1999): *passim*.

4   Mind, Matrix, and Metaphor
Integrating Patterns of Experience

As the previous chapters have demonstrated, there is a need for a different theoretical framework to examine magical consciousness. Many scholars, as we have seen in Chapter 2, have sought to adopt a "methodological parallelism" between psychological mental phenomena and physiology. This approach can be seen in the classic psychological work of William James, who saw the brain and mind as two closed but correlated causal chains, linked metaphysically rather than through scientific understanding. The overall task before us in the present work is to enlarge the horizon of cognitive science to include an analysis of magical consciousness. Neuroscientists Francisco Varela, Evan Thompson, and Eleanor Rosch, in their book *The Embodied Mind*, take inspiration from Maurice Merleau-Ponty, who in turn, drew on Edmund Husserl's philosophy in his *General Introduction to a Pure Phenomenology* (1913). In this work on phenomenology, Husserl reflected on consciousness as philosophical introspection and wrote about the importance of the direct examination of experience. However, Husserl's philosophy ignored the embodied aspect of experience; it was too theoretical and could not overcome the rift between science and experience. This was also the case for Merleau-Ponty's phenomenology of lived experience.[1] Varela, Thompson, and Rosch argue that even philosophers who critique or problematise reason do so by means of arguments or demonstrations of abstract thought, an issue they seek to address through an examination of Buddhist meditation as an experiential practice.

Frederic W.H. Myers, by contrast, as we have seen in Chapter 2, attempted to bring a scientific method to his study of the continuity of the universe. Here all phenomena—mental, physical, and metaphysical—were continuous, coherent, and amenable to the empirical methods of science. Myers's belief was that scientists should investigate all phenomena, particularly those that did not fit into current views.[2] This is certainly true of the work of anthropologist and psychologist Gregory Bateson, whose pioneering quest was to find a new conceptual space to break down the dichotomies of mind/body and mind/nature within an intercommunication of disciplines. Constructing a picture of how the world is joined together in its mental aspects, Bateson asked, "How is logic, the classical procedure for making chains of ideas, related to an outside world of things and creatures, parts and wholes?"[3] He later described choosing to examine a metaphorical language as somewhere between what he termed "the Scylla of established materialism, with its quantitative thinking, applied science, and "controlled" experiments on one side, and the Charybdis of romantic supernaturalism on the other."[4] Searching for a metaphorical matrix that could incorporate holistic as well as specific orientations of different types of knowledge, Bateson was particularly interested in the knowledge gained through what he termed "abduction," the intuitive process of reasoning through metaphor. He recognised metaphorical patterns in dreams and poetry, as well as in science and religion. In this chapter we explore Bateson's work, particularly though his reading of Jung's "Seven Sermons to the Dead," in relation to metaphorical patterns of connection. Although Bateson did not deal with magic as an issue of consciousness, or with notions of a "self" or subjectivity in relation to a non-material dimension of experience, his work on metaphorical patterns is useful for thinking about creating bridges between different types of knowledge. We then go on to incorporate a study of a non-material dimension to experience through a discussion of neuroscientific and anthropological work on certain Asian methods of writing about "subtle body" processes as a way of coming to understand the ethnographic experience of magical consciousness.

DIVERSE KNOWLEDGE

Perhaps Bateson's search to understand different forms of knowledge was initiated by his 1930s New Guinea anthropological fieldwork recorded in his ethnography *Naven*.[5] Describing his own ethnographic field notes as scrappy and disconnected in fitting what he described as "*ad hoc*" observations together, Bateson noted that he was faced with a mass of diverse material put together by natives rather than by a logical classification of scientific thought.[6] Maybe due to this experience, Bateson's emphasis in his later work was on finding connections between hugely different areas of knowledge, including diverse academic disciplines, and whole areas of life, such as religion, science, ethics, and grace. Although Bateson's last home before he died was at the ecological center Esalen, the "world-wide network of seekers that look beyond dogma to find spiritual possibilities,"[7] located at Big Sur on the Pacific coast of California, he could not totally incorporate a non-material dimension to his work, nor did he engage with qualia, emotions, "the self," or issues of subjectivity. In consequence, Bateson's model of different types of knowledge was largely materialistic. Perhaps this was a legacy stemming from his father, the distinguished geneticist William Bateson, who named his son after Gregor Mendel, the founder of genetics.[8] As was current at the time in anthropology, Bateson adopted a typical Durkheimian, socially-orientated approach to magic, seeing it as an individual practice rather than the social events of religion, as in ritualised rain dances, for example. Rejecting Frazer's conception that magic was the first stage of an evolutionary development preceding religion and then science, Bateson considered magic a result of individual decadence with which he was out of sympathy.[9]

Nevertheless, Bateson's vision of connecting different forms of knowledge in a pattern of relationships offers a basis for a different theoretical understanding of magical consciousness. It is his interest in the work of Jung that shows his commitment to exploring different types of knowledge. Jung, who had come from a family of psychics, had a vision of a monstrous flood of water that turned to blood and engulfed most of Europe, leaving civilisation crumbling just before the Great War. A short time after his vision of the flood, and during the war, Jung started a process of self-exploration. He carefully recorded his dreams, fantasies, and visions. During this time he experienced more visions, heard voices, and underwent what he called active imaginations, recording all that had happened to him. Jung described this time as the important nucleus of his work that would underpin his later psychological theories. A reading of Jung's *Red Book*, written between 1914 and 1930, seems to point to the fact that it was his personal experience of a psychological breakdown that led to his own mystical experience unfolding in a region beyond images that was nevertheless expressed in images.[10] It was to Jung that Bateson would turn as a starting point to overcome the theoretical dichotomies of thought, as we will explore shortly.

THE MIND IN NATURE: CONNECTING LIVING SYSTEMS

In *Mind and Nature: A Necessary Unity*, Bateson looked for a theoretical model that would provide a language, a metaphorical vocabulary of relationships to describe the nature of consciousness within an epistemology of living systems. He thought that mental processes were organisational and accessible to study in a monistic and unified way of looking at the world.[11] Concerned with the interface between different kinds of mental subsystems, including between people and between human communities and ecosystems, Bateson sought to reunite the Cartesian separation of mind from matter, the basis of the Enlightenment focus on certain conceptions of reasoned thinking.

Interested in cybernetics, the science of communication in machines and living beings, Bateson looked at the nature of mental processes and the relationship of communication between thought and the material world in terms of the interconnection and interdependence of ecosystems. In this manner, the mind is immanent in the whole system of the organism in its environment; it is "immanent in the active, perceptual engagement of organism and environment."[12] He was interested in the "connections between living things, between crabs, people, problems of beauty, and problems of difference,"[13] and saw that everything was a part of a pattern of life evolving. Patterns, for Bateson, were not fixed but integrated in nature—they were indeed minds in nature.

Thus Bateson's exploratory work was concerned with the interfaces between different kinds of mental subsystems, including between persons and between human communities and ecosystems, especially in relation to finding such an epistemology.[14] Trying to overcome the Enlightenment legacy that drove a wedge between mind and matter, he conceptualised the mind as inseparable from its material base, and as including multiple organisms as well as nonliving elements; his central thesis being that the patterns that connect organisms are part of a metapattern.[15] The relationships of the patterns could occur in a multitude of varying ways through mytho-poetic thought and critical thinking. For Bateson, the notion of the mind was to be apprehended as immanent in the whole system: the mind was therefore not strictly associated with a particular body; minds could merge and overlap. Seeking an "ecological epistemology" in his later books *Angel's Fear* (1988)[16] and *A Sacred Unity* (1996),[17] Bateson aimed to build bridges of communication between all branches of the world of experience—intellectual, emotional, observational, theoretical, verbal, and wordless.

Consequently, for Bateson, there was a need to study environmentally situated activity with the mind not being "in the head" or "out there in the world," but rather within the ecological contexts of people's interrelations with their environments. If the concept of the "mind" was extended to a mind participating in the environment, it overcame the limited Cartesianist division between the body and mind. Further, if the mind was defined as the personal aspect of the individual process, and "consciousness" as an intrinsic quality of the wider universe of which the individual was but one part, then the mind and consciousness were linked through a process of patterns of connections. All of this is amenable for a study of magic. In his experimental thought searching for a relational epistemology as "the science that studies the process of knowing,"[18] Bateson saw the mind as having an organisational characteristic; he thought it could be defined as an arrangement of material parts interacting. In this perspective, all organisms have a mind, and all parts of organisms have a degree of self-regulation and functioning, e.g., as cells and organs, whereby there was no requirement for a clear boundary like a skin or membrane.[19] As he was interested in "systems," this could include some living and some non-living parts which were likely to be a component or subsystem of a larger, more complex mind, as an individual cell may be a component in an organism, or a person a component in a community.

In *Angel's Fear* (1987), Bateson explored themes of aesthetics, religion, beauty, and "the sacred," steering away from either materialism or supernaturalism. He was convinced that responses of awe and recognition involved responses to a pattern as a kind of knowing; this led to respect for the systemic integrity of nature in which "we are all, plants and animals alike, part of each other's environment."[20] And so it is with ideas about "grace," which are fundamentally a problem of the integration of diverse parts of the mind, especially levels of consciousness and unconsciousness. He asserted that "[f]or the attainment of grace, the reasons of the heart must be integrated with the reasons of the reason."[21] Bateson did not want to decode a particular cultural message, such as that found in a work of art, a sculpture, or a cave painting, but rather to explore the rules of transformation by which the code transmits metaphorical *meaning*. In this sense, meaning is a pattern of connections.[22] It is a pattern of patterns. It is that metapattern that defines the vast generalisation, indeed, *it is patterns which connect*."[23] Patterns are not fixed: "In truth, the right way to begin to think about the pattern which connects is to think of it as *primarily* (whatever that means) a dance of interacting parts and only secondarily pegged down by various sorts of physical limits and by those limits which organisms characteristically impose."[24]

It is interesting to note that this approach is not so dissimilar to the Aristotelian notion of the psyche as the animating principle of the universe, the principle in living organisms, be they plant, animal, or human, that makes them alive. For Aristotle, the souls of different living organisms differed according to their varying functions: the psyche of plants, for example, was vegetative, constituting distinctive capacities for nutrition and reproduction; while animals had a sensitive soul with an awareness of their surroundings and the ability to experience pleasure and pain; and human beings had an immortal, rational soul that gave abilities of passive and active reason. For Aristotle, the soul was regarded as the principle of biological, sensitive, and rational life, but most importantly, it was not reducible to the human mind and individual reasoning.[25]

Looking for patterns of connections, Bateson sought to take consciousness from the realm of the individual and to overcome the divide between mind and body, mind and matter, mind and nature; he also searched for connections via the unconscious spaces in between that were almost impossible to express in analytic terms. Seeing mammalian interaction as occurring primarily in the idiom of primary consciousness, and only with difficulty being translated into "rational" terms, Bateson took an opposing view to Freud, who associated primary consciousness with the unconscious, which was like a cellar or cupboard of repressed fearful and painful memories. Bateson held to the opinion that unconscious components are continually present in life in all their multiple forms. Indeed, in our relationships we continuously exchange messages about unconscious materials, and "it becomes important also to exchange metamessages by which we tell each other what order and species of unconsciousness (or consciousness) attaches to our messages." Those familiar with clinical depth psychology, by comparison, are trained to attend to such metamessages and unconscious communications and recognise that they become important parts of the therapeutic and developmental practice. That is, they are known to be potent movers of both the psyche of the patient and therapist. The characteristics of primary consciousness are a communicational system between organisms—"the artist, and of the dreamer and of the prehuman mammal or bird."[26] Such human activities as art, allegory, or dance then became exercises in communicating the species of unconsciousness, "[o]r, if you prefer it, a sort of play behavior whose function is, amongst other things, to practice and make more perfect communication of this kind."[27]

A TIMELESS MATRIX: A "HEALTHIER FIRST STEP"

Breaking many traditional disciplinary boundaries, Bateson drew on various and mixed examples to explain patterns of connections. For instance, Shakespeare's magician Prospero in *The Tempest* was used to illustrate the notion of a transparent connective matrix wherein all patterns of psychic growth and movement might be understood:

> Prospero says, "We are such stuff as dreams are made on", and surely he is nearly right. But I sometimes think that dreams are only fragments of that stuff. It is as if the stuff of which we are made were totally transparent and therefore imperceptible and as if the only appearances of which we can be aware are cracks and planes of fracture in that transparent matrix. Dreams and percepts and stories are perhaps cracks and irregularities in the uniform and timeless matrix.[28]

The idea of a timeless and invisible holistic matrix, as an originating, "womb-like" environment for development, presents an alternative metaphorical pattern for understanding how magical consciousness might be understood and examined. Bateson's notion of a matrix of psychic unity, "the stuff of which we are made," is fluid, associative, and embraces diversity and difference as part of an encompassing whole.

In the 1960s Bateson had come across Jung's "Seven Sermons to the Dead"[29] ("Septem Sermones ad Mortuos"), the result of Jung's three evenings in 1916 of psychic exploration of dreams, visions, and reflections channelling the early Gnostic teacher Basilides of Alexandria, the city where "East and West meet." Bateson considered Jung's work on "Seven Sermons" as a "much healthier first step" than Descartes's separation of the mind from matter.[30] In this work, Jung had outlined differences between *pleroma*, the Greek word used in various forms of Gnosticism to mean a totality of divine powers, an eternal unstructured realm containing all opposites and all qualities, and *creatura*, an individual ego, a part of pleroma that created difference and distinctiveness in space and time. Whether intentional or not, Jung's "Seven Sermons" actually bear closer resemblance to the Neoplatonist view of the universe, rather than the Gnostic. After his reading of the "Seven Sermons," Bateson used the notion of pleroma as a metaphor for a unitary "territory," and creatura as another metaphor to describe how that territory has been variously named, mapped, and classified.

After his exploration of his psyche, Jung wrote, in a quasi-religious language, that the pleroma was both the beginning and the end of created beings:

> It pervadeth them, as the light of the sun everywhere pervadeth the air. Although the pleroma pervadeth altogether, yet hath created being no share thereof, just as a wholly transparent body becometh neither light nor dark through the light which pervadeth it. We are, however, the pleroma itself, for we are a part of the eternal and infinite. But we have no share thereof, as we are from the pleroma infinitely removed; not spiritually or temporally, but essentially, since we are distinguished from the pleroma in our essence as creatura, which is confined within time and space[31].

These speculations share much in common with Plotinus's description of the way in which each individual soul derives from and contains The One, which the pleroma resembles. For Jung, the ego required independence from pleroma. Growth required differentiation and this led to *individuation*, the process whereby the undifferentiated became individual. This process eventually led to a state of psychic harmony, represented for Jung in the mystic figure of Abraxas. The word "Abraxas" comes from the Greek, and in Gnostic cosmology the seven letters in its name represent the Sun, Moon, Mars, Venus, Mercury, Jupiter, and Saturn, the first archetype of all things; and it was creatura's way of understanding the immensity of pleroma.

Jung's understanding of the connecting principle of synchronicity makes it clear that in his notions of pleroma and creatura he was referring to a non-causal (in the mechanical sense), associative, psychological connecting principle.[32]

Bateson's metaphorical views on Jung's work have not been without criticism, however. Tim Ingold, who considered Bateson a "great dismantler of oppositions," nevertheless calls his use of the pleroma and creatura "two-faced" by seeing it as a field of matter and energy (pleroma) that is separated from a field of patterns and formation (creatura). These, Ingold contends, correspond to two ecologies: the first of material and energy exchanges; and the second an ecology of ideas, an ecology of the mind. Ingold holds that an organism in its environment is not a compound of two things, but one indivisible totality.[33] Arguing that human activity is not an operation of the mind based on the bodily data of the senses, he says it is an intentional movement of the whole being within its environment, an active and exploratory process with cognition being embedded within the practical contexts of people's lives.[34] However, Ingold's critique of Bateson does not engage with the dynamic process that connects the pleroma and creatura;

this is not a dualistic ecological connection, but rather a recognition of the differences and *ultimate unity*, of two modes of states of being. Both are part of a total field of relations, not two separate domains. It is through the map-making and classification process that we come to understand aspects of the totality; though "fissures in the matrix." For Bateson, creatura has to stand outside of the pleroma to start to map and to comprehend the process of connection, and he was keen to emphasise that "the map is not the territory," the name is not the thing named, and the name of the name is not the name. The mind was not a layer of being or consciousness over and above that of the life of organisms.

METAPHOR: A TRANSPERSONAL PROCESS OF REASONING

In the "Seven Sermons," Bateson found an incorporative vision of the human psyche, which was one that could be extended into an exploration of an integrative world.

Developing Jung's ideas, Bateson saw Abraxas as arising out of the homogeneity of the pleroma and the distinctiveness of creatura.[35] Jung's model provided a *metaphorical language*, a vocabulary of relations and a tool of abductive comparison. Abduction was the intuitive process of reasoning through metaphors, of recognising the patterns in dreams, parable, allegory, poetry, even the whole of science and the whole of religion.[36] This process of abduction occurred through the notion of *ideation*, the term coming from "ideate," to imagine and conceive ideas in the mind. For Bateson, minds were "aggregates of ideas," but ideas were "much wider and more formal than is conventional."[37] Ideas were not somehow separated from the world; rather, they evolved out of organisms communicating within an "ecology of ideas" in their environments. Ideas emerge from the primary process, and the discourse of the primary process was abductive and fundamentally metaphoric.

In his search for an epistemology of living forms in patterns of recursive, non-linear systems, Bateson took the mythical figure of Abraxas as a transpersonal metaphor for biological unity and the mind in nature. Here, he is concerned with the relationship between structure and process, particularly in his ideas about maps—how creatura creates structures for classification and meaning and reuniting with the process of pleroma, the matrix. Mythical thinking about gods and other such supposedly otherworldly beings gave Bateson the ability to be able to "wobble ideas around."[38] He was interested in the patterns of communication and interaction arising in relationships between phenomena, and saw a metaphorical bridge or pathway for messages between pleroma, creatura, and Abraxas. Accordingly, for Bateson, Abraxas was a movement of communication between metaphors, and a shift from the duality of the Cartesian mind and matter. Myths and stories could form maps of meaning to understand the totality. The pleroma could be translated into the language of creatura through mythical metaphor, "the organizing glue" of the world of mental process within nature. Jung's Abraxas is just one metaphor among many for such a relational attitude to the environment, as we will see later in this volume.

In this regard, myths can be understood as metaphorical patterns of analogical reasoning that can give meaning. Claude Lévi-Strauss pointed out that myth was a way of reaching universal mental structures of the unconscious, but using Bateson's conception of metaphorical patterns, we can engage with the magical components of the thinking process. Lévi-Strauss, influenced by Freud, was interested in examining myth as a process of the transformation of the underlying unconscious. Through searching for the logical structure of myths, he sought to find their complex symmetry on different levels.[39] However, Lévi-Strauss adhered to the analytical tendency in modern anthropology due to a reaction against the mysticism and supposed irrationality of Lévy-Bruhl's mystical mentality. By comparison, rather than focusing on the logic of myth, we can see that myths might become a medium for the expression of the *analogical* magical processes of mind.

AN INSPIRITED UNIVERSE: SUBJECTIVE EXPERIENCE

An important issue for our study of magical consciousness is the theme of patterns of connection between the material and non-material dimensions of experience. In this sense, magical thought processes are considered in the contexts of people's interrelations with their environments, and through a lifelong history of involvement with others.[40] Here, magic can be explored as related types of connecting metaphorical thought patterns, but Bateson himself is less helpful in extending understanding to an inspirited world, or to notions of an individual self and questions of subjectivity. Unlike Myers, who, as we saw in Chapter 2, thought that there was a "Superliminal Self" that had its roots in a transcendental environment,[41] Bateson stops short on this point. Looking at the nature of mental processes and the relationship of communication between thought and the material world of the interconnection and interdependence of ecosystems, Bateson did not engage with any sense of a non-material dimension, or how this could affect subjectivity. By taking consciousness away from the realm of the individual, he left the issue of "the self" in relation to its environment largely unexamined. Such a materialistic consensus undergirds mainstream psychology, neuroscience, and also, to a lesser extent, anthropology. The problem relates to the difference between the private, subjective world of individual mental life, with its relationships with non-observable and non-material entities, and the public, observable, and objective world of physiological events. As we have already seen in earlier chapters, scientific disciplines have struggled to reconcile both.

THE NON-MATERIAL ASPECT: EXAMINING EXPERIENCE

Varela, Thompson, and Rosch, in their book *The Embodied Mind*, turn to a non-Western philosophical tradition to examine Buddhist mindfulness meditation as a method for examining experience. If cognitive science is to include human experience, it must have a method for exploring what that human experience is. How can the mind become an instrument for knowing itself? It then becomes a purpose to calm the mind through Buddhist media-tion, to render the mind able to present itself to gain insight into its own nature and gain periods of more panoramic, perspective awareness. This involves the cutting of untamed habits and an attitude of letting go, then the mind's natural characteristic of knowing itself, and reflecting its own experi-ence can "shine forth"—this is beginning of wisdom (prajña). The aim is to become one with one's own experience; this is not an abstract attitude, nor is it knowledge "about" anything—there is no abstract knower of the expe-rience separate from the experience itself.[42] In the West, a similar approach involving "detachment" was advocated by the Neoplatonists, particularly Plotinus, though this practice did not develop into enduring schools of prac-tice in the same way that Buddhist mindfulness did.

Virtually all human cultures have, or have had in the past, some kind of concept of the mind, spirit, or soul as distinct from the physical body and various practitioners—shamans, medicine men, and healers—have sought a direct experience of a realm of spirit or some other divine reality (within what we have previously described as animistic worldviews in Chapter 2 of this volume). This non-material aspect of human existence can also be seen clearly in Indian and Tibetan Tantric traditions and similar Chinese practices that involve an internal "subtle physiology" of the body or rather body-mind complex.[43] If we take the practice of Tantra as an example, we can see how it interweaves the material and non-material dimensions of life. Tantra is a complex and problematic label says Geoffrey Samuel in *The Origins of Yoga and Tantra* (2010), but in the most general terms it is concerned with a disciplined and systematic technique for the training and control of the human organism, and also as a technique for "the reshaping of human consciousness towards some kind of higher goal,"[44] as well as the environment as "mind in nature." This approach is exemplified in Samuel's work on Indian and Tibetan Tantric traditions, and similar Chinese prac-tices, that involve an internal "subtle physiology" of the body.[45]

Samuel, in a study of the history and evolution of Tibetan Buddhist phi-losophy, points out that Tibetan Tantric practitioners understood that the universe had an underlying non-dualistic divine reality. This divine real-ity was concealed, but it existed within all phenomena and provided the inner logic and meaning of the phenomenal world. The role of the indi-vidual was to connect with this divine reality and in the process, not would they only transcend their individual identity, but the divine nature of the awakened being would be revealed. This view is not dissimilar to Jung's notions of pleroma and creatura, and also Bateson's metaphorical ideas of an all-embracing matrix from which we create meaningful patterns of connections, but Jung's and Bateson's conceptions are necessarily limited by the need to embrace a scientific perspective absent in the Asian conception. Samuel describes how the "inner yoga" practices of Tantra developed in India from the seventh and eighth centuries onward, and how they developed in a variety of ways through a standard ritual sequence in which the practitioner visualises and imagines a divine form. The deity, the "wisdom being," or *jñ na-sattva*, is invited to merge with the *samaya-sattva*, and the two become a unity.[46] Practitioners, by transforming themselves imaginatively into Tantric deities and through this process of transforming the world into the Tantric mandala, are practicing experiencing the world in its essentially divine and awakened nature.

Samuel sees this process as a practical application of panentheism, a shift from animism to seeing a deity within all of nature. He examines the concept through a specific set of Tantric longevity techniques from the Indian alchemical tradition, along with elements that he suggests are of Himalayan shamanism, such as soul retrieval; these are closely integrated with Vajrayāna Buddhist procedures. A description of one specific cycle of longevity practices, the *'Chi med srog thig* (or "Seed of Immortal Life" text), forms the basis of an ongoing lineage of practice, passed down from teacher to student, and associated with the Tantric deity Amitāyus, an aspect of the Enlightened Buddha. The *'Chi med srog thig*, according to Samuel, uses four components of long-life practice: *tshe* (lifespan); *srog* (life force); *bla* (separable life essence or protective energy); and *dbugs* (breath). Other factors that may be involved include *rlung rta* (good fortune) and *dbang thang* (personal power). Samuel notes how these components for long-life practices form part of a body of Tibetan terms that occur both in popular discourse and in a variety of learned contexts, including medicine and astrology. In astrology, *srog*, *bla*, *lus* (body), *rlung rta*, and *dbang thang* are correlated with the cycles of the five elements of metal, wood, water, air, and fire that are fundamental to the Chinese-derived system of Tibetan astrology (*nagrtsis*). Samuel explains that *bla* is a particularly significant factor, as it appears to have a direct derivation from the pre-Buddhist Tibetan ideas of a separable soul or life essence. Such souls can generally be lost, and the work of shamanic practitioners is often conceived of in terms of its recovery.

The body in longevity practice, Samuel points out, is seen as open to the surrounding environment and intimately connected with it, and the practice itself, like other Tibetan Tantric practices, can be seen as a reworking within a sophisticated literate culture of ideas of lost or stolen souls. Here, *bla* may pertain to social groups or regions in addition to individuals; specific places, plants, or animals in the environment may be thought of as the external homes of the *bla* and their vitality as linked to the vitality of the linked person or group. The *bla* have remained quite alive in popular understandings and easily shade over into ideas of relationships to local deities: thus, the *bla ri* (*bla* mountain) or *bla mtsho* (*bla* lake) of an area is also the home of its guardian deity. Thus, the health of the *bla* might be conceived in terms of maintaining good relations with the local deity.[47]

The central feature of the *'Chi med srog thig* cycle is a specific revelation or series of revelations, focusing around forms of Amitāyus and his consort the goddess Candalī, who is also a "harlot" or "low-caste woman,"[48] who are in turn surrounded by a *mandala* of, among others, four further Buddha figures with female consorts in the four directions; six goddesses of sensory enjoyment; eight offering goddesses; and four door-keeper goddesses with consorts, along with various symbolic supports for the aspects of the life force.[49] Samuel notes that it is the imaginative recreation by the practitioner of this mandala of deities that effectively defines the practice of the *'Chi med srog thig*. None of the individual deities is unique to this cycle, but a primary function of the initiation into the cycle is to introduce future practitioners to this specific constellation of deities, which, according to Samuel, they invoke and bring into being through visualisation and active imagination. This practice will allegedly link up the internal aspects of the associated meditational practice, as well as the ethical and affective elements to direct internal flows through the subtle body of the practitioner with the aim of assisting in the attainment of Buddhahood. Samuel points out that within the wider context of Tibetan Vajrayāna Buddhism, these techniques can be put to a wide range of uses, including "the attainment of Buddhahood, prosperity, and guiding the consciousness in the context of death and afterlife." The *'Chi med srog thig*, with its emphasis on accessing the vitality and restorative power pervading the universe, represents a form of panentheism that is very directly grounded in the everyday and pragmatic,[50] and represents a non-dualistic relationship with an inspired universe.

A PATTERN OF MAGICAL EXPERIENCE

To fully understand the essence of magical consciousness is to understand how it works at an individual level. In the chapters that follow, Greenwood gives a direct fieldwork account of her experience of the process of magical consciousness. Magical experience is intrinsically personal: not every aspect of the magical imagination is "sacred"—what makes any part of a network of connections special is its relation to a synchronous pattern of connections. Meaning comes through a process of associations; experience changes how magic is perceived. Rather than engaging in any traditional mantic practice such as Tantra, Greenwood uses the "raw" data of her own "untrained" mind. Through writing a narrative of her own life that examines the process and deeper aspects of magical consciousness, she engages with an animistic, as well as a panentheistic-type practice, but it is not contained within a prescribed series of cultural practices. Greenwood engages with magic as narrative, by focusing on how she relates to various phenomena through intuition, imagination, synchronicity, and other qualities abundant in the right-brain hemisphere orientation. She revisits periods in her life: to the land where she was born, and meditates on the coastline of southern England, amongst other locations encountered during fieldwork with British practitioners of magic. Connections between different types of knowledge—those coming from a reading of the history of a place and gained through her own alternative mode of consciousness, prompt her recall of experiences, memories, feelings of location; "way markers" from the past act as synchronous connection points through time. Inspired by Bateson, she examines her mind through the story telling process of abduction, of finding metaphorical connections located within specific environments. For Bateson, the notion of the mind was not strictly associated with a particular body; minds could merge and overlap through the shape-shifting of metaphorical reasoning. Where Abraxas was a Batesonian example of a transpersonal metaphor for the unity of the mind in nature, Greenwood senses "the dragon" as a metaphorical attractor point for the feeling, structuring, and classifying meaning process of magical consciousness. The next chapter starts the section of the book that brings the specific features of magical consciousness to life through the experience of the anthropologist.

NOTES

1. Francisco J. Varela, Evan Thompson, and Eleanor Rosch *The Embodied Mind* (Cambridge, Massachusetts: The MIT Press, 1992): 16–19.
2. Emily Williams Kelly, 'F.W.H. Myers and the Empirical Study of the Mind-Body Problem' in *Irreducible Mind: Toward a Psychology for the 21st Century* Edward F. Kelly, Emily Williams Kelly, Adam Crabtree, Alan Gauld, Michael Grosso and Bruce Greyson (eds.) (New York: Rowman and Littlefield, 2010): 60–64.
3. Gregory Bateson *Mind and Nature: A Necessary Unity* (New York: Bantam, 1988): 20.
4. Gregory Bateson and Mary Catherine Bateson *Angels Fear: Towards an Epistemology of the Sacred* (New Jersey: Hampton Press, [1987] 2005): 8, 64.
5. Gregory Bateson *Naven: A Survey of the Problems Suggested by a Composite Picture of the Culture of a New Guinea Tribe from Three Points of View* (Cambridge, UK: Cambridge University Press, 1936): 1–2.
6. Bateson *Naven*, 257–259.
7. Esalen 2014 webpage http://www.esalen.org, Jeffrey J. Kripal *Esalen: America and the Religion of No Religion* (Chicago: University of Chicago Press, 2007).
8. David Lipset *Gregory Bateson: The Legacy of a Scientist* (Boston: Beaon Press, 1982).
9. Bateson and Bateson *Angels*, 56.
10. C.G. Jung *The Red Book* (*Liber Novus*), edited and introduction by Sonu Shamdasani, translated by Mark Kyburz, John Peck, and Sonu Shamdasani (New York: W.W. Norton, 2009).
11. Bateson and Bateson *Angels*, 21, 37, 50.
12. Gregory Bateson *A Sacred Unity: Further Steps to an Ecology of Mind* Rodney E. Donaldson (ed.) (New York: Cornelia & Michael Bessie Book, 1991).
13. Bateson and Bateson *Angels*, 18–19.

14. Bateson and Bateson *Angels*, 18–19.
15. Bateson *Mind*, 10–11.
16. Bateson and Bateson *Angels*, passim.
17. Gregory Bateson *A Sacred Unity*, passim.
18. Bateson and Bateson *Angels*, 20.
19. Ibid., 18–19.
20. Bateson 'Foreword' to *Steps*, xi.
21. Bateson *Steps*, 129.
22. Ibid., 130.
23. Bateson *Mind*, 10–11.
24. Ibid., 13.
25. Brian Morris *Western Conceptions of the Individual* (Oxford: Berg, 1991): 11.
26. Bateson *Steps*, 135–140.
27. Ibid., 135–137.
28. Bateson *Mind*, 14.
29. Bateson *Angels*, accessed online on July 21, 2012 http://www.oikos.org/angelsfear.htm
30. Bateson and Bateson *Angels*, 20.
31. Carl Jung 'Seven Sermons to the Dead' in *The Gnostic Jung* selected and introduced by Robert A. Segal (London: Routledge, 1992): 182.
32. Jung *Red*, 370–371; C.G. Jung 'Introduction' to the *I Ching, Book of Changes*, The Richard Wilhem translation (London: Penguin Arkana, 1989): xxiii; Anthony Stevens *On Jung* (London: Penguin, 1991): 169, 266.
33. Tim Ingold *The Perception of the Environment* (London: Routledge, 2000): 16–19.
34. Ingold *Perception*, 167.
35. Peter Harries-Jones *A Recursive Vision: Ecological Understanding and Gregory Bateson* (Toronto: University of Toronto Press, 2002): 3–9, 98–99.
36. Bateson *Steps*, 139.
37. Ibid., xxiii.
38. Ibid., 237.
39. Susan Greenwood *The Anthropology of Magic* (Oxford: Berg, 2009).
40. Ingold *Perception*, 171.
41. Adam Crabtree 'Automatism and Secondary Centers of Consciousness' in *Irreducible Mind: Toward a Psychology for the 21st Century*, Edward F. Kelly, Emily Williams Kelly, Adam Crabtree, Alan Gauld, Michael Grosso and Bruce Greyson (New York: Rowman and Littlefield, 2010): 363–364.
42. Varela et al. *Embodied*, 23–26.
43. Geoffrey Samuel and Jay Johnston (eds.) *Religion and the Subtle Body in Asia and the West: Between Mind and Body* (Oxford: Routledge, 2013): 5.
44. Geoffrey Samuel *The Origins of Yoga and Tantra: Indic Religions to the Thirteenth Century* (Cambridge: Cambridge University Press, 2010): 2.
45. Samuel and Johnston *Subtle Body*, 5.
46. Geoffrey Samuel 'Panentheism and the Longevity Practices of Tibetan Buddhism' draft chapter for *The Idea of the Divine: The Panentheist Model: The Divine as Both Immanent and Transcendent* Loriliai Bernaclei and Philip Clayton (eds.) (Leiden: Brill, 2013): 91–92.
47. Samuel "Panentheism," 90–91.
48. Samuel *Origins*, 286.
49. Samuel "Panentheism," 1.
50. Ibid., 96.

Part Two

An Ethnography of Mind

5 The Anthropologist's Story
Prologue

> There come thoughts now
> knocking my heart, of the high waves,
> clashing salt-crests, I am to cross again.
> Mind-lust maddens, moves as I breathe
> soul to set out, seek out the way
> to a far folk-land flood-beyond.
> —Anonymous, Early English[1]

Placed in a bog, probably as a ritual sacrifice for the spirits of water thousands of years ago, the Iron Age wooden ship, even though it is in fragments, is the most powerful ship I have ever seen. It has a ghostly presence in the half-light; it is partly here and partly in the otherworld. I am watching the reflections of light on the protective glass in the National Museum of Denmark as people walk past or stop for a few minutes to look at the ship's construction, or ponder its meaning. I'm visiting this museum again on another research trip to Copenhagen, and this time I have just given a keynote lecture on magic to the Rethinking Shamanism Seminar organised by the University of Copenhagen's Nordic Network for Amerindian Studies. The atmosphere of the seminar's academic debates behind me, my mind slips into a magical consciousness orientation here at the museum. I start to feel patterns of connections to the invisible—the parts of the ship that are unseen guide me into a feeling of the moment. In that liminal space I can feel the ancestors who have passed that way and whose spirits call me, as reflections in the glass of the people who walk past the ship; I sense that I am bound by an ancient magical rhythm. This experience with the ghost ship in the Danish museum marks the start of my own experimental ethnography of mind. As I stared at the Iron Age ship in the Danish museum there was no contradiction of death in life—I sensed ancient ancestors in the liminal space between the living and the dead in that moment. Within the shadow of the ship, spectres of the past, images, and feelings arose, as I wrote in my notes, "The ghost ship sailed through time and space, Silently." According to Gregory Bateson, stories are "patterns of connectedness" that have meaning. These patterns of connectedness are what make up the participatory mode of magical consciousness that extends further than the individual mind. As we saw in the last chapter, Bateson saw the process of abduction, the reasoning through intuition and seeing metaphorical patterns of connections between things, as an imperceptible transparent matrix underpinning all "the stuff of which we are made." Stories, along with dreams and percepts, are "perhaps cracks and irregularities in the uniform and timeless matrix."[2] Bateson argued that thinking in terms of stories does not isolate human beings as something separate from other beings in nature, such as starfish, sea anemones, coconut palms, or primroses. Thinking in stories, he thought, must be shared by all of the mind or minds, "whether ours or those of redwood forests and sea anemones."[3] Meaning in a story is given through context. This is true of all communication, of all mental process, of all minds, "including that which tells the sea anemone how to grow and the amoeba what he should do next." There is an analogy between the context of partly conscious, personal relationships and contexts in much deeper, more archaic processes.[4] In this chapter, I shall outline the context in which I came to examine my own ethnography of mind. Anthropological fieldwork is considered to be a narrative by some anthropologists, whereby the anthropologist seeks intimate knowledge behind the scenes, behind the masks and roles, behind the generalities and abstractions, and the anthropologist's task involves finding some convincing ethnographic access to this narrative.[5] The stories that form such life narratives are built into the very being of a person through patterns and sequences of childhood experience. Past experiences are shaped and transformed through memory. In narrative, particular images are recollected, abstracted from memory's stream: memory recalls the past to the present.[6] My narrative is the form in which I experienced and organised my experience of magical consciousness.

A CHANGE OF PERCEPTION

In the silence in the Danish museum was another mode of perception; in my mind, the one suggested in Samuel Taylor Coleridge's *The Rime of the Ancient Mariner*, where the ancient mariner sees water snakes beyond the shadow of the ship. The water snakes "moved in tracks of shining white, And when they reared, the elfish light Fell off in hoary flakes." Coleridge's ancient mariner watched the snakes as they coiled and swam; their blue glossy greens and velvet blacks were like a flash of golden fire. Sensing a connection with the water snakes, it seemed, in this magical orientation, as if my sense of being had travelled forth across the waves. There in the museum, in the material world, I also felt as though my awareness was taken elsewhere. My mind seemed to cascade into other realities in my imagination. I felt as though I skimmed as a bird toward the sun, and swam with the snakes caught in the reflection of the golden light upon the sea. Having read this poem at school it had a deep resonance; something about the ship and the water snakes kindled an old memory. In a flash, I recalled a picture that had hung on my bedroom wall when I was a child—a brown-robed Saint Francis of Assisi stood with hands outstretched amid various birds, squirrels, and other wild creatures. Underneath were Coleridge's words from the same poem: "He prayeth best who loveth best all creatures great and small, for the God who made and loveth us made and loveth all." I thought about the synchronicity: this felt like an important connection linking my past with the present. In this poem the ship is in dire straits, the decks are covered in the corpses of sailors who have died of thirst, but the ancient mariner survives to tell the tale, despite the fact that his killing of an albatross was the event that caused the ship's misfortune, the dead bird having been hung around his neck as a poignant reminder.

A meaning of the poem lies in the ancient mariner's change of perception. When a spring of love gushed from his heart, he blessed the water snakes. At that moment of pure emotion, brought about by dire circumstances when faced with his mortality, the albatross fell from his neck in his recognition of a unity in the multiplicity of being; his connection with nature was restored.[7] The Danish ship in the museum seemed to encapsulate that moment of reconnection with the life and death process of nature: of Saint Francis and the animals that I had loved as a child, and particularly of snakes, which were to become important magical creatures in my imagination. The snakes seemed to embody the transition of one state of being to the next and would later open up my mind to "the dragon" as a powerful metaphor for my experience. Here, I realised, death was present in the midst of life. All I had to do was change my awareness. At that moment in the museum, I could feel the raw emotion of death in life and a unity in the multiplicity of being. It was instants like this that made me want to explore more about this magical mode of mind. The start of the process involved going from an "inside" opening of subjective perception to a more detached, objective "outside" position of the anthropologist.

My ethnography of mind narrative started with the Iron Age ship in the museum in Copenhagen and the ship and its associations became, in Bateson's terms, a little knot of connectedness that had relevance. As an anthropologist researching magical thinking, I came to understand how magical meaning was relational and depended on selection, combination, intentionality, and context. In this research, I subject my own experience of magical consciousness to a critical analysis in which the mind and matter are continuous: consciousness has a material aspect, but it is less solidly material than ordinary physical matter.[8] The specific value of emotions and affective feelings drive an intrinsic part of the magical process of expanding awareness into an environment that includes visible and non-visible properties. The spirit form of existence can then be seen in its effects on the mind of the anthropologist, whereby assumptions of divisions between inner and outer orders of experience—such as nature and culture, mental and material, material and immaterial, real and imaginal—can be suspended. Here, there is no split between what the "native" thinks and what the anthropologist as social scientist "really" thinks when informed by scientific discourse—there is no distinction between "native" and "non-native" in magical synchrony.[9]

Like every other undergraduate anthropology student, I had learned about Evans-Pritchard's classic account of the Azande's collapsing granary as an example of synchrony, but it was Jung's use of the concept of synchrony—to refer to a non-causal connecting principle when powerful psychic components are activated—that interested me. In particular, Jung's observation[10] that the ancient Chinese mind "contemplates the cosmos like a modern physicist, as a psychophysical structure," in which synchronicity refers to an interdependence of objective events and includes the subjective states of the observer.[11] Here, then, was a link between objectivity and subjectivity—one so fraught in the natural and social sciences—that I needed to engage with the dragon. It was only through coming to feel the pattern that the dragon had made in my life, unbeknownst to me at the time, that I could develop the idea of using the material for further examination in my research. I wanted to show how I had come to understand the dragon as a source of another perspective, one long obscured. And so I decided I would experience what happened to me as part of my research into magical consciousness.

MAGIC EXAMINED DIRECTLY

Over the years, as an anthropologist, I have addressed the issue of the examination of magic directly. Rather than presenting magic as some form of instrumental or emotional manipulation of esoteric forces or energies, my aim was to show magical thought processes. Having searching questions regarding the positions of women in religious traditions, a concern for the environment, and an interest in spirituality as an individual process, I initially decided to study social anthropology in the hope of finding some answers. Experiencing magic, firstly as a practitioner in a witchcraft coven and then later as an anthropologist, I discovered that by engaging with seemingly random magical feeling states that they had an emotional and sensory presence that was not at all random. Rather than being odd or rather bizarre single occurrences, these affective states formed patterns of synchronous meanings that came to have deep relevance. I developed the term *magical consciousness* as a form of shorthand to describe the mode of awareness that then predominated. The problem was that I could not integrate my own experience of magic with my more objective anthropological data. As the previous chapters in this volume seek to explain, two very different mind-body orientations were at work, and a theoretical framework of explanation allowing for both was sadly lacking. This lack, however, has provided the necessary spur for this collaborative project.

As we have described in earlier chapters, magical consciousness is a diffuse and associative mytho-poetic mode of mind, characterised by a sense of permeability of the boundaries between material and non-material perceptions of reality. It is a mode of thinking that is present to varying degrees in everyday thinking, though it often goes unnoticed. As we have shown, however, thinking of causation in terms of "who" rather than "what" is a kind of magical thinking. We have even seen how it can be shown as the inevitable conclusion of analytical thought when one takes subjective, conscious experience seriously. Rarely, however, is this kind of thinking acknowledged, or spelled out with any degree of specificity or clarity, except to dismiss it as not valuable.

ENCOUNTERS WITH AN "OTHERWORLD"

My increasing academic involvement with magical consciousness developed slowly. It started with my doctoral research, undertaken during the 1990s. In this work, I sought to create communication between scholarly analysis and the magical spirit panoramas of my informants, who were initially British witches and ceremonial magicians. An ultimate objective was to examine encounters with "the otherworld," a non-material, anomalous reality that was difficult to articulate using conventional social scientific frameworks that tended toward reductive, materialistic explanations. I chose not to look primarily at the rationality of magic, or the instrumentality of such thought, and instead, my research concentrated on the examination of the dynamic process of magical thinking. This aspect of a living anthropology, says Paul Stoller in his work with Songay sorcerers, can transform our conceptions of who we are, what we know, and how we apprehend the world.[12] If we fail to acknowledge the contingency of experience, we avoid the indeterminacies of the between—the ambiguities, the tangential experience, and the sensuous processes of our bodies—but if we do accept the contingency of experience, we present ourselves fully in the vortex of "the between," and we demand a fuller sensual awareness.[13] By moving into a more holistic perceptual awareness that incorporates all of life, including the emotions and dimensions of spirit, my hope has been to open up another conception of magic.

Along with the work of Bateson, Lévy-Bruhl's notion of participation as a social psychological perception of the world based on a mystical mentality, the emotional association between persons and things in contact with a non-ordinary spirit reality,[14] was especially helpful in this research. In sum, the concept of participation involves a holistic orientation that makes affective connections and associations with a non-material dimension. An early example of my own participatory attitude is of an occasion when I was standing in a long queue to pay at the checkout of a multi-national chain store. It seemed to take forever to be served. As I was waiting, I idly studied the advertising display in front of me. And then, something in my mind seemed to shift. Looking through the display, I sensed that I was going back in time. Looking upwards, I noticed the old elaborate plaster coving on the ceiling of the shop, a remnant from a bygone age. The decorative plaster had only been partly concealed by the advertisement and it was still possible to see the original ceiling of the building.

Different feelings came flooding into my mind—I felt like I was participating in several places at once and in varying realities. I seemed to be able to feel through time. It was a strange moment, as my ears gently buzzed and my awareness expanded and I felt connected; I was participating in something that felt both larger and beyond. Afterwards, I interpreted the experience as an awareness arising from my subconsciousness, behind and beyond an ordinary, everyday, more analytical perception. I gave this perception the name of "the dragon," as a form of shorthand for the whole body occurrence.

THE DRAGON

In essence, the perception of the dragon had a physical reality through my body and actions in the world.[15] Of course, I did not physically become a dragon—I did not somehow manifest into a fire-breathing monster—but nevertheless, the dragon had a form of corporeal as well as imaginal reality. I experienced it as a dance of synchronous interaction, among other things. This is what shaped what I have come to understand as the dragon, that aspect of me that remains connected and capable of transformation. As we can see, the dragon is itself only something that can be fully perceived when contemplating the world as a whole through the magical modality of thought. Within the concept of the dragon, we can see the abstract qualities of whole-making, intentionality, unity-in-multiplicity, and "shape-shifting," the blurring of subject and object, which are characteristic of magical thought. That is what the dragon "looks like" when viewed in the analytical mode. Tim Ingold points to the tendency in modern Western societies to detach dragons from reality. Rather than being a part of real life, they are carefully separated off in an imaginary, non-real world. A troubled sleeper who has a nightmare of a dragon may be calmed by the phrase, "It's only a dream," and then the boundary between the imagination and the real world is reassuringly restored. This historical separation of imagination from everyday life was, according to Ingold, achieved during the religious upheavals of the Reformation and the development of early modern science. As an early scientific pioneer in the seventeenth century, Francis Bacon railed against traditional ways of knowing that continually mixed up the reality of the world with its configurations in human minds. For Bacon, the mind distorted images. The result was that the realms of the imagination and reality were not to be confused. This separation has had lasting effects and the imagination has been "left to float like a mirage, shorn of its creative impulse."[16] When viewed in the magical mode, however, the dragon takes on all of these qualities, but also retains its ineffable quality—a quality that cannot be completely characterised in the analytical mode because that is not the purview of the analytical mode. Like qualia, the analytical mode comes to the limits of its powers when it reaches the irreducible whole, the ineffable quale, and the unity-in-multiplicity of participation and the inter-projection of the self. It also retains its essential aspect of the "mind"— causality becomes shaped by mentality rather than mechanism, and the dragon retains its "thought," its ability to choose, its awareness, and its intent—these are qualities that cannot be captured by the analytical mode, which simply proclaims that such qualities do not exist.

I came to make dragon associations in my mind. When I first started my anthropological fieldwork, I had a dream that went something like this: In the dream, a friend handed me a basket that another friend had given her. I took the basket and removed the embroidered flowery lid; a white snake rapidly unwound itself from inside the basket and sprang out upon me. It fastened its fangs into my arm . . . I awoke feeling that it was a very profound experience. Being bitten by a white snake in the dream seemed like a form of initiation to me. I did not know what the experience meant then, but more recently, I came to realise that it was a stirring of the dragon as a sort of elemental awakening. The dream took me back to memories of my childhood. I had kept grass snakes as pets and was captivated by their beautiful, smooth, zigzag patterned bodies, and their abilities to glide across the ground and swim through water. I loved letting them slide over my arms and legs as I watched their black forked tongues flicking neatly in and out as they smelt the air. I was also fascinated by earthworms and spent time playing in the wild and overgrown end of the garden. Uncovered all year, the sand pit became the home of all sorts of wildlife: from millipedes and woodlice to wriggly ginger wireworms, but most especially for earthworms. I watched how they changed shape by contracting and then extending their bodies, and how they gradually transformed the sand and the earth in the sand pit. Snakes and worms share some of the dragon's qualities of transformation: snakes shed their skins, representing cosmic renewal and rebirth following death; worms transform the earth. It was Charles Darwin who noted that worms are better at tilling the soil than us; they swallow the earth, ejecting what they do not need for nutriment in a fine tilth that cannot be matched by human ploughing. The message from this dream was that some form of transformation had started, as I synchronously recalled during my time with the Iron Age ghost ship in the Danish museum.

Coming to comprehend these participatory connections, I gradually came to discover more about the process that was occurring. I realised that I was having a strong emotional connection with nature, and also that I was being able to sense a non-material quality or feeling of spirit. As time went on—as I was trying to express the feelings with a more analytical approach as well as a direct experiential immersion—it felt imperative to name the sensations. I came to consider these collective experiences as "the dragon," and I devised ways of their further unraveling. Initially, the dragon was a feeling that started with a sense of awe in nature; it was not simply an objective symbol, or a logically based classificatory metaphor, or a recognizable, material dragon artefact. In my mind, it emphatically did not represent a simple, literal understanding of some monstrous beast, although I was to find out that it did have monstrously terrifying qualities. The dragon that I was experiencing was more complex.

Being the mainstay of many fantastic encounters in myth, legend, folktales, film, fiction, and theatre, dragons are part of popular culture all over the world, especially in China, where they are the potent, auspicious symbols of fertility and immortality. Here, dragons have a multiplicity of forms, sometimes with a horse's head and a snake's tail, or a camel's head with stag's horns and the eyes of a demon; alternatively, a dragon might have the neck of a snake, belly of a clam, carp scales, eagle claws, soles of a tiger, and the ears of a cow. However, the dragon in Western societies has a chequered past, and its power has come to be seen as something rather contradictory. Vanquished by Saint George, this dragon is a fearful, evil force to be destroyed, as encapsulated in rather stereotyped images of the saint rescuing a maiden in distress from the clutches of a reptilian monster. The dragon has also been portrayed as a symbol for good, for instance, in popular the Merlin and King Arthur stories, in which it is pitched against malevolent forces. Dragons, it seems, can represent many things to many people, and the dragon that I felt was all of these and more.

"The dragon" for me came to represent an alternative perception that I associated with the process of magical thinking. In my continuing quest for the sensory experience of the dragon I would have to search the between, the non-manifesting, internal links of the associations shaped by intuition and synchrony. As my research progressed, my initial feeling of the dragon as a participatory force of nature came to be more formalised through my fieldwork research amongst British practitioners of magic. Pagans generally refer to the dragon as an underground-dwelling, winged serpent symbolic of the elements of earth, air, fire, and water, as well as spirit. The dragon is a positive life force that has been repressed by Christianity, and is more akin to the Chinese and Japanese portrayals. The dragon became a participatory being residing in the relationships between one thing and another in my mind. Chameleon-like, it could not only change from creature to creature, transmuting into many things, but was a raw, primal, participatory force of nature running through all. The multifarious nature of the dragon seemed to represent well the complex of emotions and sensory experiences that I was having. Being also drawn to the Australian aboriginal mythological idea of time as an ancestral serpent that linked all life though its breath, I came to feel the dragon as a being of many manifestations and possibilities that could move through time and space. To experience this ancestral being, I felt that it was imperative to be able to dream, to enter the equivalent of a mythological dreamtime. The dragon represented a feeling state, a participatory association that would guide my research into what seemed like distant deeps and skies of the imaginative and synchronous worlds of magic. The dragon entity, it seemed, had been lurking in my subconscious since childhood, but it was only when I came to deliberately examine the process of magical thought that it seemed to make itself manifest. It appeared that my awareness of this entity emerged gradually, much as a tendril of dragon smoke. The more I became involved in thinking about the connections and associations of participatory magical thinking, the more I knew that I recognised magical worldviews from much earlier in my life.

WRITING THE DRAGON NARRATIVE

Beginning to see another dimension to my academic work, one that was becoming increasingly hard to write about, I came to the awareness that I was making all sorts of synchronous connections that seemed to be telling their own story. A central characteristic of participation is that affective connections and associations with a non-material dimension come through a language of a story, and in time, my exploration of my "data" on the dragon led me to write about the encounter as a narrative. When I decided to open myself up to the experience of the dragon, my objective, in academic terms, was to further research on a participatory aspect of human cognition as it melded with the non-human and non-material. As my awareness of the dragon gradually increased, this spirit being seemed to come through me as a distinct presence. Like analytical thought, magical thought rewards practice. Eventually, I started to grasp its fuller significance. Subsequently, I came to understand the dragon as an entity that was simultaneously of me and not of me. I wanted to explore the possibility that this non-material being had decided to work through me, for whatever reason. It was only though coming to understand the pattern that the dragon had made in my life that I could really develop the concept of magical consciousness. In so doing, I discovered that it was methodologically important to pay attention to moments that might be overlooked during more conventional fieldwork, and to develop sensitivity to subtleties for working with such entities. By temporarily holding in abeyance my analytical, classifying mind for the duration of the interaction, I could start to make sense of this communication.

As to why the dragon had shown itself to me, I could only guess. Perhaps it was due to my rather lonely childhood, during which I had formed close attachments to nature rather than any organised religious affiliation, or maybe because as an anthropologist, I was working with altered states of consciousness and was open to this sort of otherworldly mediation, or even because some people are more sensitive to spiritual communication from non-material realms than others. At this stage, I could only speculate. I started writing thoughts and meditations down in the format of a narrative. In the physical production of words—on the computer screen and in my body-mind through meditation—these themes became woven into the story of my life. As I wrote, they seemed to take on a life of their own through a stream of consciousness, a type of intimate recording of the everyday minutiae of life made popular by Virginia Woolf, especially in her novel *Mrs Dalloway*. This mode of writing, so different to the formal academic style, seemed to reach different parts of my awareness and my memory. I did not want to write objectively, as this would destroy the subjective experience of magic, which I slowly came to realise was central to its understanding. A pressing question was how to write about my own experience of the dragon. My reflexive approach to fieldwork had a big impact on my writing, presenting me with a challenge. I had recorded in the introduction to *The Nature of Magic* that Virginia Woolf had once written that the main thing in beginning a novel was not to feel that you could write it, but that it existed on the far side of a gulf that words could not cross. This was a little how I felt about writing about magical consciousness. It existed "out there," but I also knew that it connected with something deep within, too.

I knew that magical consciousness existed—intuitively, I had known about this as a child—but trying to put it into words was like crossing a chasm or an abyss to bring the meaning through, and then only incompletely. The problem was how to express the inexpressible, or what psychologist William James famously termed "the ineffable." Woolf thought that the novel had to be "pulled through in breathless anguish," but when I was writing that book—during one seemingly mad summer—it felt not as though I was pulling it through but that it was creating itself through me. Surely, I wrote at the time, no one admits to writing anthropological fieldwork in this way, this approach is much too subjective[17] (although I later read that Tim Ingold, in his introduction to his *Lines* book, wrote that he was not sure if it was him writing his Rhind lectures or the Rhind lectures writing him).[18] Woolf had said that words are full of echoes and associations, stored with meanings and memories. She sought to create change through words, seeing them as being created anew through being out and about in the streets, fields, and everyday life in a will o' the wisp form of a stream of consciousness. This seemed to resonate with my experience of the dragon. I also sought to create change, a change in attitude, that allows a more open approach to the social scientific study of magic in all its dimensions—social, political, psychological, and also incorporating a non-material and ecological aspect.

The participatory patterns form stories that have individual, social, and cultural meanings that can be conjured through relationships, as Tim Ingold notes in his *Lines* study, "Here the weaving of "relation" has to be understood quite literally, not as a connection between prelocated entities but as a path traced through the terrain of lived experiences."[19] Every relation forms part of a meshwork of interwoven trails. Telling stories concerns a process of relating the past and creating the new, "To tell a story, then, is to *relate*, in narrative, the occurrences of the past, retracing a path through the world that others, recursively picking up the treads of past lives, can follow in the process of spinning their own."[20] The lines of the narrative might be seen as metaphorical threads, roots, rhizomes, or fungal mycelia; they take us to the underworld and internal and external psyche of magical participation, a many-layered manifold of different aspects of knowing. These are the storylines or song lines woven through myths that connect people with the landscape, with temporal, human, and non-human relationships, like a quivering aspen grove. Aspen trees are clonal organisms that grow from a single-root network that can be literally tens of thousands of years old. They thrive on forest fires, which clear out everything and make way for new aspen trees to grow. Meanwhile, the root network survives, in some cases up to a million years by some estimates.

My relationship with the dragon was a communication with an imaginal spirit entity. Of course, this raised the anthropological dilemma of a belief in spirits: they might exist in people's imaginations, but not in reality—it was not really "real." I had realised from my previous work that when a person is experiencing magical consciousness, it makes no difference whether they believe in spirits or not. It does not matter how the experience is labelled, it is the experience itself that is important. This is another aspect of magical thinking that is important to remember: only the analytical mode is occupied by a quest for "objective" truth. This is because the essentially blurred nature of subject and object in magical consciousness obscures the meaning of "subjective" and "objective" contents of thought. Because subject and object become identified and the self becomes diffused across the universe in the magical mode of thought, the concept of objectivity becomes incoherent. This occurrence is merely a logical consequence of the fact that, in the magical mode, indexicality is blurred; it is not "I" that experiences something that may or may not be objectively true "out there." Rather, I-it-they "is experienced." Experiences occur to the manifold-in-unity. This is why the idea of subjective belief and objective truth becomes incoherent in the magical mode.

Once this essential fact of the way belief is comprehended in these two modalities is understood, we can see how misguided the application of rigorous logical, analytical, self-other boundaries to magical thought really is. It results in large-scale category errors. This realisation, of course, does not diminish the idea of a true and false belief in a well-defined subject. It merely modifies it: beliefs can only be true or false when undergirded by a stabilising framework of analytical self-other boundaries. As the self-other boundary is an important tool for rigorous analytical thought, it is not negated or destroyed by the existence of another mode of thought in which such boundaries simply do not exist. Rather, it simply provides a complementary set of ordered relations. This resolves the quandary of belief—it becomes non-relevant to concern oneself about it in the magical mode because experience is simply experience. It only becomes "real" or "imaginary/hallucinatory/etc." when one returns back to the analytical mode and evaluates the experience from that standpoint. As ever, we argue that a balance between these modes is the ideal human position. We argue that a more comprehensive understanding of human experience values both modes and applies them each in their appropriate context—magical thinking is not appropriate for solving engineering problems or physics equations, and analytical thinking reaches its limits when approaching the ineffable qualia of experience, religious or altered states, or when facing the greatest and most terrifying existential realities, such as death and eternity, realities which are universal to all humankind.

Thus, it matters not a jot if spirit communications are categorised as psychological—if they are explained as a part of a person's own internal thought processes—or whether the non-material entities communicated with are considered to be independent, with a spirit being and existence of their own. Whilst participating in a magical aspect of consciousness the question of belief is irrelevant: "belief" is not a necessary condition to communicate with an inspirited world.[21] How this communication is viewed by the person themselves, and their culture, is another matter of course. For my work, however, questions of belief or the reality or non-reality of spirits, while themselves interesting, are a "straightjacket" for an alternative perception afforded by communication with non-material entities. The issue for me was one of a different perception.

During an experience of magical consciousness it feels like spirits share a degree of corporeal materiality and possess mind. I reasoned that the minds of entities—in whatever form—and ours could meet in a wider consciousness. "The problem" of understanding an inspirited world is one of our own Western, scientific making, as the evidenced alternative conceptions show. One such example is in Tibetan Buddhist philosophy, where spiritual power is seen to pervade the universe[22], as described in the previous chapter. Of course, we know that this was a view common before Descartes. Aristotle, for instance, thought the soul was equivalent to the psyche—it was the principle of life that animates. This view was one that William Blake tried to re-invoke on the cusp of the scientific revolution. Harking back to the earlier view, Blake, who "saw through his eyes, not with them,"[23] envisioned a world in which every creature was an inspirited person living within the total freedom of its Imagination.[24]

I reminded myself time and time again that the view that all of life is infused with spirit, soul, and consciousness was common in the ancient world prior to the dawning development of the rationalising scientific worldview of Blake's time. Recall, however, that this essentially panpsychic perspective rested at the end of even so analytical a thinker as David Chalmers as noted in Chapter 2. Panpsychism is a basically magical approach—it is therefore interesting that it was a very natural possibility resulting from a very simple principle: a commitment to taking subjective conscious experience seriously and non-reductively.

The period from the seventeenth century to the present in the Western world seemed to me as just a "blip in time" and one that could be transformed again—not back to some so-called Golden Age, but as a paradigm change for a broader conception of consciousness that integrated a spirit dimension. In this respect, I came to be very inspired by Blake's work; it seemed to take me back to a place of what he would call a child-like innocence, one that has been described. Deciding to write using poetry and a stream of consciousness style to "bracket" my analytical thinking, I tried to access the participatory and synchronous language of magic working through the themes the dragon had conveyed to me.

NOTES

1. *The First Poems in English* translated by Michael Alexander (London: Penguin, 2008): 56.
2. Gregory Bateson *Mind and Nature: A Necessary Unity* (New York: Bantam, 1988):13–14.
3. Ibid., 14.
4. Ibid., 15–16.
5. Anthony P. Cohen and Nigel Rapport 'Introduction' in *Questions of Consciousness* (ASA Monographs 33) Anthony P. Cohen and Nigel Rapport (eds.) (London: Routledge, 1995): 7–9.
6. Ibid., 7–9.
7. Gregory Bateson and Mary Catherine Bateson *Angels Fear: Towards an Epistemology of the Sacred* (New Jersey: Hampton Press, [1987] 2005): 74.
8. Geoffrey Samuel and Jay Johnston *Religion and the Subtle Body in Asia and the West: Between Mind and Body* Geoffrey Samuel and Jay Johnston (eds.) (Oxford: Routledge, 2013): 1.
9. Kirin Narayan 'How Native Is a 'Native Anthropologist?' *American Anthropologist* (New Series) 95(3) (Sep. 1993): 671–686.
10. *I Ching*, Richard Wilhem translation (London: Penguin Arkana, 1989): xxiii.
11. Anthony Stevens *On Jung* (London: Penguin, 1991): xxiv.
12. Paul Stoller *The Power of the Between: An Anthropological Odyssey* (Chicago: University of Chicago Press, 2009): 4.
13. Ibid., 33.
14. Quoted in Stanley Tambiah *Magic, Science, Religion and the Scope of Rationality* (Cambridge: Cambridge University Press, 1991): 91; Lucien Lévy-Bruhl *The Notebooks on Primitive Mentality* of Lucien Lévy-Bruhl, Peter Riviere (trans.) (Oxford: Basil Blackwell, 1975).
15. Susan Greenwood 'Toward an Epistemology of Imaginal Alterity: Fieldwork with the Dragon' in The *Social Life of Spirits* Diana Espirito Santo and Ruy Blanes (eds.) (Chicago: University of Chicago Press, 2014): 6–7, 12.
16. Tim Ingold 'Dreaming of Dragons: On the Imagination of Real Life' *Journal of the Royal Anthropological Institute* 19 (2013): 735–736.
17. Susan Greenwood *The Nature of Magic: An Anthropology of Consciousness* (Oxford: Berg, 2005): xii.
18. Tim Ingold *Lines: A Brief History* (London: Routledge, 2007): x–xi.
19. Ibid., 90.
20. Ibid.

21. Susan Greenwood *The Anthropology of Magic* (Oxford: Berg, 2009): 140.
22. Geoffrey Samuel 'Panentheism and the Longevity Practices of Tibetan Buddhism' in *Panentheism Across the World's Traditions* Loriliai Biernacki and Philip Clayton (eds.) (New York: Oxford University Press, 2013).
23. Gregory Bateson 'Foreword, 1971' to *Steps to an Ecology of Mind* (Chicago: University of Chicago Press, [1972] 2000): xxi.
24. Kathleen Raine *Golgonooza: city of Imagination* (Ipswich, Suffolk: Golgonooza Press, 1991): 11–12.

6   Looking Into the River

There are no peoples however primitive without religion and magic. Nor are there, it must be added at once, any savage races lacking either in scientific attitude or in science, though this lack has been frequently attributed to them.

—Malinowski[1]

The first Great Western train travelling from London to Totnes, a small town on the estuary of the River Dart in Devon, meandered its way along the coastline of the Jurassic south coast of England. Sitting in a window seat watching the coastline zigzag in and out of view, I was on my way to visit Jardani,[2] a Gypsy *chovihano*, for a shamanic healing ritual. I had first seen Jardani, a small, dark man of around forty with a twinkling smile and a red kerchief around his neck, when he was talking about his healing work to a group of academics at a conference on Shamanism held by the University of Newcastle, in northeast England. Listening to his account of his shamanic healing work, I was intrigued in the light of what I already knew about Gypsy culture. I wanted to find out more for my research on British practitioners of magic and their relationships with nature. Jardani and I spoke briefly after his talk and exchanged contact details. During the course of our exchange of lengthy letters, I told him how I felt cut off from my ancestors, and we discussed the importance of ancestors and spiritual healing. When Jardani offered me a shamanic healing ritual, I decided to take him up on his offer, hence my trip to Totnes.

Having done some preparatory reading, I knew that Gypsies were a diverse wandering people of Hindu origin from the north of India, and that they had absorbed many cultural influences in their travels before arriving in Europe in the fourteenth century. I also knew about the romantic fascination that many people have for their nomadic wandering life, as well as the fear and dislike that they engender in some people. Being already familiar with the work of Victorian writer Charles Godfrey Leland (1824–1903), who had written on witchcraft, and knowing that he had also written on Gypsies, I had searched out his book *Gypsy Sorcery and Fortune Telling*, first published in 1891. I discovered that Leland saw the Gypsies as priests of a practical peasant religion of the "old faith" of witchcraft. Although I was aware that Leland's interest came from a romantic and stereotyped view of Gypsies, this nevertheless fascinated me. I had also read the work of the English author of novels and travelogues George Borrow (1803–1881), who was not immune to such stereotyping too. Borrow developed a lifelong empathy with wandering Gypsy nomads, and, being a bit of a wanderer himself, visited their encampments in London, Spain, and Russia. He wrote that Gypsies awakened feelings that were hard to describe. I felt that I had something to learn about magic and these hard-to-describe feelings. Deciding to take my own experience of magic further in my research, I felt I was indeed flowing alongside the sea towards another part of my life; a part that I would discover helped connect me with something vital to my increasing understanding of magic, and particularly shamanism.

Taking shamanism as a general term for "the regulation and transformation of human life and human society through the use (or purported use) of alternate states of consciousness by means of which specialist practitioners are held to communicate with a mode of reality alternative to, and more fundamental than, the world of everyday experience,"[3] I had found that this concept and practice aligned closely with my research on the experience of magic. It also gave my work a potentially panhuman focus, the notion of "shamanism" being seen to relate both to Western and non-Western peoples. Indeed, the shamanic healing ritual that I was about to experience would introduce me to something fundamental about magic. It would not only reconnect me with one of my ancestors, but also help me make connections that would later have great magical significance. I would come to the realisation that some notion that transcends the physical body in time and space, and beyond and between lifetimes, is indeed essential to thinking magically due to the fact that it is the core element of relational and participatory awareness. Above all, this experience would show me how much magic is, at its most fundamental, an emotional, personal experience.

Here, in my participant observation of the ritual, I had to intentionally open myself up to the emotion. I had to knowingly become receptive to the notion that spirits can flow through a body, and in the process bring a change in perception. It was through becoming more open to this exercise that my relationship with the spirit of my grandfather became real, and how I subsequently came to make associations with horses, snakes, and finally, the dragon. As Susanne Langer pointed out in her *Philosophy in a New Key*, a study of symbolism first published in 1942, "The limits of thought are not so much set from outside, by the fullness or poverty of experiences that meet the mind, as from within, by the power of conception, the wealth of formulative notions with which the mind meets experiences. Most new discoveries are suddenly seen things that were always there."[4] The experiences that resulted from the healing ritual with Jardani certainly did seem as if they had always been there, but that somehow I had come to disbelieve in a childhood sense of magic, or forgotten how to access it.

* * *

Jardani was waiting at Totnes railway station. As the train pulled in I saw him standing on the platform. Dressed in a sweatshirt and jeans, he did not look out of the ordinary. On closer inspection though, I saw that he did have a slightly otherworldly, elfish, or *bitte foki* (little folk) look to him, as he had a mischievous face that crumpled into a grin at the slightest opportunity. He told me later that it was the fact that he had a slight squint and a hand turned the wrong way when he was born that had marked him out by his family as a future *chovihano*—a person who would form a special communication with the spirits. Such marks are pointers towards a shaman's vocation in many shamanic cultures. Instantly I felt at home as we made our way a short distance up the hill to the flat in a converted brewery that he shared with Maggie, his partner at the time and *patrinyengri*, or herbalist assistant. Our conversation was relaxed, and I felt it was easy to chat about magic; there was much laughter and I was told that the Gypsies were a child-like, fun-loving people.

A short time after my arrival at the *chovihano's* flat, we started my healing ritual by sprinkling salt around and over us as protection against bad spirits. Red wool, also for protection, was tied to our wrists and also hung from the frame of Jardani's tambourine. Maggie waved a *ran*, a birch wand, decorated with a painted green vine interspersed with gold and silver dots representing the otherworld; the small bells tied to the end tinkled to keep away bad spirits. I knew that shamanic practitioners do not understand the magical world in terms of good and evil, but they do consider there to be good and bad spirits. It is important to know which is which. I have come to understand bad spirits as not being evil in themselves, but rather as "beings out of place." It is the *chovihano's* job, like any shamanic healer, to sort out which spirits should be where. The three of us sat around a single candle flame that flickered as we gently rocked in tune with the rhythm of the Gypsy's tambourine. All three of us gradually moved deeper into a trance and the air became thick with emotion. The sound of the jingling wand permeated the atmosphere. A white goose feather and a black crow feather sat on either side of the candle to represent light and dark, and a glass and a bottle of whisky was placed alongside. This whisky was for the Ancestor, the Gypsy's ancestral spirit guide, when he arrived in spirit through the *chovihano's* body.

The Ancestor, speaking through the *chovihano*, started talking about the spirits of sickness as he sipped the glass of whisky that had been poured for him:

> The spirits of sickness these days are very comfortable. They know what they can do, they know what they can achieve; they know all the tricks.

So it's a matter of breaking all this down and making them realise that they can't stay here because this life cannot sustain them. They will be far better off going somewhere where they can be as they want to be.

It is the modern attitude that allows the spirits of sickness to invade people; it is this attitude that sees everything as a part of a whole, whereas by comparison, the old Romani way sees the spirits as separate and external to the self:

The modern attitude to the spirits of sickness is not a healthy one; sounds quite funny when I say that [laughter]. You need to start to see yourself as being independent from them, so that they can realise they're not a part of you. The spirits of sickness do not realise that they're attacking you; they are such a part of you. They fit quite comfortably; this is their home.

A change needs to be made, and it is important to see them as being very separate spirits. The Ancestor advised, "Start externalizing these sicknesses that you have and start understanding that they do have their own beings." The Ancestor started speaking kindly but sternly to me:

The way I see your soul, if you'll allow me to say this, is that your soul is busy looking into the river but not at its own reflection. Your own reflection is crying out and is saying, "Look at me, look at me."

The *chovihano* was channeling his spirit ancestor to heal me of my soul loss. My task was to find my soul. Using the rhythm of the tambourine to go into a trance, the *chovihano*, as he later explained to me, had allowed his own everyday identity to become malleable—like a doughnut with a hole in the middle—thus providing a space for the Ancestor to come through. The *chovihano* rocked backwards and forwards, going deeper and deeper into a trance as the Ancestor inhabited his body. His visage and tone of voice changed and I sensed a distinct presence in the room. The Ancestor, via the *chovihano's* body, placed his hand on my head and commanded the spirits of sickness to depart—they were told to find their own place and to leave me. The Ancestor continued:

You need to look into the river and see your own reflection . . . That is not simply a Romani way, that is the way of all souls . . . Your soul is what you're looking for.

In many shamanic traditions there is a notion of a whole soul; spirits of sickness cannot invade whole souls. In my case, the Ancestor told me that I had spent too much time looking at other souls and that this was why the spirits of sickness had found their way into me. My soul was looking at the reflections of others and seeing their suffering and it was crying out for my attention, for it was lost to me. Here, deep in the heart of this magical ritual, my own soul loss was being reflected back to me. But what was my soul and how had I lost it? I had become disconnected with a part of myself.

When the Ancestor had had his say, and had drunk his whisky, it was time for him to retreat back into the otherworld. He said his goodbyes, saying how fond he was of us all. The whole process seemed to be part of an everyday occurrence, as though an elderly and respected relative had just dropped in for a quick drink and a chat. The *chovihano* lay down on the floor while the Ancestor was departing and after a few minutes, Jardani returned to join in the ordinary conversation that had started after. There was a minimum of fuss as the candle was gently blown out amid laughing and general good humour as we continued talking into the night.

Communicating in this way with the spirit of the ancestors opened my awareness. I knew that I would have to open myself up to the experience emotionally; otherwise, I would not learn what I needed to about magic. Most importantly, it made me focus on the soul, or spirit essence of a person, as opposed to the physicality of the body, as a central component of a magical perspective. A participatory pattern of connections was starting to form in my mind as glimmerings of awareness, gradually gaining in more clarity.

The following day Jardani, Maggie, and I walked down into the pretty Devon town of Totnes. En route, Jardani stopped at a birch tree growing by the side of the road and talked to it, as was his usual habit. Gypsies have an animistic worldview in which everything is alive and has consciousness, and so everything can be spoken to—from the trees in the road to the kettle as it is boiling to make the everyday cups of tea. This birch tree in particular was special to Jardani. He would chat to it each time he passed, asking it how it was, and filling it in on any news. On this occasion, he introduced me to the tree and asked its permission to take one of its small sprouting twigs that were growing from its base. Cutting off one such thicker twig with his penknife, he presented it to me as a gift from the tree. Later, he decorated the end with red wool and it became my own *ran*, or birch wand. It was a special moment and I sensed a real magical connection with Jardani and Maggie, as well as the birch tree.

A few days later, ten people, mostly academics from the Newcastle shamanism conference, were arriving for a ritual to celebrate the eclipse of the sun by the moon, an important moment in Gypsy legend. I stayed on to experience the ritual too. In Romani mythology, Gypsies were born of the mating between brother *Kam*, who became father sun, and sister *Shon*, who became mother moon, during an eclipse. Jardani told us that this was our ancestral family, informing us that *Kam* and *Shon* loved and would look after us, and that all our ancestors welcomed us. This time in the ritual, the group had a very deep effect on me and I realised my ancestral connections—both with my blood relatives, especially my grandfather, but also my relationship with the natural world, as expressed through the sun, moon, and particularly the birch tree from which my little wand had come, and all birch trees.

The Romani ritual was an expression of cyclical time as seen through a connection with ancestors located in the natural world, as a family. The sun was a small boy in the morning, a young man during the eclipse when he mates with the moon as a young woman, and he dies at night before being reborn the next morning. During the eclipse, the sky was grandfather and the earth grandmother to their incestuous children. The transition of the sun during the day is a common theme in various mythologies. In Egyptian mythology, for example, the sun god Ra sails his boat across the sky during the day, before sailing through the underworld at night to rise again to the sky each morning, and this is a similar pattern to that indicated by Scandinavian rock carvings made thousands of years ago (to which I will return in Chapter 14). According to Jardani, brother sun and sister moon grow during the course of the day into a young man and young woman, and mate during the eclipse before the rising and dying order of the sun is returned. The eclipse is therefore an extremely potent magical time.

Previously, I felt that I did not have any spiritual connection with my ancestors, but through my healing ritual and the eclipse ritual I did start to get a sense of a magical world opening up. I kept in touch with Jardani, and some months later, I came to further develop my relationship with my grandfather.

* * *

During some Gypsy Hallowe'en trance journeying, or "spirit travelin'" as the Gypsies used to call it, I met my grandfather in spirit, Hallowe'en being a time when ancestors are said to come close. Jardani and Maggie had moved from Devon to East Sussex in the intervening time and they held a group shamanic journey at their house, a cottage belonging to a local farmer and surrounded by fields. Six of us—all of whom had, in one way or another, been involved with Jardani—were going to experience some more trance work on this Saturday morning. There was a relaxed atmosphere as we sat down on the floor around a candle and Jardani told us about how the Gypsies saw the otherworld as shapeless—it had different heights, sises, and directions, and shifted from one form into another; it was also timeless and was an "expansion of mind." The otherworld formed a different reality to that of the ordinary, everyday reality. It was the realm of the imagination and it was real; it had a life of its own and was not just fantasy. Jardani explained that otherworldly spirits did not always use words, but could use signs, language, music, writing, or feelings to communicate, and that in days gone by, the group would help to interpret a person's experience of the otherworld. For the Romanis, there was a special road or *drom* to the otherworld, and this world of everyday reality was only a temporary home—human spirits were "only passing through this civilization." Jardani's portrayal of the otherworld had simplicity and he encouraged us to be child-like in our understanding of it—it was expressed in uncomplicated everyday language as ordinary as bread and butter. We were encouraged to accept its child-like straightforwardness. I knew that I would have to immerse myself fully into it if I was to understand the experience to the best of my ability.

That evening, we were going to journey to the "edge of the world" in our imaginations. Although we were told that this journey nevertheless had a reality, it was not "just our imagination" as something "unreal," an issue to which I will return in Chapters 9 and 12. We were handed a tarot pack and told to draw a card to give us information for our journey. I drew the Death card; there was an image of a skeleton carrying a scythe, a symbol of the Grim Reaper. This card is usually interpreted to mean that the end of one life stage is occurring in preparation for the next; it does not always represent physical death, but it could mean physical death too. I even felt a bit afraid, although I would come to understand later that fear was important for opening up my emotions. I was familiar with using tarot cards from my research and was learning to understand their symbolic significance. The cards seemed to tell me that I had to make changes in my life, but before that could happen, I had to let go of the present.

Jardani and Maggie prepared us for our trance journey by asking us to lie down on the floor, close our eyes, and open up our imaginative inner world. We had to observe ourselves as the spirit was leaving our body—"turn around and look at your body, touch it, and then walk out of the door, or through the wall, leaving your body sitting there." We were told to go in our imaginations to a familiar place—to the end of a walk with which we were familiar. To go out of the house along the road to the "end of the known" and then somersault—leap in the air around and around, or spin round and round. Jardani, as the *chovihano*, would help us on our way through by shaking his tambourine; he would call us back to everyday reality by changing its rhythm. I followed the instructions in my journey.

In my imagination, I walked out of Jardani and Maggie's house down the lane that we had all walked down the previous evening in material reality, past an oak tree that was a special magical tree, and to the point in the lane beyond which we had not gone in the physical world, where it was no longer familiar. I did a somersault and then waited for something to happen. The Death tarot card came into my mind, and eventually, a skeleton with a dark cloak came as my spirit guide. We travelled through space and into nothingness—there was complete sensory deprivation in my journey. I had left everything behind. Then I remembered that I was supposed to take out the sacred objects found from a previous trance journey on Friday evening as preparation for the weekend's trance work. I had found a sand egg timer, a seagull feather, and a strange fruit during the course of my journey, but my spirit guide told me that they meant absolutely nothing. I had nothing.

We went on through eternal space and eventually, I could see a glimmering of something beyond—just glimmerings—a land, people, experiences, grey, dark—but nothing to "grab hold" of, that I could identify with, or link with anything. I felt that I had to wait for any feeling or message. It felt very frightening. I asked for help from my guide, and the message was that the end is the new beginning.

Eventually, I heard the *chovihano's* tambourine change rhythm, the message to come back to everyday reality. I hovered above the room as a spirit in my imagination, looking down at the bodies that were lying on the floor, seeing them as part of the living—they had warmth that I did not have. It took a long time to feel that I was back in my body, and to feel that I was alive again. This felt very disturbing, but it also made me feel more aware of being alive, more fully alive. I appreciated that in a way that I had not done before, and I realised that my research was taking me deeper into the emotional experience of magic.

Back at home in London a couple of weeks later, I started experiencing what seemed to be the gates of my consciousness opening. Ancestors flooded though as presences during dreams and quiet reflective times. I felt as though something inside me was releasing. I sensed that I had made a connection with my grandfather in spirit. It felt healing. The ancestors invited me to go beyond the known in another trance journey. I felt compelled to let myself go to discover more. As in the journey at Jardani's, I went beyond the next gate, the next field, a bit further up the lane, out of the copse . . . further in my imagination. Through darkness—like the death journey at Hallowe'en—I found myself in deep space, among the stars, looking down at the spinning planet Earth. I saw the Earth as consciousness, though time and space . . . all the thought that ever was; all beings therein were a part of this consciousness, all together, yet all separate at the same time, spinning through space. Somehow it all seemed to fit into place within that eternity of the moment, and I felt the Gypsies' child-like laughter ripple through space.

Fragments of a conversation I had had with Jardani about Gypsy attitudes towards death came into my mind. He had told me that after a death, nothing is kept of the person's belongings—everything is burned, including their wagon, like in the old days. Something made me tell Jardani that I had kept my mother's ashes, and it was eight years since her death. Rather shocked, he told me I had to deal with them as soon as possible to let her spirit move on. When she had died, I had not known what to do with them, telling myself that I would wait until the time felt right. Now I was in agreement with Jardani that holding her ashes was not allowing either of us to fully acknowledge her death. So on an afternoon in mid-November, a friend helped me to conduct an ash-scattering ritual. My mother used to visit a local park to exercise her dog every morning, and I knew she loved the place, as she had very strong affinities with nature. A few days previously, I had visited a small copse of young beech and oaks that surrounded a larger storm-ravaged beech tree at the far end of the park. The copse had felt inviting and I thought it would be an ideal place to scatter her ashes. On the afternoon of the ritual, I gathered together rosemary and rose petals from the garden, and some wine and chocolate, as an offering for the nature spirits of the copse, and my friend and I walked the short distance to the park. As the light faded, I scattered the rosemary and the rose petals before following suit with the ashes. As I shook the ashes out of their container, I wished her peace and sent love.

A couple of weeks later, I started experiencing ancestors flooding into my awareness as spirit presences. On one occasion, the ancestors invited me to go beyond the known in a journey. I felt compelled to let myself go. I felt as though something inside was opening up and releasing. It felt healing and I sensed my grandfather, who was my mother's father, in spirit and that "he cared about me and would make sure I was okay." The spirit ancestors thanked me collectively, not in words but with a feeling, for letting my mother's spirit go to where it should be, saying that she was now at peace.

During one such trance period I found myself at the top of the old beech tree in the copse. After a visit in everyday reality to the copse, I felt the large beech tree was communicating with me. It told me that it was in the long transition between living and dying. It gave me a beechnut case with which to journey "beyond the known" and three of its fallen branches. It felt as if the ancestors were a distinct presence; they were all around, and I could feel them in my body too as many wraith-like figures clamouring to gain access to my mind amid circles of swirling energy. I made a drawing of my experience at the time, which appears below in Figure 6.1.

I went into the beech tree in my imagination and felt its transition—the process of being in between the living and the dying—of how one merges into the other, without absolute distinction, and very different to a view that life and death are separate.

It was after these rituals and the spirit communication with my grandfather that his story telling came flooding back in my memory. I realised his importance to my early life. I felt a sense of relationship that had previously been missing and it increased my feeling of connectedness. Something significant had occurred in my understanding of magic.

During the ritual spreading my mother's ashes, I had picked up three fallen branches of the old beech tree that it had indicated it wanted me to take. I gave one to my friend for helping with the spreading ashes ritual for my mother, I kept one, and the third I was determined to give to Jardani for helping my connection with the ancestors, particularly my own grandfather. For Maggie, I had a small patchwork bag containing some of the beechnuts. Some days later, I travelled to Sussex to give them their gifts from the beech and tell them enthusiastically of what had happened as a direct consequence of their healing work with the Ancestor. To my surprise, my news was greeted coolly. Jardani and Maggie received the gifts, but I could tell, by their faces and actions, that they were not welcome. This was confirmed to me when at a later workshop they were still distant, and Jardani told

Figure 6.1 The Ancestor Tree

me that he had left my magical staff in the field outside their window. I felt totally confused and emotionally upset. I still have no conclusive evidence for their actions and have not had the opportunity to talk to them about what occurred, either. I am certain that Jardani saw anyone as a potential threat to his power and magical authority. I had crossed the anthropological divide at that moment, having become truly immersed in the culture and magical practice that I was studying. However, it did teach me the emotional power of such experiences. It was at this point that I realised the full implication of my involvement in my research. I needed to regain my objective distance, but importantly, not devalue the vital information that I had gained from the experience. The shamanic rituals that I had undergone seemed like catalysts that freed up unconscious material in myself. This was a crucial lesson in learning how to achieve a balance between magical and analytical thinking.

A general suspicion might or might not have been a part of the estrangement between Jardani and myself. Reflecting on the cause of this rift, I remembered how in the early days, Jardani had talked to me of Gypsy culture. He told me how he had been brought up to be suspicious of everything, especially non-Gypsies, and how a central part of Gypsy life was tricking people. Much kudos was given to anyone who could outwit another. The example Jardani gave was how it would be a family challenge to manage to get the last piece of cake on a plate. Whereas non-Gypsy politeness and etiquette would demand that the remaining piece was offered around the table, in Jardani's case it would be a challenge to get it by subterfuge, or other such means, politeness being taken as weakness. When we were in Totnes, he had taught me how to outwit people in a supermarket by hypnotizing them. This, he said, one could do by focusing energy on a person and willing them to move in a certain direction, such as leaving a queue at a checkout to speed up the process of paying for goods. By concentrating on the back of the head of the person in front, it was possible, so he said, that the idea could be implanted in them that they had forgotten something that they needed, the result being that they left the queue to go and get it. This was a magical way of waiting for less time at checkouts. When I tried it, it did seem to work, as people intuitively seemed to sense when someone was focusing on them. I learned that a lot of magic is about very mundane matters, but actions like queue shortening can make a practitioner of magic feel very powerful, and power is a central issue in the applied practice of magic, as I have discussed elsewhere.[5] Jardani also taught me how to *dik* and *shoon*, how to open up my awareness to notice things that most people would not notice, as a type of animal sensory perception. For example, he told me that you could catch a rabbit or a hare, firstly by developing an animal sense to track it, and then secondly by mesmerising—keeping it within your stare—and finally, throwing a hat over the creature to trap it. I was sure that Jardani had never done this himself, but nevertheless, it did demonstrate to me the opening up of an awareness of the senses, an aspect so fundamental to the experience of magic.

In the intervening years, Jardani and Maggie set up a foundation that promoted Jardani's idea of "Jal" as the indigenous culture of the Romani people, describing it as "the religion that became lost," as a way of promoting their ideas and workshops. The early days when I had known Jardani were long gone. He appeared to organise his responses to people, and became more of the workshop leader, travelling internationally and making up a romanticised Gypsy culture as a background to entice people into his workshops. I found that the draw of the nomadic, romantic Gypsy was very potent among those participating in Jardani and Maggie's workshops, it did indeed seem that people were searching for a way of life that had become lost in modern, technologically driven societies. However, despite falling out with Jardani, the essence of what he taught me via his Ancestor, about "the way of my soul" from looking into the river at my own reflection, and his reconnecting me with my own spiritual ancestors, has been fundamental to my knowledge of magic. If I were to be very generous, I would say that maybe he knew this all along, and perhaps this was a part of the Gypsy mode of tricking. The role of the trickster, one such as Loki in Northern European mythology, who acts as a provocateur, a challenger of assumptions and boundaries, is well established in shamanic traditions.

After Jardani's healing ritual, where his Ancestor reintroduced me to my soul by telling me to look at my own reflection in the river, I knew that shamanic healing worked on a magical level. I had become more aware of my own soul rather than being too questioning, to the point of denial, or being too concerned about what other people were doing in the various groups practising magic that I was working with as an anthropologist. Jardani had taught me an important magical "truth:" the soul, or some other conception of a non-material component of life, is the uniting principle that connects the individual with his/her self and the wider cosmos in a magical worldview. Such a conception is a vital component of a participatory and animistic worldview. In addition, I was also more acutely aware of the essential need to keep a balance between my affective magical experience and the more objective, analytical thought of the anthropologist. An overall aim was to bring both perspectives into balance to reveal the deeper dimensions of psychic unity as a state of mind, as well as a lived experience.

NOTES

1. Bronislaw Malinowski *Magic, Science and Religion* (Garden City, New York: Anchor Books Doubleday & Co. 1954): 546.
2. Jardani and Maggie are pseudonyms.
3. Geoffrey Samuel *Civilized Shamans: Buddhism in Tibetan Societies* (Washington: Smithsonian Institution Press, 1993): 8.
4. Susanne K. Langer *Philosophy in a New Key: A Study in Symbolism of Reason, Rite and Art* (Cambridge, MA: Harvard University Press, [1942] 1979): 8.
5. Susan Greenwood *Magic Witchcraft and the Otherworld* (Oxford: Berg, 2000).

7   Grandpa's Magical Desk

When I turn the key in the lock of an old oak roll top desk, in my memory, the snake-like wooden shutters rise upwards, revealing pigeonholes and tiny drawers crammed full of letters, notes, correspondence—reminders of a life tidied away. The desk is still alive with the spirit of the past and full of the spirit of the present. This desk is my Grandpa's desk. After my spirit journeys enabled by Jardani, I felt much closer to my late Grandpa and strongly drawn to him. I wanted to understand more about him. As a psychic event, magic brings causally unconnected, anomalous events together in an especially meaningful way, and as I explored I would discover that Grandpa's desk would become for me a repository of memories. Here, we see one of the essential characteristics of magical thought—the tendency toward whole-making; its atemporal, nonlocal, free-associating nature allows connections to be made and wholes formed from what would in the purely analytical mode be considered isolated, independent parts or entities. We also see an animistic quality coming into play as well, linking the physical reminders of Grandpa with Grandpa's now nonphysical intentionality. Gaston Bachelard, in *The Poetics of Space*, his study of intimate places, notes that "desks with their drawers" along with furniture such as "wardrobes with their shelves" and "chests with their false bottoms" are "veritable organs of the secret psychological life." Bachelard draws on Arthur Rimbaud's poem "Les étrennes des orphelins" to convey the magical quality contained within such furniture to suggest that they have mysteries lying dormant between their wooden flanks, and distant and vague joyful murmuring occurring from within.[1]

According to Bachelard, one must be receptive to the image the moment it appears to experience the "very ecstasy of the newness of the image." This newness makes a "sudden salience on the surface of the psyche" that reverberates with an archetype lying dormant in the depths of the unconscious; the relationship, Bachelard emphasises, is *based in reverberation, not causality*.[2] Stories are built into the very being of a person through patterns and sequences of childhood experience, and learning happens within an experiential sequence of what important others do, and transference is a principle of shaping past experiences.[3] My childhood experience with my grandfather at the magical desk was one of these shaping moments, one that I would come to realise later. My discovery was that Grandpa and his magical desk had shaped a formative part of my psyche.

With this in mind, I recollected how my grandfather used to tell me stories about the horses he rode and looked after during the Boer and First World Wars while I sat on his knee at this desk. Now when I return to this at Grandpa's desk, I find that it was the start of my magical thinking. Susanne Langer, as we have already seen in Chapter 6, made the point that most new discoveries are things that have always been there, but which we only become aware of through different experience.[4] While Grandpa was filling my young imagination with stories, he showed me exciting things inside the depths of the desk. These were my first memories of what felt like magic. The strangely shaped objects —mundane in the every-day, grown-up world—were new and curious to me. Letters in different coloured envelopes nestled in pigeonholes; bottles of ink and pots holding pens stood guard like sentries over the treasure-filled drawers. Periodically pausing from his tale, Grandpa allowed me to choose to look inside one of the tiny drawers. When I had made my choice, Grandpa would slowly slide the drawer out of its place in the desk and, after much dramatic ado shaking its contents around while I waited, transfixed with excitement, he would eventually show me inside. I could look at the drawer's contents but not touch. If I was lucky, that drawer contained a boiled sweet, its brightly coloured wrapper hiding amongst the paper clips, rubber bands, pen nibs, and drawing pins. Taking the sweet and putting it in my mouth helped to make everything connected with those moments enchanted in my memory.

Recalling this memory of my grandfather brought to my mind Jardani's Ancestor's admonitions delivered during my healing ritual to connect with my soul. Also, Hermann Hesse's novel *Steppenwolf* seemed to resonate with the Ancestor's words. Hesse's protagonist Harry Haller's search for his soul struck me as particularly significant, especially in these words:

> It did not last long; but it returned in a dream, caught a glimpse now and then; Sometimes for a minute or two I saw it clearly, threading my life like a divine and golden track. But nearly always it was blurred in dirt and dust. Then again it gleamed out in golden sparks as though never to be lost again and yet was soon quite lost once more.[5]

Was my soul like a divine and golden track threading through my life, as Hesse's writing suggested? Had this track become blurred in dirt and dust? So far, I had learned several important features of magic: that death in the form of the ancestors was very much a part of life; that there was a unity in the multiplicity of being; and that the way into this alternative reality was through the "between," a liminal space. Now, it seemed I needed to find a sense of "soul" as a non-material part of me that perhaps could connect with my own magical consciousness. As the above suggests, I sought to find it through a rekindling of my relationship with my grandfather. My spirit connection with him became manifested through my passion for horses. These creatures would become a bridge between the man, his stories, and my sense of my non-material essence. Further, horses would lead me deeply into a synchronous experience of magic. Being intrigued by Carl Jung's notion of synchronicity as a non-causal connecting principle,[6] I thought that the term could be used to describe the association points between ordinary everyday and magical awareness. The concept of synchronicity—an essentially magical thinking process—was useful to help me associate things that would otherwise be separate in an analytical mode of mind, and to provide associative magical links to aid in the interpretation of meaningful events. Horses became for me a synchronous link with my grandfather, and a connection with the dragon.

In time, I would come to realise that for millennia, horses and dragons have had mythical associations. In Chinese and Japanese mythology, for example, the dragon is also a dragon-horse. According to K'ung Ngan-kwoh, a famous scholar in the reign of the Chinese Han emperor Wu at the turn of the second century BCE, a dragon-horse is the "vital spirit of Heaven and Earth" with a horse's body with dragon scales.[7] A Japanese aphorism states, "In heaven a horse is made into a dragon, among men a dragon is made into a horse."[8] The dragon-horse is also connected with water. In Chinese legend, the dragon is a "benevolent horse, the vital spirit of river water. . . its neck is long, and its body is covered with scales. It has wings at its shanks, and its hair hangs down its sides. Its cry consists of nine tones, and it walks on water without sinking."[9] Mythologies such as these, while not speaking to the analytical mind, speak directly to the magical mind; they provide a linking synchronicity that connected with my sense of a non-material essence. Meditating on this, I found myself drawing dragons, the meanings of which were totally unconscious to me at that time, but when I look now at the example image in Figure 7.1, now it does have horse-like qualities, especially around the head, eyes, and ears.

At the beginning of my research on magic I had been largely unaware of the dragon as a shaping force in my life, but gradually, as I got more involved with studying and writing about magic, I began to link one thing with another. I started having anomalous experiences, ones that I would later put together as meaningful to my dragon narrative. Initially, horses became magical vehicles, so to speak, of my increasing insight into the connections between my experiences. Horses would come to shape my life in everyday reality as well as preparing the foundation for my work on magical consciousness. Horses were an important link in my understanding of synchronistic patterns of magical relationships and connections. The more I became involved in thinking magically about the dragon, the more I recalled what at the time seemed like odd experiences. The dragon spoke to me in small moments of stillness

Figure 7.1   Drawing of Horse-Dragon

and reflection, and in dreams, hopes, and fears that gradually I came to interpret as having meaning. I had to learn to listen to the dragon's voice. I needed to hear the dragon speak from its so-far silent realm, to tell its story. My task was to explore deeper into my individual experience of magic to see how the process of magical thinking unfolded within an inspirited and connected reality. I hoped that this would shed light on more indigenous cultures that had ongoing relationships with spirit worlds. It seemed especially important that I should do this to demonstrate that magical consciousness was indeed potentially inherent within the human psyche, and not just in supposedly irrational individuals or "primitive" peoples.

Later, I would come to write that Grandpa's legacy to me was a passion for horses; his stories about horses would reverberate through my everyday life. Due to this influence, I would come to own horses in the everyday world. By working to afford what would otherwise have been an impossible fantasy, and through a pattern of synchronicity, two horses in everyday reality became especially important retrospectively. Each of them was significant in assisting me in examining the deeper process of magical awareness.

* * *

Casting my mind back into my memory of long ago, I recalled my relationship with my grandfather. In the imagination of my magical consciousness he opens one of his small desk drawers and inside I see a dragon's egg, shining like mother of pearl. This egg contains all my life experiences that will one day add up to me writing this story. The memories cascade into my psyche from such experiences. Once formed, they create their own moving, fluid crystal, the facets of which gleam and glow as the dragon's eye reflects in darkness, there to linger for a moment and then be gone, forming and re-forming across aeons. The dragon's egg is a sacred gift of active imagination guided by intuition. Connecting and weaving, as if in a dream, it is like entering another world of unfathomable and exciting mysteries as I look back to that time. The memory of the desk takes me into the future in and outside my mind—to see the future is to see the past through the words that tumble into consciousness. I want to explore the dragon that is out and about in everyday life. Here the stream of time flows in circles; the past and the future become caught in perceptions of the present. Time in magical thought has an essentially atemporal or anti-temporal quality: the past and the present are contained in the future, and the future is contained in the past. Time takes on a different meaning—it no longer progresses from past, present, and future, but exists in an entirety in the moment.

The words unlock an experience that allows participation in the moment, to be inside the moment: to participate in the life of the moment as I sit with my grandfather looking backwards in time as if through a cut glass crystal, as in a photograph collage I made (see Figure 7.2).

My memories are mute until I can give them a voice. Those moments at Grandpa's desk lay dormant for me until now, but the magic is always

Figure 7.2   Grandpa and the Anthropologist as a Young Child

present. It surfaces from time to time and, dragon-like, it now comes through my mind:

> The memories lie dusty in a drawer
> glimpsed through a crystal half darkly.
> Distant time brought to light
> an image recalled
> and passing once again
> into
> obscurity.
> Fond memories of time past,
> of being held
> close and warm.
> Darkness through the years of living memory
> to return once more
> on this sunlit, silent shard.
> Connecting, weaving as a dream
> they come to mind this time
> to have voice.

The dragon is speaking to me. Now I am listening. . . The anthropologist in me wonders whether the dragon has come to express that which was previously silent. It feels so. I need to know another way of knowing to connect with my past in the words of Hesse's dusty golden soul track.

* * *

As a way of trying to get closer to my grandfather, and to understand the affinity between us, I did some investigation into certain material artefacts to discover more about his life in the military. Searching dusty piles of old, unframed photographs, I found one of him as a young army corporal mounted on one of his horses.

Forgotten and uncared for, this picture looked as though it might hold the key to the mystery of something deeper. A clue to my grandfather's life, some insight into another realisation might be found if I searched and imagined. Perhaps this horse was Punch, the horse that liked to be tickled behind his ears, as Grandpa had told me at the magical desk? I read that the Blue Cross, a charity formed to help the millions of horses injured during the Great War, gave out information booklets to soldiers to help them look after their horses, and part of their advice was to gently stroke the horse's ears to relieve stress. Perhaps this is what Grandpa did to the horses that he looked after. Perhaps they comforted each other on the lonely, terrifying battlefields miles from home? Examining the image for minute details, hoping that they would take me into Grandpa's world, I sensed that I would find out more about the dragon in the shadows cast in the picture—in the spaces between the known and unknown. Grandpa wears regulation khaki serge service

Figure 7.3   The Anthropologist's Grandfather as an Army Corporal

dress: a tunic, cut loose with two patch pockets on the chest and the two stripes of a corporal on the arm, breeches, puttees (spirally wound bandages covering the lower part of his leg from the ankle to the knee), a round cap of blue cloth, and a brown leather bandolier over his left shoulder. The military saddle, bridle, and other horse harness are hung with the accoutrements of war; by his side is a long sword, safely sheathed in a scabbard. In his hand, Grandpa holds a rolled banner carrying the regiment emblem. I learned that when this was unfurled, it was a command for his troops to follow him.

Looking for more clues about Grandpa's life, I discovered some old medals in a box of jewellery and trinkets. By holding his medals in my hands and examining them closely, I saw that one was for the Boer War when he enlisted to go to South Africa at age seventeen, and three were for the Great War. Growing up, I had not taken much notice of the medals, even dismissing them as associated with British colonialism and warmongering. But now I had the sense that I needed to overcome my hatred of war to find out about this part of his life. Even a justifiable and necessary war as an act of defence against an aggressor is brutal, bloody, and shocking, but I knew that I had to try and understand the significance that this war had for life—and death. As I turned the four gleaming metal medal decorations on their brightly coloured ribbons threaded on a metal bar, I noticed a small metal oak leaf pinned to the rainbow-coloured ribbon. This indicated, as I later found out, that Grandpa was mentioned in Dispatches in the House of Commons for honourable service. By looking closer and reading the small written inscriptions on the medals, I saw a synchronistic link: Grandpa was in the

Second Dragoon Guards. Through further research, I found out that the name dragoon came from a type of early short shotgun called a "dragon." Viewed analytically, of course this is simply "coincidence:" a meaningless co-occurrence of seemingly related but actually unrelated events. Viewed magically, however, here was my connection with the dragon!

Initially carried by dragoons of the French Army (there is no distinction between the words dragon and dragoon in French, Portuguese, or Spanish), this firearm was issued to mounted troops that needed a lightweight, easily handled weapon. Early versions of the shotgun were decorated with dragon's head carvings around the muzzle, giving the impression of the fire-breathing monster. It is also thought that the mounted infantryman, with his loose coat and the burning match used to ignite the priming charge of the firearm, resembled the mythical dragon at a gallop. The Dragoons were a class of mounted troops that originated in the seventeenth and early eighteenth centuries as fighting-trained infantry who rode on horseback but dismounted to fight on foot. Later, the Dragoons evolved into cavalry (from the old French *chevalier*, a "knight"), soldiers or warriors who fought mounted on horseback, but they retained their historic title of dragoon. So it dawned on me that the Dragoon Guards was a synchronistic connection with the dragon. The dragon was there as a magical connection linking a theme of associations between my grandfather, the horses he rode, his army regiment, the firearm, and the mythical beast.

This contemplation of the synchronistic connection between the ancestral dragoon and "the dragon" highlights the binocular vision one must adopt in order to balance the analytical and magical ways of understanding these events. In the analytical mode, these two things are causally unrelated to one another. Here, they remain distinct, isolated, and unconnected. In the magical mode, they are "connected" via meaning, both personal and universal. They give an uncanny feeling of purposefulness to events, and we sense the presence of a nonphysical mind behind it (in the same way, albeit more prosaically, that we saw the presence of a mind behind Bozo's pie throwing events). The magical mode creates whole feelings, whole mental entities, and subjective, whole qualia. It is also intimately tied to subjectivity itself. These things, subjectivity and whole forming, are things the analytical mode functions poorly at doing. To maintain a balance, then, we must keep the tension of both views. We know they are causally and analytically unrelated, and at the same time they are magically, meaningfully, and holistically related.

The Great War had such a huge impact in every imaginable way. For my grandfather, it remained as a silence seen in the sadness in his eyes; and for me, the horror of the war was the start of the experience of the dragon via my grandfather's horse stories. Although I was spared the carnage and emotional scarring of the physical reality, the process of understanding took me deeper in my search for meaning in life and death. The elements of the dragon were there in my past, lingering in the memories of Grandpa's stories, his experience in the war, and the associations that came to my mind when I realised that by synchrony his army regiment was named after the dragon. Somehow, perhaps, I had picked up these psychic connections from a very young age at the magical desk.

Horses did not come into my life easily. Our family was not rich and my parents struggled to buy me the odd riding lessons and, on a couple of special occasions, riding holidays. All my pocket money was saved to buy anything remotely connected with horses. Owning a pony of my own—a dream of many young girls—was completely out of the question, and way beyond my parents' means. Occasionally, there were hoof prints in the mud along the alleyways behind the house where I grew up, probably left by an old rag and bone man taking his cart along the back entrances hoping to pick up other peoples' junk to sell, and I would follow the tracks, hoping to catch a glimpse of the horse that had left them. The leaving of such a trail excited me and I felt that I could sense the presence of the horse. I imagined riding the horse that had left the tracks so close to my heart.

My dreams of owning a horse of my very own came true when I started my first job as a junior medical photographer at University College Hospital Medical School in Gower Street, central London. With my first pay packet, and with a loan from my father-in-law, I bought a horse. From then on, my life would be interwoven with looking after horses, but two really transported me synchronously into different realms, both in the everyday and magical reality. The first was a thoroughbred racehorse called Karamai, and the events surrounding her purchase and training showed me the process of synchrony in action. Cielle, the second horse, would also teach me about synchronicity, but by taking me deeper into the unknown in a magical reality. In both cases, the horses would transport me into other places in the seen and unseen or non-manifested worlds.

KARAMAI: SYNCHRONY IN ACTION

Standing in the middle of Chantilly Forest, in the Bois de Boulogne, France's premier racehorse training centre, forty kilometres from Paris, I watched as an immaculately turned-out dark bay thoroughbred racehorse cantered past me on the piste, or training gallop. The horse's lithe muscular beauty was in total harmony with the jockey perched on her back.

The sight made my heart swell with pleasure. I was in my mid-twenties and I felt as though I was in an enchanted woodland; there were manicured sand tracks stretching into the distance, and amid the clearings stood elegant châteaux, the like of which I had only imagined in fairy tales. I had to pinch myself to make sure I was not dreaming, for this was actually my horse. Looking at the picture now, I recollect standing in the racing paddock on Karamai's maiden race at Chantilly on 14 July 1977 with the other owners and Jacques, my jockey and trainer, dressed in his racing silks. Karamai

Figure 7.4   Karamai in Training at Chantilly

was to run in the sixth race of the day, the Prix de la Breteche, for fillies of three years who had never won a race. To see the rather scruffy, gangly foal that I had bought at Newmarket transformed into the most elegant and beautifully turned-out, high-speed equine was to see the ugly duckling turned into a beautiful swan. Karamai performed well, coming eighth in a field of eleven potentially classic fillies. The events that led to this experience hinged on one moment of synchrony.

However, my racehorse experience started quite by chance, or so it seemed at the time. Looking back, I understand it now as a synchronous event in the pattern of my life. In search of a future brood mare for my Arab stallion, I visited Tattersalls racehorse auction, at the famous racecourse at Newmarket in East Anglia. I was toying with the idea of breeding an Anglo-Arab—an Arab/Thoroughbred cross. As I walked around the auctions, I realised that this was the big business of the racing industry—it was far beyond what I could ever have imagined. The digital display indicating the amount that was being bid for each horse rocketed into millions of pounds, what were to me unimaginable figures. The prices at Newmarket were mostly sky high, but the bidding on one lot, a late-foaled bay filly born in April rather than the preferred January, was very slow. Thoroughbred foals that are destined for flat races rather than jumping "over the sticks" are ideally born in January or February, as this gives them the most advantage in terms of growth for when they start racing, usually at two years old. I bid for her and, as no one else seemed very interested, she became mine under the hammer for 300 guineas, a very modest sum. And then something happened that I thought strange at the time but later attributed to synchrony. A man with an Irish accent who said that he had made a mistake with the bidding approached me outside the saleroom. Saying that he was acting on a client's instructions, he had bid for the wrong horse, and he offered to buy my foal. This made me determined to keep the filly—if this man was interested in her, then she might have racing potential. Wild thoughts ran through my head that I would not mate her with my Arab stallion but try and race her. This seemed like an impossible dream because I had no money, no connections, and I knew next to nothing about racing.

When I got home I did some research on the foal's bloodlines and found out that she was sired by Karabas, a well-known Washington DC International winner who stood at stud in Ireland, and her well-bred dam had successfully raced too. We named her Karamai. The more I learnt about Karamai's breeding the more I came to think that she might indeed have a future in racing. Working for the Medical Research Council as a medical photographer at the time, I had the opportunity to get to know some of the research scientists, and after we had been talking about a photographic job that one had requested me to do, we started chatting and I jokingly asked him if he wanted a share in a racehorse. Then came another moment of synchronicity. Not expecting him to be interested for a moment, I was dumbfounded when he told me that he had been to a party the previous weekend and had met a French girl who had told him that her brother had recently been a champion junior jockey, and was starting to train racehorses in France. This seemed like an unbelievable coincidence, but it was what I now understand as synchronicity.

Enthusiastically, I told the scientist about my thoroughbred foal, and he was very keen to ask the girl if her brother would be interested in training my filly. Jacques, the French jockey-turned-trainer, was indeed interested in training my filly. Jacques was impressed with her looks and breeding when he came over from France to see her. His father owned a small market flower stall in the centre of Paris, and it was this stall that financed his son's training of two racehorses in Chantilly. When she was old enough, we took the filly to France and she started her race career. The deal was that the trainer's father would pay for her training and we would split any winnings.

It was here that I was called upon to help train the horses in Chantilly. Life was divided between the hustle and bustle of Parisian city life and the quiet beauty of Chantilly. Jacques put me into training. I learnt many of the skills required to turn out a first-rate racing animal. Karamai went on to race a couple of times in the south of France, but eventually, there were problems. Jacques had been too outspoken about the conditions for jockeys as a champion junior jockey and he had upset some influential people. They made it impossible for him to obtain a trainer's licence and the horses had to run under another trainer's name. And so Karamai's short racing career ended. I gave her to Jacques, who eventually sold her, as it became impossible for him to train her or any of the other horses. Nevertheless, the experience with Karamai taught me to believe in the seemingly impossible, to allow synchrony to become manifest.

CIELLE: SYNCHRONY THROUGH ASSOCIATIONS

The second horse that had a huge impact on my understanding of synchrony was a bay Arabian mare that would steal my heart and would transform my imagination by turning into a dragon-horse during a shamanic journey many, many years later. The first part of this horse's synchronous story I describe here, the second part, where she takes me deeper into magical consciousness, will come later in the volume. This horse, also a bay mare, but unlike Karamai—who helped me understand synchrony through certain events as I have just outlined—took me back in time to Lord Byron, a Romantic poet, who discovered a connection with nature. The bay Arabian mare's bloodline connected with the English aristocracy through Byron; she was a descendant of a horse owned by Lord Byron's great-great-granddaughter, and it was this that started an association in my mind. Byron had embarked on a grand tour from Europe to the Middle East between 1809 and 1811. During this two-year journey, he wrote "Child Harold's Pilgrimage," an autobiographical Romantic poem describing his travels as a "childe" (a medieval name for a young male candidate for knighthood) through Portugal, Spain, Gibraltar, Malta, Greece, and Albania. Although he was said to be "mad, bad, and dangerous to know" in human society on his grand tour, Byron developed an affinity and companionship with nature and from this point of view, he would come to have a close connection with my own travels in magical consciousness. Once again, a horse would provide the synchronous connecting point. For now, the important start to this relationship is as follows.

My magical connection with Cielle started in my memory when I read a news article about a 1721 Stradivarius violin, the "Lady Blunt," owned at one time by Byron's granddaughter Lady Anne Blunt. The violin, which was advertised for sale by the Nippon Music Foundation, was to be sold at a forthcoming auction. This highly valued musical instrument was being sold to raise money for the crisis in Japan following the 11 March 2011 earthquake, tsunami, and nuclear crisis. I followed the news of the violin and three months after the initial auction, another advertisement read that the violin raised £9.8 million ($15.9 million) for aid to Japan. The sale of this violin took me back in my memory to the circumstances of my magical connection with Cielle. Seeing the name "Lady Blunt" in a news article, I remembered that a long time ago, during the 1970s, I had met Lady Anne Blunt's granddaughter, Lady Anne Lytton, the great-great-granddaughter of Byron, when I had been visiting her Arabian stud while searching for a stallion to mate with my chestnut mare Bisara. At Newbuildings Place, in

Shipley, part of the beautiful Sussex Wealden landscape, Lady Anne Lytton had shown me her bay Polish stallion Grojec. I can still remember Lady Anne's enthusiasm for the horses even though she was very old, frail, and walked with the aid of a stick. Not being able to afford Grojec's stud fee, I decided to send Bisara to be bred with one of his sons, the grey Sky Crusader. Owned by the Marchioness Townshend of Raynham, Sky Crusader stood at stud at Raynham Hall in north Norfolk. Lady Anne's stallion Grojec's genes were dominant in the bay filly foal that was the result of that mating; this seemed like a biological and magical synchronous association in my mind as I thought back to my connections with this horse.

The bay filly, which I had named Cielle, was not brave. She would dart back to Bisara and hide behind her at the slightest hint of anything unusual; it would take time for her to pluck up the courage to investigate anything. Although it took me ages to approach her, when I eventually gained her confidence, we formed a close relationship.

Cielle relied on people. This was shown clearly when her first foal was born. When I arrived at the stable in the morning I was greeted by the mare,

Figure 7.5   Cielle

which had given birth to the foal during the night. I immediately saw that there was a problem. The foal would not get up and Cielle, instinctively knowing something was wrong, was anxious for human assistance. The foal's fight for life was short-lived, and he died a couple of days later. Cielle's process of grieving for her foal was plain to see; she was so distressed. The National Foaling Bank, an organisation that matches orphan foals to foster mares that have lost their own foals, advised leaving the dead foal with the mare for two days. We did as the foaling bank suggested and took the stiff foal, curled up as though he was asleep, in and out of the stable and the field with Cielle as if he had been alive. During this period, the mare never left the foal's side, although she knew he was dead.

Much later, I came to the realisation that it was this experience of Cielle's that would make a special connection between us—she seemed to understand something profound about the experience of death. Some time previously, I had decided that I could not manage looking after horses as well as studying anthropology. Not being able to bear to sell Cielle, I arranged for her to go on permanent loan to a woman who had bought one of my other horses. It would be some time before I would make contact with the mare again. One day, many years later, when Cielle was twenty years old, I had the phone call I had been dreading. A vet was asking my permission to put her down. She had severe colic and none of the relaxing drugs had worked. Cielle's death had a very great impact on me—I was overwhelmed with sadness and grief. However, it was through Cielle's death that I would really come to understand the profundity of magical consciousness as she helped me to travel in the dark realms of the magical imagination, but that would come later, much later, as I shall describe in Chapter 14. Before that part of the process could happen, I needed to return to the place of my birth to find what lay in store regarding my connection with the land through an understanding of its history, as well as its magical inspirited aspects, in relation to my developing narrative of the dragon.

NOTES

1. Gaston Bachelard *The Poetics of Space* (Boston: Beacon, [1958] 1969): 78.
2. Bachelard *Poetics*, xv–xvi [our emphasis].
3. Gregory Bateson *Mind and Nature: A Necessary Unity* (New York: Bantam, 1988): 15.
4. Susanne K. Langer *Philosophy in a New Key: A Study in Symbolism of Reason, Rite and Art* (Cambridge, MA: Harvard University Press, [1942] 1979): 8.
5. Herman Hesse *Steppenwolf* (New York: Bantam, 1927): 34.
6. C.G. Jung *The Red Book* (*Liber Novus*), edited and introduction by Sonu Shamdasani, translated by Mark Kyburz, John Peck, and Sonu Shamdasani (New York: W. W. Norton, 2009); C.G. Jung 'Introduction' to *I Ching, Book of Changes*, The Richard Wilhem translation (London: Penguin Arkana, 1989): xxiii; Anthony Stevens *On Jung* (London: Penguin, 1991): 169, 266.

7. Marinus Willem De Visser *The Dragon in China and Japan* (New York: Cosimo, [1913] 2008): 58.

8. Francis Huxley *The Dragon: Nature of Spirit, Spirit of Nature* (London: Thames and Hudson, 1989): 20.

9. De Visser *Dragon*, 57.

8   Dragon Source

During my healing shamanic ritual, Jardani's spirit Ancestor told me to look at my own reflection in the river to find my connection with my soul. In order to explore this admonition further, I returned to Carshalton, a small town in southern England known for its spring waters, the place of my birth. I thought that perhaps these waters might reflect to me something essential to my continuing understanding of magical consciousness. Through researching into the pre-history and history of the place, I gradually came to relate to the land and its mythology, and started to open up my emotions in relation to its waters. Carshalton stands on a spring line at the foot of the North Downs, and there are numerous springs and watercourses in the area. These waters may have given the area its name, Cars-Aul–ton: "Cars" coming from the watercress that grew in the water, "Aul" meaning well or spring, and "ton" meaning "enclosed farm," deriving from the Anglo-Saxon "Aewelton," a "settlement by well or spring". In ancient times, springs and wells where life-giving water trickled from a hillside or welled up from the earth were regarded as sacred places between the everyday and spirit worlds. Most likely, this was a place of healing then. As well as watercress, peppermint, thyme, lavender, chamomile, liquorice, rosemary, hyssop, and other herbs were grown, all of which have medicinal properties. Watercress has antiviral, anti-bronchitic, and tonic attributes, while peppermint is still used today to treat the common cold, cough, inflammation of the throat and sinuses, and respiratory infections. Perhaps Carshalton was similar to Flag Fen, near Peterborough, in East Anglia, a pre-historic 3,500-year-old causeway of timber posts stretching across a watery Fenland basin. Flag Fen was a likely a ritual site of healing where votive objects, such as swords and daggers, were placed in the waters. It does not take much to imagine that Carshalton was the same, and that people from all around visited its sacred waters for healing. It seemed to me that the waters could open up my awareness.

Carshalton is still a place of water; it lies near one of the sources of the river Wandle, a tributary that flows into London's River Thames. Coursing from its source through pools and springs, the Wandle was diverted into canals, ornamental lakes, and the ponds in Carshalton, where it was landscaped in the eighteenth century as part of a large landed estate. Synchronistically, in relation to my magical connection with horses, in the seventeenth century, racehorses were led past the waters of the ponds on their way to the adjacent stables at the Greyhound public house to be prepared, inspected, and paraded before being taken to race on the nearby Banstead Downs. Nearby, Epsom was to become the home of the most famous racecourse in the world, where the classic races the Oaks, named after a local estate and the first run in 1779, and the Derby, which started the following year, are run today, nearly two hundred and fifty years later. I felt as though I would have to look deep into the waters at Carshalton to sense the meaningful connections that would lead me to greater insight of my own essential being.

* * *

Standing looking into the water at Carshalton, I remembered dawdling home from school between the ponds when I was thirteen years old. Each day, my friend and I would point to some enormous old ivy that was twisting itself around the massive boughs of a yew tree and say in unison, "That's ivy, you know," bursting into giggles at our own silly joke. For every day, we would say the same thing, and every day, we would share that moment in a peal of laughter, in a daily ritual. The ivy—that I now see as dragon-like in its serpentine embrace of the tree—guarded the ponds. I also have fleeting reminiscences of school days where the rector of All Saints, the church opposite the ponds, fought to teach us irreverent girls religious knowledge. And later, when I was eighteen, of dancing, draped in gold and silver tinsel, on the tables in the large backroom of the Greyhound, an old public house adjacent to and overlooking the water where the racehorses were stabled in the past. Now, many years later, as I reflect on Carshalton, the old dragon-ivy is now gone. The yew tree has been cut down, but young ivy tendrils entwine themselves anew around the yew tree shoots. The stump shines skull-like, hinting at its past as the ivy tendrils beckon into the future. I somehow sense that the new ivy growing around the base of the yew tree would lead me deeper into the spirit of the place. Ivy is tenacious; it clings on regardless, gradually growing and spreading its coils like a dragon sentinel for the waters here. Intersected by a road bridge and bounded by a park, the church, and the Greyhound, the waters reflect the images of the dragon-ivy as well as all the life that has moved in and around the area through deep time. I feel that the waters of Carshalton still hold a mystery as I look into the water and see my own reflection as the dragon staring back at me.

This seemed a positive start, but I needed to do some research on the place to find out what I could to guide my search of what appeared to be the magical properties of the water.

Today, the church of All Saints stands facing the ponds. Carshalton's written history starts with the Domesday Book of 1086, and it records that "aultone" was a "farmstead at the source of a river" with a church listed.

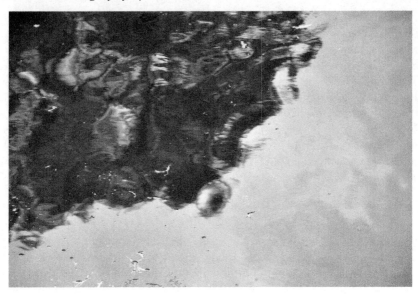

Figure 8.1   Dragon Reflected In Water

It is well known that early Christians in this land built churches on pagan sites. With the advent of Christianity in the seventh century, the church had tried to eradicate or take over pagan beliefs about the sacredness of places where waters emerged from the earth. In the eighth century, Bede noted how Pope Gregory I gave instruction to Augustine in 602 to encourage the christianisation of the pagan practice of decorating sacred places, and so springs and wells gradually became holy wells. In Anglo-Saxon times, the church would originally have been made of wood and converted into a stone structure during the eleventh century; the earlier wooden churches were replaced by stone ones to protect the increased wealth of the religious foundations. Furthermore, new monastic rules had introduced bell ringing, which required strong church towers.[1] The land of Carshalton was taken from the Anglo-Saxons by William the Conqueror after the Battle of Hastings in 1066. William gave the five separate holdings recorded in the Domesday Book to Geoffrey de Mandeville for services rendered in the battle. These five holdings were consolidated into one and Geoffrey de Mandeville became the first Lord of the Manor of Carshalton.

Just outside the All Saints churchyard wall, and also adjacent to the ponds, is Anne Boleyn's Well, known locally in the seventeenth century as the Bubbling Well. Queen Anne Boleyn was the second wife of King Henry VIII and mother of Queen Elizabeth I, and according to local legend, the well was so named when her horse kicked a stone and a spring of water appeared. It is also said that the name of the well is a corruption of Notre

Dame de Boulogne, after a chapel dedicated to Our Lady of Boulogne built near the well, the Count of Boulogne being Lord of the Manor of Carshalton in the 12th Century and ancestor of Anne Boleyn. Boleyn, or Bullen, is a corruption of Boulogne. It is from the name "Boleyn" that the well popularly became known as the Bubbling Well, although it is probable that earlier, the well was named after St Anne, as the cult of St Anne was popular in England. During the sixteenth-century Reformation, such Catholic holy places were secularised, and this is probably when the legend of Anne Boleyn was established, this being a time of political upheaval when Henry VIII broke from the Catholic Church in Rome. Henry's wish to annul his marriage to the Spanish Catherine of Aragon and marry Anne was the primary reason that sparked the formation of the Church of England. With the Dissolution of the Monasteries in 1536, all religious houses, monasteries, and priories were closed, the monks and nuns dispersed and the buildings, their possessions, and lands, were seized for the benefit of the throne.

It is almost certain that the well had even older associations as a pagan spring dedicated to a female deity. The name "Anne" comes from Annis, a Celtic goddess of rivers, or Ana, a Celtic goddess of fertility who is likely the same deity as Danu, the ancestress of all gods. In my imagination, the Anglo-Saxon Angurboda, a nature spirit with primal connections, might also derive her name from Ana. Surrounded by railings and overgrown with lavender, the well is now neglected. Buses and other traffic thunders past. Probably not many people are aware of the well—quite a contrast to earlier times when people drew on its waters everyday, and maybe came to the wellspring for healing.

A stone's throw from Anne Boleyn's Well is another wellspring, named Margaret's Well by the art critic, social commentator, artist, and poet John Ruskin (1819–1900) after his mother. This spring was previously, according to an 1868 Ordinance Survey map, called the Waterhouse Pond. Ruskin bought the spring and landscaped the area, mentioning it in the introduction to his book *Crown of Wild Olive* (1872). An engraved stone by the spring reads: "In obedience to the giver of life, of the brookes and fruits that feed, and the peace that ends. May this well be kept sacred for the service of mews, flocks and flowers, and be by kindness called Margaret's Well." This dedication is more in line with an older veneration of the waters, but now it is rather neglected too. It is clear that the waters of Carshalton are not valued today, unlike in earlier ages. The water was seen in ancient times as the source of all life, and it was associated with women as the bearers of life. I need to know more about the ancient sacred relationships with water. Anglo-Saxon and Norse mythology reflect a regard for the creative power of water. The cosmos is created from water: the Élivágar are eleven rivers that exist in Ginnungagap, the primeval void that arises from Hvergelmir, a bubbling, boiling well beneath the third root of the cosmic tree Yggdrasil in the cold realm of Niflheim. From the meeting of the ice from these frozen rivers

Figure 8.2   Anne Boleyn's Well

and fire from Muspellheim, the fiery realm, water is created. From water, the cosmos is formed from toxic rime. Such is the importance of water in this creation.

* * *

It is easy to understand the mythological language of the Norse or Anglo-Saxon peoples, the echoes of which still linger in the land at Carshalton, as remnants of dragon-ivy tendrils in memories. Thirteenth-century Icelandic historian and poet Snorri Sturluson describes the cosmic Yggdrasil as a mythological ash tree that unites the celestial realms, the everyday world, and the underworld (as described in Chapter 2). In the *Poetic Edda*, a thirteenth-century collection of Old Norse poems contained in the Icelandic medieval manuscript *Codex Regius*, he tells how its branches spread out over the world and extend across the sky.[2] Yggdrasil reaches upwards to the skies, and downward deep into the earth. Sturluson says that the tree's roots also extend very, very far. The first root leads to Asgard, the land of the Æsir gods, while the second root goes to Midgard, the human world. The third root of Yggdrasil goes to Helheim, named after the goddess Hel, sometimes also called Niflheim, an underworld realm of freezing mist and darkness, the land of the dead. It is in Helheim where Níðhöggr the dragon bites the tree's roots. Underneath the root in Asgard, the land of the gods, is *Urðarbrunnr*, a well of destiny adjacent to the assembly place of the gods; under the root in Midgard is a well of wisdom called *Mimir*, into which Odin sacrificed an eye for knowledge; and underneath the third root is the well *Hvergelmir*, the source of the eleven rivers called the Élivágar. Thus, wells and water have a significance of destiny, wisdom, and primal creation, and some scholars consider these three wells to be the same well.

At the sacred well *Urðarbrunnr* dwell three sisters, three shadowy female representatives of fate. One is named Urðr, who spins the past, another is called Verðandi, a weaver of the present, while the third is called Skuld; it is she who cuts that "which might become." Together they are the *nornir*. In the mythological worlds of Scandinavian cultures between 800–1200 CE they were regarded as three in one, or as one *norn* representing past, present, and future all at once.[3] The nornir are mighty in wisdom and set the fates of human lives.[4] Here was a connection with the dragon of the waters at Carshalton. Perhaps the dragon that I had seen reflected in the water was Níðhöggr, the "corpse tearer" dragon that dwelt at the bottom of Yggdrasil, near the well with the nornir. Every day, the nornir water Yggdrasil from the primeval fountain so that its boughs remain green. In modern interpretations, the nornir are *wyrd* sisters who spin, weave, and cut subtle threads of each person's life pattern. Each individual is a part of an interwoven cosmic tapestry, "a vibrating and shimmering web."[5] The sisters are mighty in wisdom and set the fate of human lives by weaving golden threads of individual fate in the hall of the moon: "And there the golden threads they wove/And in the moon's hall fast they made them."[6]

The golden threads woven in the hall of the moon are the weavings that shape everyday life. Urðr and Verðandi spin and weave destiny, but fate is not fixed in the mythological imagination; destiny can be changed by the weaving of alternative patterns in an instrumental act of magic. Here, perhaps, the dragon-ivy took me at the significant age of thirteen—the classic time of a girl's first menstruation—through the healing waters of Carshalton to the hall of the moon. There it felt that my destiny was woven by the nornir. Perhaps this was my first initiation into the dragon. Symbolically, the moon is linked to water and emotions. The web painting that I did subsequently expressed to me the magical weavings that would guide my synchronous exploration of magical consciousness (see Figure 8.3).

It seemed that it was the Anglo-Saxon Angurboda who spoke to me as I thought about the connections of web patterns in my mind. Angurboda is the mother of the serpent Jörmungandr, fathered by the trickster god Loki, who encircles middle earth. Angurboda is a primal energy manifesting as a creative female force, a terrifying mother, a nurturer and healer of sorrows. These words came to me:

> The waters hold me in their embrace;
> give birth to me
> as I am. Now.
> My skin sheds, layer
> after layer,

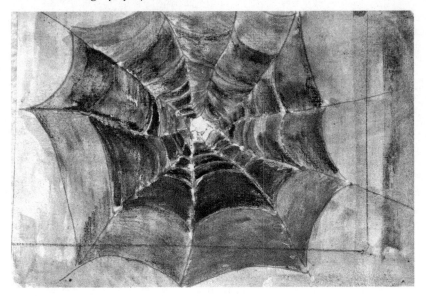

Figure 8.3   Web Painting of Hall of the Moon

Until I come home.
Dark is its hold
in the cradle of life
And death
until I return
once more.

The moon spirits of the waters at Carshalton seemed to bring me home to the source of the dragon.

Here we can see how the magical mode has its own landscape. To call it a "subjective" landscape is to use analytical language to describe magical realms and risks category error. Magical thought, rather, through its processes collects, interprets, and generates data to form its own kind of reality. From the analytical mode we can label it as a subjective world of the mind, of the imagination. But from the magical mode, this nomenclature is incoherent. It simply is. It is the spirit world or the otherworld. Though the otherworld(s) has/have many names depending on what tradition one looks at, the Welsh name for the otherworld is most appropriate: *Annwn* means "not-world." The otherworld is the World that is the Not-World. The name is a lovely paradox, and one that makes sense only in the magical mode, which is real from its own perspective, but not real from the analytical perspective. My thoughts turned to an examination of the world of the magical imagination, which I shall explore in the next chapter.

NOTES

1. Anne Savage, translation of *The Anglo-Saxon Chronicles* (London: Guild Publishing, 1988): 152.
2. *The Poetic Edda* Carolyne Larrington (trans.) (Oxford: Oxford University Press, 1999): 6, stanza 19.
3. Karen Bek-Pedersen *The Norns in Old Norse Mythology* (Edinburgh, Scotland: Dunedin Academic Press, 2011).
4. *Völuspá*, 'The Wise Woman's Prophecy', in the *Poetic Edda*.
5. Brian Bates *The Real Middle Earth: Magic and Mystery in the Dark Ages* (London: Sidgwick & Jackson, 2002): 179.
6. *Helgakviða Hundingsbana I*, (the *First Lay of Helgi Hundingsbane*) in the *Poetic Edda*.

9 Imagination

The feeling that the dragon-ivy of Carshalton had initiated me into the watery realm of creation was certainly significant, but what could it tell me about my imagination?

Magical thought with its mythological language has its own landscape and its own reality formed through the imagination. Analytically, it can be described as the subjective world of the imagination, but it is real in a magical perspective. The dragon for me was real in this perspective. J.R.R. Tolkien said, in his 1936 Sir Israel Gollancz Memorial Lecture, that the dragon, as a potent creation of the human imagination, is "no idle fancy" and that it is "richer in significance than his barrow is in gold."[1] The imagination is indeed rich in significance, but to the analytical mind, the dragon is not really real in the everyday world. The problem is that in Western cultures the imagination is seen as unreal, and people believe that there are no such things as dragons, but the actions of dragons in the magical imagination have an effect on people's lived realities. Indeed, what could be more real? The dragon was certainly working through my imagination, and so I turned to the work of the poet and artist William Blake to try and find out how I could understand more about this through his perception. When William Blake wrote in 1790 that "[i]f the doors of perception were cleansed everything would appear to man as it is, infinite" in *The Marriage of Heaven and Hell*, it inspired generations of people to explore the poetic imagination. Blake's unified vision of the cosmos was encapsulated in the belief that heaven could be felt in the joyous opening of the Imagination (with a capital "I"). In the 1950s, Aldous Huxley wrote in his classic work *The Doors of Perception* (1954) that he thought that mescaline would allow him into Blake's visionary world. However, Huxley discovered that the visionary world he saw was not some fantasy realm but the everyday world seen differently—it was his awareness of it that had changed.

Influenced by William Blake, I sought to develop my own experience of magical consciousness, not through mescaline or some other psychotropic substance, but by deepening my awareness of "the infinite" through my imagination. For Blake, the Imagination was both infinite and eternal: it could be found even in seemingly ordinary things, such as a grain of sand or a wild flower, as in the first four lines of his "Auguries of Innocence" poem:

> To see a World in a Grain of Sand
> And a heaven in a Wild Flower,
> Hold Infinity in the palm of your hand
> And Eternity in an hour.

This visionary moment seemed to me to be encapsulated by the idea of holding infinity in the palm of my hand and eternity in an hour—what an amazingly mystical feeling that must be! Having long been interested in the work of Blake, I decided to explore more of his work as a possible entry point into the imaginary aspects of magic, particularly the more fearful dimensions, as alluded to in his poem "Tyger Tyger:"

> Tyger! Tyger! Burning bright
> In the forests of the night,
> What immortal hand or eye
> Could frame thy fearful symmetry?

In this poem, Blake seems to search for the distant deeps or skies from which this terrible creature arises: from what dread furnace did its deadly terrors clasp? Blake had found himself within some frightening places that filled him with terror, "In what distant deeps or skies Burnt the fire of thine eyes?" and this process of exploring the dark recesses of his own imagination had fuelled his visions. The Tyger, like the dragon, is a creature of fear and destruction; it is a predator of the night that haunts the deepest and most fearful terrains of the imagination, but for Blake, unlike in our contemporary Western thought, the Tyger was real (a subject to which I will return in Chapter 12).

In my quest for understanding more about the dragon, I decided to find out more about William Blake's ideas that all life existed within the Imagination. After I read that Blake had spent three years at Felpham, a small village near Worthing on the south coast of England, I decided to pay a visit to see whether I could glean any inspiration from the place that would deepen my understanding of magic. Here, perhaps, I could get to feel the landscape that inspired him, the places where he had the visions that had fuelled his imagination. Travelling to one of Blake's homes, at Felpham, I started to try to connect to the poet as a spirit ancestor of the Imagination. These experiences helped me to get into the "realm of the dragon." I had already read that the first record of the word *imagination* dates from the fourteenth century as a "faculty of the mind that forms and manipulates images." It comes from the Old French *imaginer*, which in turn comes from the Latin *imaginary*—to form a mental picture—and from *imago* (image), and also from *imaginare*—to form an image of, or represent something. Imagination is a key to creativity, and creativity is central to magical consciousness. Creativity is a faculty of the imagining mind and, as neuroscientist

Antonio Damasio points out, it involves a process of rapidly combining and re-combining an assortment of ideas, the most plausible juxtapositions of which are then remembered through a strong generation of representational diversity. A variety of novel combinations of entities and parts of entities as images are brought to the conscious mind through the interactions of internal processes or external stimuli.[2] However, imagination is usually perceived to be "in the head" and there lies the problem. If a wider perspective on the imagination is taken, it is possible to conceive an interactive space of magical consciousness where communication with imaginal entities might occur. I needed to explore Blake's world as much as I could.

The essential issue here is that of the source of the imaginary images. There are primarily two sources. One is volitional, and the other is not. Volitional imagery is that which we can conjure up at will: think of a pink elephant, there it is. But to truly engage with the "world of the dragon," one has to depotentiate the volitional aspect of the imagination and allow it to play out non-volitionally. This requires some practice, and is greatly enhanced by the mantic techniques that appear cross-culturally, such as privation, entheogen, ritual, drumming, dancing, etc. Doing these things immerses the subject into a non-volitionally directed landscape of imagination that is the referent of such words as Annwn or the Otherworld(s). These practices allow us to experience the imaginary world and grant it a verisimilitude that is sometimes so convincing as to make the subject feel it is a world more "real" than the physical world. It grants this imaginary world an objective quality. It is in this state where we can actually discover things and interact with nonphysical beings that have their own motivations, thoughts, and intentionality. This imbues it with the kind of reality we are familiar with when we interact with the physical world—objects and people move and interact in a way separate from our own volitional control. This cultivates magical thought through a non-directed imagination that the subject can then interact with. The familiar objection that this imaginary world is "not real" when viewed in this light becomes pale and rather meaningless: non-physical, sure, but still "real" in the sense that it has consequences, causes, effects, intentions, etc. It might be objected that such a world cannot affect one's physical body, which makes it unreal. Tell that to someone suffering from severe posttraumatic nightmares, whose blood pressure is elevated, heart rate increased, and stress hormones worked into overdrive. These are physical effects brought about by interactions with the (in this case violently insistent) non-volitional imaginary world. Here is where we see the potential dark side of this world, and must tread with caution.

TO "SWEET FELPHAM"

When William Blake and his wife Catherine travelled to Felpham from London in 1800, it took them seventeen hours and seven changes of horses.

Blake had never seen the sea before. On my journey to Felpham, three hundred and six years later, I decided to take the coast road from Brighton, which lies about thirty miles to the east. The day in February was quite bright as I started out, but as I drove through the industrial estates, wharfs, and commercial harbours of the West Sussex coast, clouds darkened the sky. A black-headed gull flew across my path; I noticed that it had just started to get its summer plumage. In winter, the gulls' heads are white, but in spring, they become progressively darker until they reach black. Reflecting on my quest, I thought of the process of the mind and the inspiration that was bringing me to this place. According to Blake, every creature lived within its Imagination,[3] even the black-headed gulls flying in the sky. All life existed within the Imagination for Blake and as I drove along the coast, I pondered my own experience of imagination. When I was an art student in the late 1960s at Wimbledon School of Art, in leafy south London, I had been particularly inspired by Marc Chagall (1887–1985), a Russian-Jewish shamanic artist. I particularly loved Chagall's images of people and animals flying through the air. Chagall represented the world of the imagination drawn from his childhood and portrayed a magical otherworld from a dreamlike state. He described painting as a window through which he could fly away to another world. He wrote about his imagination as an unfinished world, a strange, unfamiliar country, a "weightless land where there is nothing to differentiate a man from a bird, where a donkey lives in the sky and everything is a circus, and where we walk so well on our heads."[4] The turning upside down of all that is ordered and where the impossible —like a donkey living in the sky—could sound like Shakespeare's "such tricks hath strong imagination," in a *Midsummer Night's Dream*, but I was excited by the different possibilities of thinking that it seemed to offer. Artists have often been likened to the insane because of the unpredictability of creative genius, but this is the power of the imagination, and it intrigued me. For Chagall, as with all other artists, the imagination is the doorway into creativity. The imagination is also the doorway into magic, but it was a long time before I would realise the connection. Recollecting this time now, I can see that this creative expression opened the way for thinking magically.

I had started the foundation course at Wimbledon, where I was introduced to sculpting, drawing, painting, photography, printmaking, stained glass making, and the history of art. I discovered that I was better at photography than painting, and I took an individual creative photography course at Wimbledon. Photography was not new to me, as I had been taught by my father to develop photographs in our blacked-out bathroom when I was young; I was given free rein to do whatever projects I chose on the photography course. My interest in various social and cultural issues pointed me towards anthropology, although I had no idea what anthropology was at that time, and I won a national Kodak prize for my photographs of race-goers at the Epsom Derby, drug addicts, street sleepers, and rich shoppers in Harrods, London's famous Knightsbridge store. In particular, I was drawn to the work of the French photographer Henri Cartier-Bresson (1908–2004), who tried to suggest larger philosophical questions about class and the meaning of life in his pictures. Cartier-Bresson revealed the world as he saw it through his intuitive sense of capturing just the right moment in time; he stressed the moment as crucial to the meaning of the photographic image. Feeling an intense need to communicate what he felt and saw, he thought that a picture must grow from a love and comprehension of people. It was the little human details of a photograph that could radiate universal meanings, and he sought to capture a beauty in the here and now of the complex human world.[5] Cartier-Bresson's photographs evoked a whole range of emotions, but all made me think about capturing the imagination in the moment; this seemed to have the potential to offer insight into the complex human world, and my own feelings. Preserving the act of living in the small details of life seemed to be a wonder in the ordinary, the everyday, and the seemingly banal aspects of a kaleidoscope life. Now I could see Blake's life of the imagination captured in a situation, a look, a juxtaposition of people, objects, light, and dark, or a glimpse into another world that appeared to lie deeper, as if just the other side of an invisible veil.

After leaving Wimbledon, I eventually decided on pragmatics rather than imagination in order to earn my living. Gaining a job in medical photography as a junior medical photographer, I started work at University College Hospital Medical School. I was called upon to photograph everything unusual: from shorn-off shotgun bullet wounds in the Accident and Emergency Department, surgical techniques in operating theatres, and post-mortem specimens to just about everything and anything on the human body—sometimes before and after surgery. Most importantly for my future anthropological work, medical photography introduced me to the objective knowledge of a scientific discipline. It also indirectly introduced me to William Blake. Spending many lunchtimes in the old, strangely musty, leather-smelling library with its vaulted ceilings and air of traditional authority, detective-like I pored over forensic medical books. Taking my sandwiches at lunchtime, I frequently visited the small Hunter hospital museum of extraordinary medical exhibits that included all manner of strange specimens. Pickled in glass jars and used to instruct the medical students on embryonic development, as well as various diseases and injuries, the museum specimens fuelled my inquisitive musings on the philosophy of life and death. Named after John Hunter (1728–1793), one of the first people to apply a rational and scientific approach to surgery, the museum fed my curiosity. Having read Garet Roger's novel *Brother Surgeons*, a story about the brother anatomists William and John Hunter that was first published in 1962, I was filled with the romance of the younger brother John's curiosity about life, in particular, his pioneering exploration of human anatomy, and felt a sense of affinity. A contemporary of John Hunter's was the artist William Blake, a darkly brilliant and erratic genius who spoke the languages of mysticism and natural science and who intrigued me. Blake,

I found out, was a poet, but he was also conversant with the technical language of anatomy.[6] Blake would reappear in my life as an inspiration some time later when, as an undergraduate, I received a copy of *The Marriage of Heaven and Hell*, from one of my anthropology professors and the synchronous connection had been made. After a promotion to medical photographer at King's College Hospital in Denmark Hill, south London, which involved more of the same type of work, I eventually moved to the Medical Research Council in Carshalton, south London, a scientific research establishment close to my birth place and where I had gone to school. Here I came to further understand the ways that medical science pursues objective knowledge. I would realise later, when I came to study anthropology, that this would stand me in good stead as background information on the workings of science. After several years working in the photographic department at the Medical Research Council, including a couple in charge of the section, I started attending an anthropology evening class. My route to anthropology had followed a circuitous path that led through art school and photographic work, both of which contributed to my understanding of the importance of the imagination in my anthropological research on magic.

As I drove along the seacoast, I was reminded that Blake thought wisdom could be found through connecting with nature through the Imagination; he would not have approved of the industrial, soul-less buildings that lined this particular stretch of road. I reflected on this as I drove into Felpham, a typical Sussex village of flint and whitewashed thatched cottages. At its heart, Felpham looks much the same as in Blake's day; the later outreaching development of modern houses had not changed the shape or character of the village. I had done some research on William Blake by reading biographies and had found out that he was born in Soho, London in 1757, and that he was baptised in the font at St. James's Church in Piccadilly, London. I had attended many talks and lectures on various spiritual themes such as shamanism and witchcraft, organised by Alternatives, a liberal ecumenical organisation based at St James's. Sitting in the pews of St James's, a beautiful church designed by the famous architect Christopher Wren, I had imagined that William's spirit wandered in the aisles. I felt I had already made some sort of a connection with the man who had made a strong impression on me; his spirit seemed to pervade that building.

As I walked past Blake's pretty thatched cottage in Felpham, a group of visitors from London had stopped to look. Unfortunately, the cottage, being privately owned, was not open to the public, but there was a pilgrimage route around the village that took in Blake's cottage, the Fox Inn, a stone's throw away, and the site of a house where Blake's patron William Hayley lived. I decided to take myself away from the Blake tour of the village and visit the Fox public house to get a feel for the place. Sitting in a seat by the window, close to the door, I sipped my sparkling water and tried to get some sense of the genius of his spirit. According to a plaque on the outside wall, the Fox Inn had been re-built after being bombed during the Second World

War, so it was not like the original building that Blake would have known. Blake had rented his cottage from the inn's landlord, and he would have had to walk past the original inn each time he went into the village. He had been arrested on its threshold for the alleged assault of a soldier and sedition due to his radical political views, and I was sitting just a couple of feet from the spot. I reflected on what I had learnt about Blake's life.

Blake attended the Swedenborgian Church of the New Jerusalem in London, and he was initially inspired by its founder, Emmanuel Swedenborg (1688–1772), a Swedish scientist, mystic, and inventor who put importance on contacting high spiritual planes. Swedenborg had had a visionary experience in which he became overwhelmed with dizziness and felt close to death, "In a dream a roaring wind picked him up and threw him on his face. A hand clutched his own clasped hand and he saw Christ." Becoming convinced that he was a spiritual emissary from God, Swedenborg considered it his duty to explore the higher planes to inform humanity; he entered ecstatic trances to explore heaven and hell. He thought that eternal life was an inner condition, and that gradual redemption occurred through the personal regulation of higher and higher spiritual states. Ultimately, however, Swedenborg opposed the spiritual world to the natural world; it was this aspect that Blake came to reject, and he was influenced by Jacob Boehme (1575–1624) in this regard. A farmer's son, who was a shepherd and then a shoemaker before becoming a visionary, Boehme tried to find a spiritual unity. Boehme had had mystical illuminations, the first of which was allegedly brought on by the sudden gleam on a tin or pewter vessel that caused him to see into the heart of nature and a concealed divine world. This gave him the sense of being embraced by divine love, as if his life had been resurrected from death.[7] Boehme thought that God manifested in contraries of good and evil and light and dark, and he sought to overcome all opposites, seeing nature as a form of revelation that brought inner transformation.

Taking the idea of exploring heaven and hell from Swedenborg and the theme of spiritual unity and inner transformation from Boehme, Blake developed his own vision—not of another world, but of this world. Believing that paradise was not a higher spiritual place but a state of being, Blake thought that one's perception of the world was what was important. Blake had developed his own visionary skills that were inspired by the spirit within nature. Envisioning a world in which all things in nature not only had consciousness and spirit, Blake believed they also had Imagination. Blake's vision challenged an idea popular in his time that only the human mind had consciousness. This was a view that claimed that the human body, as opposed to the mind, just acted from mechanical instinct, as did animals. By contrast, Blake thought that everything in the world had consciousness and every creature was an inspirited person living within the total freedom of its Imagination.[8]

Blake lived during times of radical political and social upheaval—the French and American Revolutions, and the growing dominance of a materialistic, scientific worldview. There was a rapid social transition, something of which we live with today in our seemingly constantly changing global world. Growing up in eighteenth-century London, William Blake was in the midst of a lot of visionary and dissenting religious teachings. Blake was a free thinker who did not follow the crowd, and his thinking was shaped by a tradition called *antinomianism*. Antinomians distrusted all institutional authority and received wisdom, and instead found authority in the individual's inner experience of faith and love. Blake saw this as a type of perennial philosophy, one that was the underlying essence of many religions.[9]

Blake was influenced by Mary Wollstonecraft's *Vindication of the Rights of Women* (1792) and wrote the poem "Visions of the Daughters of Albion" in 1793 to illustrate his view that the conventional views of sexuality veiled understanding of the true nature of reality—sexuality, as well as everything else, was holy. In this poem, the young maid Oothoon loves the chaste Theotormon, but is raped by the lustful, passionate Bromion. Theotormon, as the name suggests (*theos* meaning "god," and *tormentum* meaning "twisted torment") is a god of twisted torment, while Bromion is Greek for "roarer." Both men reject Oothoon, according to the patriarchal social convention of the time, but Blake's poem ends entreating the reader to know the deeper reality of life, that everything is holy:

> And the wild snake the pestilence to adorn him with gems and gold; And trees, and birds, and beasts, and men behold their eternal joy. Arise, you little glancing wings, and sing your infant joy! Arise, and drink your bliss, for everything that lives is holy!

It was important for Blake to trust the inner wisdom gained through the experience of participating in the holy life of the Imagination; he thought that this restored an original unity of being that connected everything.

Notwithstanding, Blake's views of dragons were contradictory. Early in the nineteenth century he had been commissioned to illustrate books from the Bible, including a terrifying four painting cycle from the Book of Revelations that depicted Satan in the form of a Great Red Dragon. This dragon has been described as "having seven heads and ten horns, and on his heads seven crowns. His tail drew one third of the stars of the sky, and threw them to the earth." Blake often referred to worms as symbols of mortality, as opposed to the divine life of the spirit, but he was also influenced by Tantric sexuality. In some forms of Tantra, originally a medieval Indian practice for bringing the individual into awareness of a divine cosmic consciousness (as we saw in Chapter 4); the snake symbolised an erotic energy force that rises up the spine, leading to spiritual illumination.[10] Consequently, Blake's work and life seemed to hover between different worldviews. On the one hand, in Christian iconography, Satan is the dragon and the source of evil, but on the other, the serpent is the source of a more holistic spiritual wisdom. Both are symbols of the material world, but reflect through their behaviour the attitude toward matter: in one it is evil and is to be warred against, in another it is a source of life.

As I thought about Blake's life, I wondered how I could sense his spirit to find something that might bring more Imagination here at Felpham. In many ways, Blake's world was a far cry from the world that I knew at the beginning of the twenty-first century, but in another sense, it was also quite similar. Sitting in the bar, it felt strange to be so close to a place that Blake would have known well; however, I did not get much of a feeling for Blake there. I needed to find another way to connect. As I sipped my water, I tried to get a sense of Blake's life, what motivated him, and what drove him to the edge of despair and what some would call madness. Just a short walk down the road was Blake's cottage. It was here in the garden that he saw fairies. Blake's earliest biographer, the Victorian Alexander Gilchrist, records how Blake asked a lady if she had ever seen a fairy's funeral. The lady apparently replied that she had not, and so Blake told her about the first one he had seen the previous night in the garden of his cottage:

> I was walking alone in my garden, there was great stillness among the branches and flowers and more than common sweetness in the air; I heard a low and pleasant sound, and I knew not whence it came. At last I saw a procession of creatures of the size and colour of green and gray grasshoppers, bearing a body laid out on a rose leaf, which they buried with songs, and then disappeared.[11]

Perhaps the fairy funeral was an omen for the future of rationalising Western cultures; the fairies were probably parodying our idea of death, too, with this procession. Blake thought that as children, we have a type of innocent wisdom. We are encouraged to think magically as children—fairy tales fascinate the imagination and animals can talk—but then, when we reach a certain age, we are expected to grow out of those beliefs. I pondered on this as I tried to connect with Blake's thinking. After a while, I had a strong feeling that the sea was the best place to experience the spirit of Blake. Surely, I would find his spirit in nature.

Leaving the Fox Inn, I took the short walk to the sea, trying to see with Blake's eyes. Many of the houses would not have been there in Blake's time, but the view of the sea was the same. The sun had come out from behind the clouds and sea and sky merged in a beautiful misty aquamarine blue. I stood and looked at the horizon; it seemed to take me into the life breath of the artist and poet. For the three years that he was at Felpham, Blake seemed to gain much inspiration from nature; he had visions while being entranced by the shifting lights of the sea. Along the shore he had seen the spirits of ancient poets and prophets as spectral bodies, as if the sea had taken human form. As he walked along the shore, he was aware of the possibility of an infinite life—an Eternity that was always present. Time seemed to condense, and "the doors of perception opened." The retreating waves had left their rippled indentations in the sand, and the sunlight lit their crisscrossed patterns as far as the eye could see. William must have stood here and seen exactly what I saw—he must have seen the world here.

In Blake's view, time was not linear. It did not start at a particular point or stop at a particular point: it was ever-present. This made it easier to connect with Blake. I had been concerned with the three hundred years that separated us, but I came to realise that a different perception of time would bring us, complete with our own past experiences, together in the present—for all existed in the present moment, the past, present, and future imbued with meaning. It was heaven. At Felpham, I could imagine how Blake viewed the world. Imagination was there in the stones on the beach, on the sand of the beach as it participated in the rhythm of the tides. I picked up a stone, trying to find a connection, and I started walking, relaxing. I felt aware of the sea: it is the same sea that Blake saw. I felt aware of the stones; they were the same stones that Blake walked on. The past and the present merged in the place. Suddenly, Blake felt closer. William Blake's thinking spoke to me, although our lives were separated by more than three hundred years. As I felt the spirit of Blake I realised that what was important was that I connected with my imagination; this seemed to be a link into a rich stream of sensations and feelings that ran deeper than the individual aspects of life. The imagination appeared to be like a current; it felt as though it tapped into the very wellspring of being. It was not that individual differences were not important, but the imagination seemed to include that particular to the individual and also what we share with others. As I walked barefoot along the sands, I knew that William Blake was someone who was in communication with other realities; he was a person who was in touch with things which most people do not even know exist. He had visited places of intense joy and despair. Blake was an individual on the edge, and some people called him mad. The boundaries between genius and madness are sometimes difficult to draw. This is the hard reality of the imaginary world—the genius and the mad person both are at times accosted by the upsurge of the non-volitional, imaginary world of dream, vision, and so forth. The difference is that where the genius can take these gifts and forge them into something coherent and powerfully beautiful, the mad person is overwhelmed by it. Blake's time at Felpham was troubled and he had much inner conflict that at times seemed to devour him. A spectre of his doubts and fears haunted him as he searched for the expression of the wisdom he had found.

If I could see, feel, and hear the world around me as alive with Imagination, I could develop a child-like wisdom. I was starting to realise how much the magical mind thinks in patterns that connect in a psychic unity. Patterns dance into magical awareness and become a shining track into other realities, much as the geometric shapes on prehistoric cave walls lead a shaman into different realms of perception and experience. The matrix seems to include all qualities and all opposites, and so it is possible to experience all of life and death, unity within multiplicity, in an encompassing whole. This psychic unity is fluid, associative, and embraces diversity and difference; it a landscape of the imagination that extends further than the human mind but also encompasses it. I felt that I had gone some way to understanding not just the monistic worldview of William Blake's thought, but the darker recesses that were hinted at in the dragon quality of the Imagination. What I had come to know, however, was that poetry for Blake was the inspired voice of the imagination, and that the dragon represented as much a certain mode of the human mind as a state of the soul.[12] The imagination was indeed a doorway into another mode of perception.

NOTES

1. J.R.R. Tokien 'Beowulf: The Monsters and the Critics' *Proceedings of the British Academy* 22 (1936): 257–258.
2. Antonio R. Damasio 'Some Notes on Brain, Imagination and Creativity' in *The Origins of Creativity* Karl H. Pfenninger and Valerie R. Shubik (eds.) (Oxford: Oxford University Press, 2001): 65.
3. Kathleen Raine *Golgonooza: City of Imagination* (Ipswich, Suffolk: Golgonooza Press, 1991): 11–12.
4. Daniel Marchesseau *Chagall: The Art of Dreams* (London: Thames and Hudson, 1998): 147, 159.
5. Graham Clarke *The Photograph* (Oxford: Oxford University Press, 1997): 197, 207–8.
6. Jane M. Oppenheimer "A Note on William Blake and John Hunter" *Journal of the History of Medicine and Allied Sciences* (January 1946): 41–45.
7. Patrick Harpur *The Philosopher's Secret Fire: A History of the Imagination* (London: Penguin, 2002): 205.
8. Raine *Golgonooza*, 11–12.
9. E.P. Thompson, *Witness Against the Beast: William Blake and the Moral Law* (Cambridge: Cambridge University Press, 1994): 5, 109–110.
10. Marsha Keith Schuchard *Why Mrs Blake Cried: William Blake and the Sexual Basis of Spiritual Vision* (London: Century, 2006).
11. Alexander Gilchrist *Life of William Blake* (London: Dent & Sons, 1863): 139.
12. Kathleen Raine 'Introduction' to *A Choice of Blake's Verse* (London: Faber & Faber, 1972): 12–13.

10 The Doors of Perception

I was encouraged by reading about the Imagination of William Blake, or perhaps it was the opening of my senses that encouraged the dragon. But in an instant, when the lightning flashed, zigzagging in forks across the blackened sky, and the thunder crashed, I recalled seeing the dragon in my memory. Slowly, the dragon appeared to uncoil from a small almond tree in the garden, its eerie outline transformed into a fiery creature. Transfixed, I watched it crawl up into the branches, and gradually I felt that I was melding with the dragon until we were one. During storms I used to sit in the open doorway to the house, huddled in blankets, watching the awe-inspiring power of thunder and lightning. My mother, sitting by my side, encouraged me to feel the warmth of being inside against the wet coldness of outside. In late winter, just on the verge of Spring, the little almond tree's white-pink blossoms had danced in the breeze, before the petals fell, giving way to green, velvet-cased nuts. Standing alone, in the centre of a neatly manicured lawn surrounded by rose beds, this dragon tree sometimes had a plastic-covered washing line with brightly coloured pegs used to attach clothes tied to it. On windy days the clothes danced themselves dry in the breeze. My mother used to hang blankets over its branches and I made a camp inside. This was a place of adventure, but it was also a place where I felt safe. The dragon *was* the tree, and from here, I could venture into different realms within my imagination. It seemed that the dragon, as a sensory awareness, had been there all along. It was my perception of it that had changed. My exploration into the reality of the imagination as a doorway into the unknown was helping me to recover magical elements of my life that I had forgotten, or previously deemed unimportant. Once my realisation had been drawn to the synchronous associations, I began to see seemingly ordinary things in a new light.

Many years later, while I was walking in the mountains just north of Periana in southern Spain, I came upon a grove of small almond trees. One in particular reminded me of my childhood almond tree. This little almond tree on the mountainside was holding its footings and its delicate branches, bearing leaves and green, velvety nut cases, fingered outward into the sky.

By the curve of its branches it looked as though the dragon has been caught by a northerly wind and frozen in time, into the dry, thistle-prickled, red earth. That morning, I had watched the dawn rising from below the mountain, gradually spreading with the heat haze that enveloped the valley in the direction of the grove. I had taken the narrow, crooked path back up the mountain. Walking further up, I had come to the little tree. Rocky outlets lay in between the narrow paths made by generations of bell-tagged sheep and goats that had made their browsing way between the trees. Sitting on a rock opposite the almond tree, I watched as flocks of sparrows and then of goldfinches fluttered through the branches. The bark on the tree formed elongated slits near the earth and as it went upward, they made a crazy-paving patchwork; the whole was covered with egg-yolk ochre and silver-grey coloured, lacy-edged lichen. My awareness took in the experience of being in the place. The air was warm and the gentle twittering of the birds allowed my imagination to meld with the presence of the tree, as it had done when I was a child during the thunder and lightening storm. A childhood nursery rhyme came into my mind: "I had a little nut tree/ and nothing did it bear/ but a silver nutmeg/ and a golden pear; The king of Spain's daughter came to visit me/ all for the sake of my little nut tree." This rhyme, as I found out subsequently, is said to relate to Catherine of Aragon, daughter of King Ferdinand and Queen Isabella of Spain and the first wife of King Henry VIII, who was divorced for his second wife, Anne Boleyn. My memory flashed to Anne Boleyn's Well in Carshalton, the place where I was born and spent the early part of my life (as described in Chapter 8). Jardani, the *chovihano*, had told me that trees are connected with each other. We had often spent time underneath trees, particularly "Old Man Oak," and he had given me a piece of this oak tree. If you speak to one, then there is always a link of interconnection with the others—it was like a magical telegraphic pathway. I always imagined the trees whispering together and passing on their gossip. The connection between this Spanish tree and the English tree of my childhood, long gone, seemed to go through time and space, as well as different lifetimes. So why had I thought about this rhyme at that moment? As I sat close to the Spanish almond tree, words seemed to arise from the tree:

> Bark, deeply crinkled, riven lines, cracks, criss-cross.
> Roots hold my place, branches sway,
> gently,
> leaf-fingers caress the air.
> Nuts in green velvet, inside hard, speckled shell enclosing secret.
> Kernel, ridged,
> leads through.

The tree seemed to be "leading me through" to another perception. Almonds are said to bring wisdom and deep spiritual insight, while fire and fidelity are qualities of the nutmeg, and the pear has associations with immortality. As the hard outer almond case cracks open, the kernel is revealed, and my senses open. I imagine the fire of the dragon rising up through the tree once again, as it had done in my childhood garden. Coiling out into the world, the dragon took me into a mythological landscape of lightning flashing quicksilver. Shifting shape and becoming many things, totally unbelievable in literal analytical thinking, it offered a vast panorama of alternative possibilities that went through many lifetimes.

Now I can understand that watching the lightning flash and seeing the dragon emerging from the little almond tree in the garden when I was a child was an expression of the dragon's mutability, how one thing can transmute into another in the magical, imaginary thought processes. The dragon and the tree transformed into each other with a fluidity of rippling, dancing water. The dragon represents the source of non-volitional imaginary content. Or, put another way, these are the thoughts of the dragon, and they are also one with the dragon. Coming to an awareness of the dragon did not happen overnight. In fact, it could be said to have happened over a lifetime as I reconnected with the almond tree. What did change was my realisation that the dragon had been there all along. All I had to do was shift the way I experienced the world to re-discover the reality of the mythological imagination that I had known as a child. Reflecting on this childhood encounter, I knew that I had not materially transformed into the fire-breathing monster, but the vivid experience had stayed with a palpable feeling deep in my subconscious. At times such as these I sensed nature's elemental power; I realised that the boundary between myself and everything else was permeable and not absolute! It was these early experiences that led me to associate the dragon with nature in my imagination. As I sat on the Spanish mountainside, I reflected on my experience of the dragon; how it had helped me to open my "doors of perception," as sought by Aldous Huxley, inspired by William Blake.

My own perception was opened further not with mescaline, but through the beat of a drum. I had been experimenting with shamanic journeying during my research with British shamanic practitioners, many of which used the drum's rhythm to go into a trance for visualisations. I had bought a drum so that I could participate in rituals and other events and experiences, but also, as anthropologist, observe what was happening at the same time. During a conference on shamanism in Cardiff, in Wales, I had had my first shamanic journey during which I became a snowy owl in my imagination.[1] On the basis of this experience, I had joined a drumming group in Vauxhall, on the banks of the River Thames in London; every month met up with around twelve people to journey on shared experiences in a community hall. This involved lying down on the floor while one member beat a drum for about fifteen to twenty minutes. During this time, we used the active imagination to propel ourselves into a magical state of mind: this is an example of a controlled decentring of the self.

These were my first experiences of opening my perception by using a drum to induce altered states of consciousness; they would lead to me to my first direct, practical contact with a feeling that I first consciously attributed to "the dragon." I had been staying in a small fisherman's cottage, in a village on the harbour at Wells-next-the Sea. I had bought a drum some time previously but had not used it. The drum had hung on my bedroom wall for a long time, waiting to be painted. I kept staring at it, thinking that one day, I would get around to it, but time came and went. And then something happened. Suddenly, I got a feeling that the drum needed to be painted and it needed to be painted soon. . . Not analysing this feeling of immediacy, I sat on the floor in the cottage with all the paints surrounding me, as I noted from my field report written afterwards: *I felt a deep presence of a dragon; it was a pulsating feeling that seemed to be coming from the base of my spine. The presence slowly took over as I squeezed some red and yellow paint onto a saucer. Picking up the paintbrush, I mixed the colours together with water, making sure that there were lots of streaks of both colours still in the paint. As the first strokes of paint met the drum it seemed to sing in response. The blood-red paint, the drum, and my whole being seemed to come into alignment; it was almost like placing the last piece of a jigsaw puzzle into position when the subtle shifting of the wooden shapes transforms the parts into the whole picture. Now I can start to see the fiery tendrils of connections that enable another awareness. The dragon was blood red. It felt primal. As the first wash of colour went onto the drum, I seemed to connect with something vaster. At the moment that the paint, the drum, and my awareness connected, I felt the dragon's tail twitch deep in my being. The air seemed to go thick and I felt a tingling in my ears. I found myself disappearing into each brush-stroke, around and around into a spiralling vortex of*

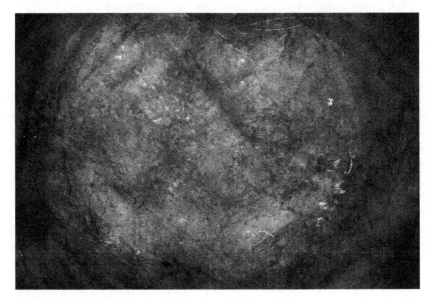

Figure 10.1   Dragon Drum

red. The dragon appeared around the rim of the drum; its coils wound ever tighter,[and] flames burst from its mouth.

I felt that I had become the blood-red fire dragon through what felt like aeons of time. I recorded that my body knew the dragon, deep down, even while I was not consciously aware. I sensed that the blood-red dragon was the fire of my passion, my energy, my life-spirit and my soul in contact with nature and what felt like primal ancestors. It was a deep realisation of an alternative perception, one not immediately apparent in the everyday world. The dragon had taken me somewhere else. Some time later, when I was in less of an altered state of consciousness, I carefully painted the rim of the drum with the fire-breathing creature that I had experienced.

* * *

An opportunity arose for further research on the dragon when Geoffrey Samuel, my anthropologist friend and colleague from the University of Cardiff, invited me to participate in a research project in Wales, the mythological lair of the red dragon. The aim was to create a "dreaming" of the River Taff. Inspired by Australian Aboriginal Dreamtime, the idea was to build up feelings and experiences as part of an ongoing mythological and historical story of the environment around the famous Welsh river. I had met Geoffrey at the Nature Religion Conference organised by the University of Lancaster in 1996, and we had corresponded and met many times, sharing an interest in alternative modes of knowing and exploring scientific theoretical frameworks for their examination.[2] South Wales was once a land of coal mines, and the Taff was so polluted that it was said to run black with coal dust: at one point, it took 100,000 tonnes of colliery waste each year. Pitheads and slag heaps once dominated the landscape, but the coal industry declined from its heyday of 620 mines in working operation to none. The last mine closed in 1994, but the remains of its industrial past can still be seen surrounding the river. I had already spent time in Brecon Beacons, the source of the Taff, and wanted to connect with this river more. The name Taff may have the same origin as the Thames, being derived from the Celtic *Tam*, with a root meaning dark, smooth, or wide spreading. Rivers are symbolic of life and death, time and destiny; they spread the waters of life.

It was a freezing cold day in February and the British Army was on manoeuvres when the small group of people that Geoffrey had invited arrived at Taf Fawr, the "Big Taff," one of the two sources of the Taff in the Brecon Beacons. Soldiers were running over the mountain in camouflage gear carrying rifles; there was an air of activity blowing across the snow-covered terrain, and this was echoed in the river, which was rushing down from the mountainside, cold, clear, and bubbling. I stood beside the river and tried to let go of all my thoughts to let the place speak to me. Rivers have hidden depths, and labyrinthine, subterranean elements; they also flow along, linking people and places. It is necessary to just have enough information from maps, history, folklore, etc. to set the scene, but not too much because it can cloud direct experience. Shifting my perspective, I started to feel the whole course of the river as it coursed downwards on its way into Cardiff Bay. A different pattern emerged, resulting from its complex history from early prehistoric settlements to the intense industrialisation of the coal mining and iron working around Merthyr Tydfil. I let the clear, cold waters wash through my awareness, my internal thought processes start to flow away, and I started to feel the raw pulse of life through the water. The rapid movement of Taf Fawr was in stark contrast to the second source of the Taff, the Taf Fechan or "Little Taff," a few miles away. All is silent and still at Taf Fechan. Here, the second source of the Taff is tamed into the Talybont Reservoir. Weirs are managed by the Wales Water Company, and the river is frozen and looks like a scene from the Artic, so different to the activity at Taf Fawr. The dark gothic architecture of the Victorian waterworks adds to the eerie atmosphere of the place. It could almost be the surface of the moon. Everything feels to be held in abeyance; there is a peace and quietness here, a time for reflection, such a contrast to the rapid movement of Taf Fawr.

The Taff, like all rivers, has accumulated its own memories, but this river has a special history because of its industrial past. The Welsh valleys were rich in coal and collieries were opened to meet the demands of the iron trade. Coal and iron were carried by canal barge down to ports at Cardiff and Newport. Working conditions were tough for the miners, who included women and small children as young as six years old. The younger children controlled ventilation systems, while the older children and women hauled coal from the face to the bottom of the mineshaft. Thousands of miners died due to underground roof falls and explosions. The situation of the miners was made worse by overcrowded housing and unsanitary conditions, both of which led to outbreaks of cholera. There is a palpable pain and deprivation in the land and its waters; it is said by some that the souls of the dead linger here. Moving on downstream is the confluence, sometimes called "the dark pool," the swirling part of the river where the Taf Fawr and the Taf Fechan meet at Cefn Coed-y-Cymmer, just below Merthyr Tydfil, home of the eighteenth- and nineteenth-century Industrial Revolution. The first train to run on rails ran here, and it was the place that gave birth to the Labour movement—the Merthyr Rising of 1831 saw between 7–10,000 workers march under the red flag as a protest at their working conditions. The confluence feels like a very powerful area due to this history, and also the meeting of different aspects of the Taf Fawr and the Taf Fechan. The meeting of the two source rivers of the Taff feels like the coming together of two opposing forces. According to Welsh folklore, "the whirlpool of the River Taff at Cardiff forms a small lake when the bed is almost dry. . . people said it was fathomless, and that in its depths a monstrous serpent dwelt, and gorged on the unfortunate victims that were drowned in the river and sucked into the pool. When any bodies were not recovered from the whirlpool, people said they had been swallowed by the serpent."[3] The place has a power, but now it has been neglected—there are lots of slag extraction piles, rubbish, and a feeling of an abandoned river. The industrialisation process has taken its toll on human beings and the land. However, rivers have different currents, eddies, and depths, and all are part of the general stream; they form their own ecological habitats, as well as tell many stories and hold feelings, memories, and emotions.

Figure 10.2   The Confluence Where Taf Fawr and Taf Fechan Meet

Figure 10.3   Pontycafnau Bridge Showing Dragon Aspect

The river holds many different ripple patterns. What images, feelings, sounds, and memories come from the water? I feel another knowing of the body through my breath and the pulse of blood through the earth. I stand on the Pontycafnau Bridge over the Taff, near the confluence, which is the first iron railway bridge ever built, in 1793, and it also served as an aqueduct. Today, the shadow of the bridge transmutes the natural habitat of the river as a reminder of the dragon in the swirling waters. I look into the depths of the water, picking up memories of the past. I feel that I can sense the dragon in the river as it makes its swirling way along the old mining valleys to the sea via Cardiff Bay. Water in prehistoric times was seen to be the source of all life, as I had learned through my research on Carshalton, the place of springs and wells and of my birth, but culturally, we have lost this sacred connection. Water is a deep and ancient force in cultural memory. We are all born of the primordial waters: we grow within a maternal amniotic sac, and water makes up most of our bodily composition, so we are physically linked.

The mind of the river holds my reflections; like the waters of Carshalton, the waters of the Taff hold me. A perspective from the other side: what would the river see?

Something trying to communicate
through frosted ice.
Spirit
to
spirit.
The land and the spirit are one.
I cannot speak for the river;
maybe I am a vague flash in its memory.
Through aeons, what do I matter?
Small, insignificant, a whisper then gone.
But then again,
perhaps the river does ken with a kenning within its unfathomable depths.
A sense of yearning to hold space;
to share the second of eternity in the moment.
In the moment we both flow as one.
And that is all that matters.

The flow is a reminder not to get stuck in the past—to go into the depths but not to stay there, to keep things moving, ever flowing. Everything changes; move onwards. The river tells me to look into my own reflection, as Jardani said, but not to become distracted or mesmerised by it. Look deeper. The river can help bring memories into the present, where they can be healed. At that moment, we both flow together where all the waters meet.

Reading about the Taff, I felt I had accumulated some of the history and the pollution of the industrialisation process of the Welsh valleys. It felt that it was important to clear up the rubbish and litter along the riverbanks, but there was also a corresponding process within me. After visiting the Taff, and back at Geoffrey's house, a couple of us went on a shamanic drumming journey. The dragon came as a purifying force to me; it appeared as the rivers of the land and took me deep down into the underground waterways. These needed a spirit purging of human exploitative activity. I was taken into a white spiral in my imagination and a red dragon emerged strongly, fiery and angry at not being recognised. It told me that the Taff is part of a whole process of extraction that has drained its lifeblood from the land without acknowledgement. The dragon manifested in my imagination as the spirit of the Taff lands and waters; it took me down in blue smoke tendrils deep into the mineshafts and caverns of the earth. It felt like the red dragon was the fury of the earth that had been plundered thoughtlessly. The dragon's smoke tendrils were messages from the earth and I could follow them down into the source of the pain. To feel the anger and to feel the pain was to experience the roar of the dragon; going snake-like into the mineshafts and dark caverns was to acknowledge the earth's hurt:

> Fire of red dragon,
> burning bright volcanoes,
> sending smoke spirals upwards.
> To follow them curling downwards snake-like,
> is to see and to heal the hurt that is done.
> The ivy tendrils grow once more.
> Now salmon swim, gone is black coal dust.

Now there is purification of the waters of the Taff: fish swim where there was once coal dust pollution.

Things are changing; renewal and healing is happening. The red Welsh dragon connects with the dragon-ivy sentinel at Carshalton. The ivy indicates resilience and tenacity, as the dragon symbolises renewal in magical consciousness. I have learnt that communicating with the spirits of the waters has opened up a process of knowing that all are connected through ripples of relatedness.

> The water holds the place
> of her deep knowing
> of the past;
> it takes me
> darkly
> through time.
> And lingers
> in her being
> to connect with ripples
> Brightly.

The spirits of the waters flow through all beings before returning once more to their source, there to be reborn and renewed in the life of the magical Imagination.

Figure 10.4   Healing Waters

NOTES

1. Susan Greenwood The *Nature of Magic* (Oxford: Berg, 2005): 102–105.
2. Geoffrey Samuel *Mind, Body and Culture* (Cambridge: Cambridge University Press, 1990).
3. M. Trevelyan *Folk-Lore and Folk Stories of Wales* (London: Elliot Stock, 1909): 9, 14. Cited in Jacqueline Simpson *British Dragons* (Ware, Hertfordshire: Wordsworth, 2001): 48.

11 A Mythological Language

Imagination requires a language to shape and express the memories, thoughts, and feelings that arise during the process of magical consciousness. This language is often shaped through mythology. Myths are the opposite of truth to the analytical mind, but mythologies provide a foundation for the development and expansion of magical thinking. In magical consciousness they offer a "geographical framework" for synchronistic occurrences and the fluid boundaries, as exemplified by the mutability of the dragon. The ability to metamorphose is vital to an understanding of the mythological language of magical consciousness, a reminder that the magical mind refers not to the material world as such, but to a profoundly subjective universe that nevertheless has great impact on everyday reality. In my case of examining my own particular ethnography of mind, I was not surprised to intuitively discover that the dragon could transmute into Freyja, a shape-shifting goddess of the northern European tradition.[1] Freyja seemed to be a "more human" manifestation of the dragon in this variable awareness. Thus, Freyja became an intermediary who would teach me about the specifically human aspects of the dragon's elemental nature. This mutable aspect of magical consciousness is not that dissimilar to Tibetan Tantric practices whereby an individual might engage in a ritual to connect with a deity, as discussed in Chapter 4.

Experiencing the goddess Freyja in magical consciousness formed a synchronous association in my mind. Cats are particularly associated with Freyja, who was said to ride in a chariot drawn by these felines,[2] and wore gloves made from their skin, and I remembered the nineteenth-century author Rudyard Kipling's *Just So* story about a cat that walked alone. The process by which the connective events between the goddess and the story about a cat became meaningful was circuitous. It came about through meditative walking on the south coast of England and involved a search for fossils on a beach. A different perception was brought about through the synchronous, interwoven pattern that was idiosyncratic and totally meaningful to me. It demonstrates, at its most fundamental level, the individuality of the system and technique of magical consciousness.

***

My opening experience with the goddess Freyja occurred many years after an academic conference on Nature Religion Today, held at the University of Lancaster campus in the Lake District in 1996. It was here that I met psychologist Brian Bates, and that meeting would change the course of my research. Brian was the author of *The Way of Wyrd*, a best-selling novel recounting the training and initiation of a Christian scribe by a shaman in Anglo-Saxon Britain. He also taught an innovative course on Shamanic Consciousness at the University of Sussex, as well as training actors, such as Mark Rylance, Kenneth Branagh, Timothy Spall, and Sean Bean, at The Royal Academy of Dramatic Art in London. From chatting together over breakfast one morning at the conference, Brian and I discovered that we had similar views on magic. We stayed in contact and when he broke his leg in an accident the following year, he asked me to teach his shamanism course at Sussex, which I agreed to do on very short notice. I then went on to teach Shamanic Consciousness for many years, first as an undergraduate interdisciplinary module in the psychology department, and later as a course in the Department of Continuing Education. I also designed and taught a sister undergraduate course on Altered States of Consciousness as part of an interdisciplinary module in the School of Cultural and Community Studies, also for the psychology department. During this time at Sussex, Brian and I developed our own shamanic research programme, and it was while we were working on this that I first encountered the goddess Freyja.

We enacted a mythodrama based on a poem first written down in the Eddic *Völuspá* in which the Norse god Odin tries to burn *Gullvieg*, a seeress equated with the goddess Freyja. Brian had included the story in his book *The Wisdom of the Wyrd*. The poem was written in northern Europe when people believed that the world was imbued with spirits and certain women were seeresses, specialists at prophecy. Named *völvas*, they sat on a raised dais during *seiðr*, a ritual during which other women formed a circle around them and chanted to draw in spirits to assist in the process of looking into the future, as described in the *Saga of Erik the Red*. We decided to enact this as a sacred drama: I embodied, or "channelled," the goddess Freyja while Brian embodied the god Odin. Freyja taught *seiðr* to Odin even though *seiðr* was considered to be women's magic and unsuitable for men. For Odin to learn such magic was evidence of his ability to transcend gender roles; while still maintaining that such roles exist and have definition, he was also able to go beyond them—this is a common aspect of ritual[3] and magical thought. Later Christian writers accused Freyja of turpitude, but this belies that she is a goddess of fertility, as she is a member of the Vanir fertility deities. Freyja is also a death goddess. Being a Valkyrie, a spirit of battle, her mission was to choose the slain in battle, those who had fallen on land or sea. She took half to her hall Sessrumnir while the other half went to Valhalla, Odin's hall. Valkyries are said to transform into ravens, swans, or "horses formed from the clouds with hoar frost or dew dripping from their glistening manes."[4] During the preparation, which took many weeks, we ran through the narrative of the poem and made practical arrangements regarding setting up the ritual—everything was carefully researched. During this time, we slowly started to feel the essence of the deities as the practical dimensions of the narrative of the myth unfolded.

A seeress had arrived at Odin's hall to foretell his future. Unbeknownst to Odin, the seeress was the goddess Freyja. The mythodrama unfolds when Freyja, masquerading as an ordinary seeress, has to impart bad news to Odin: he is not going to be so successful as a warrior as he had thought. He is furious with the seeress, and orders her to be burned. Obeying Odin's command, his soldiers put the seeress to death. However, the seeress, who is of course Freyja, rises from the ashes twice before being finally killed a third time. This unnerves Odin, and the mythodrama explored the feelings that arose between god and goddess and the wider mythological meaning for the cosmos. An extract from my notes of the ritual, as I experienced it:

[T]he Seeress waited outside the hall. Wearing a black cloak with a strap studded with precious stones reaching to the hem, she melted into the growing darkness. Around her neck were three amber necklaces; she held white cat skin gloves, and on her feet were long, laced-up, calf leather boots. The warrior god Odin had summoned the Seeress. She could hear him and his men now inside the hall; there was laughter and shouting and general merriment, and tales were being told of victorious battles, each aspect dramatised and relived. The Seeress felt nervous as she ran her fingers down her staff; the smooth feel of the wood comforted her, reminding her of her magical connections. She knew she was in touch with her magical power—she felt it as she felt the blood coursing through her veins—but she also knew that she faced a challenge, for she was to conduct a divination for Odin. . . .

When all was correctly set out ready for the Seeress, she was invited inside and courteously escorted to the table to feast on mead, honey, dates and also the heart of a wild boar. She partook of the hospitality offered, and the conversation was respectful and polite. Six magnificent gold rings were put before her, and she greedily placed them on her fingers, holding out her arm to admire their shine in the firelight. This Seeress loved gold; she lusted for it. A platform had been constructed with a high seat strewn with furs, on which she was to perform her divination, and when she had satisfied her longing for gold, she mounted it. She was an impressive presence; the room fell silent, waiting to see and hear what would come next.

As she climbed into the high seat, she started to slip into trance, and as she looked down at the small circle of women who had been gathered to sing her into the spirit world, and the assembled crowd of warriors below, she felt them drawing into her, Odin in particular. She settled herself into the seat, feet planted firmly apart and staff before her; it supported her with its twisted shaft formed by the growth of honeysuckle in its formative years, the falcon feathers bound to its tip gently swaying. She leaned forward, the staff taking the weight. Going deeper into [a] trance, she felt the energy inside her move up and down the staff; she was riding it. Her back tingled, and there was a buzzing in her ears. Her body became a channel as, rocking, she soared upwards in spirit to the sun; the falcon was still circling lazily in the sky. The warmth of the sun filled her being as she felt herself expanding outwards. She lost sense of herself into the greater cosmos. After a while, she drew the solar energy into the conduit formed through her spine and the staff, holding it together with the energy of the gathered crowd at her feet. Then, in spirit, she descended to the depths of the earth, deep, deep into the dark and down into a cave behind a well, a well of wisdom of the source of all being. This was the cave of the female ancestors—the matrix of being. A circle of shaggy brown bears greeted her spirit; they were sitting in the cave around a fire, and they held the collected wisdom on which she drew. This was ancient knowledge. The Seeress felt connected to her source. She opened her heart; she was ready to perform her work. . .

As soon as three more magnificent rings were placed in her palm, she felt a shiver run through her, and she was frightened. Seeing into the future, as predicted by the current threads of fate, she would have to tell the company about the dissolution of the world and the final battle of the gods. . . . It challenged Odin's power, and he was mortified, and then his shock turned to anger. How dare this impostor make such a pronouncement! She must be a witch!

Odin had commanded his men to kill the witch, but after two attempts, she still rose up. After the third attack, however, she moved no more, and the breath passed from her body. Mortified, Odin was filled with remorse and, finding Freyja's burnt and bloody body, he reached for her heart, kissed it, and then ate it.

The wind was roaring outside the hall, and the rain was pouring down; the trees were waving in the gale outside. The goddess Freyja started to feel the energy moving through her. It wasn't fierce, but gentle, and the wind seemed to be calling her. It took her to a beach, and she remembered the golden rings that Odin had given her; she saw them beneath the rippling waves of the sea, and the sea melted into her. She saw the sun reflected in the water, and the rings sparkled in golden rays; the sea beckoned her deeper into its greenish blue, shimmering depths. Freyja felt the primal power of the water and her connection with the deep well of wisdom outside the cave of the ancestresses. Then she felt again the power of the wind, and she knew it was the spirit of Odin. The wind howled as it raced through the treetops, as Odin came whistling through every fibre of her being and they descended together into the dark of the cave under the sea.[5]

In these passages, one can see the very "process" of how magical consciousness takes everyday events and memories and weaves them into a powerful imaginary narrative that is real in a different way from how things are real in the analytical mode. It is always important to remember that the deities encountered in these interludes have intent and personality, memory and desire, but they cannot be engaged unless one is immersed in a magical mode of thinking, whereupon they take their most potently affective quality. From the time spend researching the "role" of Freyja and meditating on her aspects, I was familiar with the goddess. It seemed as though she was calling me into an understanding of the dragon, one that was only possible through a more "human friendly" and intimate association. Called the "wild woman" of Northern myth due to her practice of magic and her free expression of sexuality, which put her outside societal norms,[6] it was her aspect of wildness that seemed to link with Kipling's wild cat. Freyja was my synchronous link between the old magic of Kipling's story and the essence of "wildness." This felt like a key to an understanding of the manner in which myths help shape synchronous connections in the mind.

It was during this time that I remembered a story about Freyja and a necklace referred to in the mythological poem *Beowulf* as the Brosings' necklace; it was a gem-figured filigree necklace forged by four *dvergr* or dwarfs, a piece of jewellery that was no ordinary trinket, but rather a magical talisman—the Brisingamen. According to this myth, Freyja saw the necklace and was enchanted. Deciding that she must possess it, the goddess went on a visit to meet Dvalinn, Alfrik, Berling, and Grer, the dwarfs that had crafted it. Freyja offered the dwarfs gold and silver for the necklace, but they would only sell it to her if she would lie a night with each of them. Magically, this can be seen as a union with the primordial forces of divine nature, one of an especially intimate nature, transforming the practitioner mentally and having very rich symbolism (as will be described in Chapter 13). Freyja wanted the necklace so badly that she agreed.

As an act of magical connection with Freyja, I had been drawn to make a talismanic necklace in the goddess's name with pieces of amber that I had collected over the years. There were rough dark brown pieces and smooth milk white ones I had found in shops when I was travelling along on the east coast of the U.S. Others were a bright clear yellow resembling pomegranate seeds that came from an old necklace found in a junk shop, and still others were rich golden brown stalactite-shaped found in a fossil shop in Britain. Threaded alongside the amber were cowrie shells and a long bone found on the beach at Hope Gap, a stone's throw along the coast from Cuckmere Haven on the Sussex coast (see Figure 11.1).

As I fingered this necklace, it seemed to take me closer to the goddess Freyja. I felt my awareness shifting into a place of communication. The goddess seemed to be present in the landscape.

Drawn to Cuckmere Haven, I could sense Freyja in the land. It was this beach that I imagined in the Freyja and Odin mythodrama when Freyja saw the golden rings under the sea. Here was the place where Odin brought Freyja back to life as part of his magical teaching to open his heart. The goddess taught him "feminine" seiðr magic, and he chose to transcend his masculine gender boundary willingly to learn from her (the idea of a great hero being taught by a magical war goddess has countless Celtic parallels as well). I felt that the goddess was there in the ancient rhythm of the land, precisely at the point of stillness between the oxbow river flowing out and the sea tide going in at the Cuckmere Haven estuary. She was there where

Figure 11.1   Freyja Bone, Amber, and Shell Necklace Seen through the Seeress's Crystal Ball of Divination

the river met the sea. I felt her palpable presence at that moment, in the same way that I had known her presence during the mythodrama. I was watching the sun in the dazzling reflections of the sea. Through the brilliance of the mid-day sun, Freyja brought the blackness of night. Freyja, while mediating the sun, is always in a relationship with darkness. Her dominant energy is solar, but always in connection with the dark, as life with death, fertility with decay, and amber with bone.

Freyja brought these aspects into manifestation within herself, and within me. Freyja had opened my heart. She was a manifestation of the dragon as a pulse of nature that rippled through my awareness. The tide came in rapidly in little eddies and rivulets—it advanced and then receded again while the River Cuckmere flowed outwards towards the sea. There was a point of stillness, when the sea was no longer coming in and the river had stopped flowing out. A strange lull in the air engulfed the eerie quietness before everything transformed as the tide turned: the water in the river changed direction and surged towards the land. The air was filled with sounds again. This was a space between different rhythms, millions of years in the making.

The mind in such a process of magical consciousness absorbs information, mythological and otherwise. The analytical and associative magical aspects of thinking are not distinct—they merge one with the other. My mind turned to thinking about how many peoples had been there at that river estuary. Early nomadic hunters and gatherers gave way to more settled agricultural life for the human inhabitants of the land surrounding the wide, fast-flowing River Cuckmere. Over thousands of years, peoples have come and gone, each leaving their own marks on the landscape, from the first settlers—who arrived from 4000 to 3000 BCE—who left flint tools, and Bronze Age Celtic peoples who created a hill fort on Seaford Head and farming terraces on the steep down land slopes some time in 500 BCE, to the Romans who worked iron around 43 CE. The chalk trackways on the land made trackways in my mind; they linked with stories that led into deeper reaches, creating chalk trackways in the landscape, much like in the Aboriginal Dreamtime. I needed to go deeper into the Dreaming of the land. Freyja had opened my heart to the place and I wanted to find out more. This would take me into the world of Rudyard Kipling and his *Just So* story of "The Cat that Walked by Himself" as a feline connection with Freyja.

* * *

Kipling was born in India in 1865 and spent much of his early days there before coming to England in 1897, when he was thirty-two years old. Living his formative years in India must have had a great impact on Kipling, and particularly on his understanding of magic. From my own experience of India, I knew how deeply culturally ingrained spirituality is in within Indian life. Having travelled in West Bengal, primarily from what is now Kolkata north to the Himalayas on the Nepalese part of the "rooftop of the world," I had felt the spirituality in the landscape, something that has been deeply overlaid in most Western European countries. In India the feeling of magic is palpable, ever-present, and alive in its peoples and the landscape; it is seemingly caught in the colourful fluttering of the ubiquitous Tibetan prayer flags as you travel further north to the mountains. Further south in Kolkata, while visiting the Kalighat Temple and participating in a puja led by a Brahman priest to the goddess Manasa, the Hindu folk goddess of snakes and mother of the Nagas, I could sense the power of the energy built up over centuries. All of life and death was at the Temple complex—pilgrims came to worship, to be fed, and to die. Forty goats and sheep were sacrificed to Kali, the principle temple deity, every morning, and buffalo were also ritually slain once or twice a year, for she had a taste for blood. I walked into the Temple through the narrow, stone-lined streets, crowded with stalls selling offerings of garlands of the red hibiscus flowers that are sacred for Kali. I had walked past many pilgrims, many ill, sick, and dying, who were coming to ask the goddess for healing, or returning when their prayers to her had been answered. Each bore offerings of hibiscus flowers. Throughout the Temple complex there were nooks and crannies, each holding a number of shrines to Krishna and Shiva, where Vedic fire pit ceremonies were held daily. Kipling must have felt the same visceral, raw power of the spirituality inherent in India. Here in England one has to work harder to feel its presence, a presence I felt was drowned out by materialism and the destruction of the earth.

Kipling, being a man of his generation, was an avid supporter of British colonialism. The evidence of this colonialism still stands in the crumbling Victorian elegance of what was then Calcutta, the capital of the British Raj in the Colonialist era; all of which I had seen in its decaying opulence, and which was symbolised by the Victoria Memorial, a grand palace built for the British Queen Victoria that she never visited. Could I get beyond the man's politics to understand his magic, as alluded to in his magical story about the solitary cat, my connection with Freyja?

Trying to get deeper into Kipling's psyche, I had visited Batemans, a seventeenth-century sandstone house further north in the Sussex Weald, the erstwhile home of Kipling when he moved from Rottingdean on the Sussex coast. Standing in Kipling's book-lined study in Batemans, I remembered that I had tried to get a deeper sense of the man. This house was a sanctuary for Kipling, surrounded by thirty-three acres of land, including a mill and a stream that was the inspiration for his *Puck of Pook's Hill*. However, I felt a sense of sadness there in the dark room where he had written "The Cat that Walked by Himself" and all the other *Just So Stories*. Penned in 1902, at a time of intense personal crisis, the *Just So Stories* were written for his daughter Josephine, who had died in 1899 from pneumonia. Perhaps they were an expression of his search for meaning during the emotional chaos and despair after her death. Kipling also lost his son John in 1915 at the Battle of Loos during the First World War, and there is a heavy feeling in the place. Did he ever recover from such a loss of his children, and is it possible to retain a sense of meaning at those times and in the face of such trauma? Was I picking up this sense of loneliness in my feelings?

Before moving to Batemans, Rudyard Kipling used to live in The Elms, a house on the village green opposite a duck pond in the village of Rottingdean. I felt drawn to the place to discover more about Freyja and the cat association. Rottingdean is a sleepy village some miles west of Cuckmere Haven, and further along the Sussex coast towards William Blake's Felpham. It was a bright, sunny, and very cold day in late January when I visited. As I crossed the busy coast road, the everyday roar of cars receded in my awareness as I walked from Rottingdean village towards the sea. The concrete promenade gave way to pebbles, and my feet crunched as I tried to hold my balance. I felt myself becoming alive to the sea, the waves crashing on the shore—louder and louder as each footstep brought me closer—the sounds resonating with the rhythm of the rise and fall of the waves. I heard the sound of the water rushing over the sand as first the wave arrived, and then retreated over the shore, as if it was being pulled like a carpet from the other direction. Looking up, I noticed a flock of black-headed gulls eyeing me further up the shoreline; perhaps they were the same ones that I saw flying overhead when I was on the way to Felpham to find out more about how William Blake viewed the imagination. Deciding that I had come just that bit too close, they took off into the air, swooping over my head, their white-headed winter plumage stark against the blue of the sky. The sun was warm on my back and the air was inviting as I walked along the beach. My mind took off in a cascade of feelings and memories, like the flight of the black-headed gulls as they wheeled and dived betwixt shore, sea, and sky. The feeling of returning to the coast overwhelmed me. The sun gave the wet stones a sparkle that brought them to life; they lay wet and glistening all around. As I looked down into the sea beneath the waves, the water sparkled as the chalk underneath gleamed bright white. Deep red sea anemones and small fish and shrimps darted between the rocks. I could imagine whole worlds in each crevice, each crack of chalk, and each particle of the sand beneath me.

The world under the water at Rottingdean seemed to invite me, Freyja-like, into an elemental awareness. By synchrony, I remembered reading Kipling's cat story by an open fire in a remote cottage at the foot of the Preselis, the mountains in north Pembrokeshire, southwest Wales (where some of the bluestones were taken to create Stonehenge over four and a half thousand years ago). Recalling the Welsh cottage as I gazed into the rock pools at Rottingdean near to where Kipling had lived, I remembered that it stood by itself at the bottom of a sunken lane. Mosses, ferns, and a hawthorn hedge gave way skyward to tall foxgloves whose pink-mauve sentinels bent downwards with the breeze, seemingly wanting to know who went forth. The small cottage dwelling had a strange oldness about it. A copy of Kipling's *Just So Stories* was on the cottage bookshelf, and I recollected that I had picked it up and started to read "The Cat that Walked by Himself." Just before reaching the end of the story, the lights in the cottage flickered, giving me a couple of minutes to quickly finish what I was reading. Then I was plunged into darkness so black that I melted into its all-consuming embrace. Slowly, the moon had risen over the mountains, and an eerie brightness cast ghost-like silhouettes that had made connections in my mind.

The flickering light kindled my memory: I was aged nine and Mrs. Butler was reading some of the *Just So Stories* to our class of forty eight or so children in primary school. We sat, arms folded on the desks, our heads on our arms, listening to how the rhinoceros got his skin, how the leopard got his spots, the whale his throat, and the camel his hump, but for me it was the cat that had haunted my imagination. The story tells of a woman who created the first singing magic in the world. It had a haunting oldness that spoke to me in ways that I did not understand then, but that I felt in the hidden-away cottage miles from anywhere at the foot of the mountains. The woman makes a home in a cave, and a man, dog, horse, and cow come to live with her. They all agree to become domesticated by providing services in return for their food, but not the cat. The woman tries to tempt the cat to do the same by singing magic with a flat mutton bone, but the cat was the wildest of all wild animals and he walked by himself; "all places were alike to him." The cat does agree to catch mice and be kind to babies in return for milk, but he retains his wildness and "on moonlit nights he roams the woods or the roofs, walking by his wild lone." What was it about the story of the cat that walked by himself that had caught my imagination as a child? Was it the eerie feeling of the woman's singing magic? Did it somehow suggest an invisible and mysterious realm to which the woman had access?

This intrigued me as I walked along the beach at Rottingdean, most probably where Kipling himself had also walked. Perhaps I was picking up something of Kipling's spirit, much as I had picked up a sense of William Blake as I had meditated on the beach at Felpham. Pondering on the thought that walking on his wild lone might have brought some comfort to Kipling, I wandered on along the coastline at Rottingdean. Did he roam along this same beach under the white cliffs where jackdaws nest and rooks fly overhead to ease his pain? The black Rottingdean windmill stands high up on Beacon Hill on the surrounding downs like a huge black crow, rather ominous now. As I tread on the stones, I reflect on walking along this hidden beach below cliffs and between waves thundering onto the shore. I am by my wild lone, as the cat in Kipling's story. My feet crunch on the pebbles as I look for signs that give me clues to what I am feeling —things that draw me to them in my imagination.

The Volk's electric sea railway, built between 1894 and 1896, used to run between Rottingdean and Brighton, some four and a half miles to the west. I can see the concrete remains of the pillars that used to support the strange, insect-like sea tram that was officially named *Pioneer*, but nicknamed *Daddy-Long-Legs* due to its being perched high up on iron supports above the waves. The railway deposited its passengers from Brighton onto the Rottingdean pier, at the end of which Kipling, accompanied by his children, used to fish. The sea tram and the pier has long since gone, and the coastline has gradually eroded, the plundering sea claiming all manner of buildings as the village has been forced ever northwards. The stones on the shingle beach are omnipresent in their myriad grey muted colours of various shapes and sizes, echoed in the swell of the waves.

As I walk along the shoreline, perhaps I can find the wildness of Freyja and the wildness of the cat in the magic of the dragon encapsulated within a stone. The Chinese say that the dragon-gods are hatched from stones, especially beautiful stones known as dragon's eggs. It is said that when these are split thunder is heard, lightning flashes, and water flows from the stone. In Chinese legend, an old woman found five dragon stones lying in the grass. Soon they split and the old woman carried the newborn serpents that had emerged from the eggs to a river to set them free. It is said that she was rewarded with insight.[7] What was this insight? The freedom of wildness, and a different perception brought about through Freyja the mythological goddess, a story about a cat, and the overall mutability of the dragon?

After walking for some time, my eyes attuned to the shapes and patterns of the stones in front of me, I see what looks like a piece of anthracite, a coal-like stone that has facets of different colours that sparkle and gleam from all its aspects. I pick it up and admire it, but put it back down again. When I was quite young I had a book that fascinated me, and the memory of it has stayed with me to this day. It was a cheaply published edition designed to keep children quiet during rainy days and it had sections for "colouring-in," puzzles, crosswords, and word games. The puzzle that I remember most clearly was a picture of a riverbed where you had to identify the shapes of different water creatures hidden amongst the stones. The challenge was to make out the outlines of fish from the water beetles and snails. I would gaze at the page for ages, running my fingers over the images and letting them take me into the bottom of the river, another world in my imagination. This puzzle had a hold on my imagination and I remember that as I searched for fish, my awareness of the other shapes diminished. If I looked for water beetles or snails, I would notice only them. This memory comes to me now and I realise that there are patterns within patterns and this is somehow important to thinking magically and to making synchronous connections with the elements.

I wander by the sea. I know this process well, and I am very familiar with the scene in front of me—the silhouetted crow windmill standing proud on top of the hill, the chalk cliffs and the circling seabirds. The tide comes in and out in its usual rhythm, regulated by the gravitational pull of the moon. As I watch, I am always drawn back to the feeling that this must have been the same scene for our early human ancestors. Nothing has changed; the sea is still influenced by the moon, as we are. My awareness returns to the stones. Really I am looking for a sea urchin fossil that can be found on this coast. Coming from the Cretaceous period, many millions of years ago, these fossils in magical thinking link back in time when we had a common life in the sea. Do the fossils, like the prehistoric painted lines in caves, penetrate the rock face and lead to the spirit realm? The Kalahari San see the painted lines as "threads of light" that come down from the sky to take their shamans to visit god.[8] Can I find a deeper insight by following the call of the marks in the stones too? For some time I have used fossils as a way of linking in with what I am feeling—as a measure of synchronicity with the dragon, a connection with an ancient wildness of spirit.

Turning to walk back, I start retracing my steps, and then have the insight that my desire to find a fossil has blinded me to seeing alternatives; maybe even that piece of anthracite has a message for me after all. The more I ponder on it, the more I think how all its facets constitute many elements—they make up a whole as a type of hologram. Rather than being open to what comes, I have been blinded by my pre-conceived ideas about finding a fossil. I walk back to find the stone, but part of me already knows that I will not find it among the trillions of pebbles on the beach. I know deep down that the message was there for me to take; I had to seize the opportunity or it would be lost forever. Now the stone seems to have retreated back into the others; I cannot find it. Feeling rather despondent, I turn to go home and as I look down, I suddenly see a sea urchin fossil half covered in sand. Reaching for it, I can make out that its distinctive star pattern takes the form of a heart. I am delighted that I have found a fossil after all! The fossil is rather like a guiding star; it represents a chalk and stone beacon on the connecting pathways of magical consciousness.

I found what I was looking for, but at the same time I realise that there many other aspects of awareness that lie beneath the pattern in my awareness. There was a message in the coal-like stone with its many facets, too. Each facet seemed to reflect a range of alternative perspectives—different views. It taught me to be open to different experiences. The issue now was how to find meaning in the fossil. The meaning was not completely in the fossil, but lay in the pattern. However, the meaning was not totally held in the pattern, either: the meaning was in the realisation that there is a pattern among other possible patterns. This requires a wildness of walking, like Kipling's cat, outside what is known to see other possibilities. The dragon is the pattern, the process of change and transformation in magical consciousness. It would take me into a place of wild elemental confrontation, as will be recounted in the next chapter.

NOTES

1. Catharina Raudvere 'Now You See Her, Now You Don't: Some Notes on the Conception of Female Shape-Shifters in Scandinavian Traditions' in *The Concept of the Goddess* Sandra Billington and Miranda Green (eds.) (London: Routledge, 1996): 41.
2. Hilda Ellis Davidson *Roles of the Northern Goddess* (London: Routledge, 1988): 51, 108.
3. Adam Seligman, Robert Weller, Michael Puett and Bennett Simon *Ritual and Its consequences* (Oxford: Oxford University Press, 2008).
4. M. Oldfield Howey *The Horse in Magic and Myth* (New York: Castle Books, 1998): 14–15, 51–53.
5. For the full version see Susan E.J. Greenwood *The Anthropology of Magic* (Oxford: Berg, 2009): 83–90.
6. Stephan Grundy 'Freyja and Frigg' in *The Concept of the Goddess* Sandra Billington and Miranda Green (eds.) (London: Routledge, 1996): 56.
7. Marinus Willem De Visser *The Dragon in China and Japan* (New York: Cosimo, 2008 [1913]). Cited in M. Oldfield-Howey *The Encircled Serpent: A study of serpent symbolism in countries and ages* (London: Kessinger Publishing, 2005): 260.
8. J.D. Lewis-Williams 'South African Rock Art and Beyond: A Personal Perspective' *Time and Mind: The Journal of Archaeology, Consciousness and Culture* 6(1) (March 2013: 45.

12 Confrontation

My task in this exploration of the ethnography of my mind was to know-ingly face my fear and lose my bearings amid a sense of controlled decen-tring, or what felt like a personal disintegration. By immersing myself in developing a relationship with Freyja through the ritual process of the mythodrama, and also by my realisation that Kipling's cat was symbolic of "the wild," I realised that my experience of the goddess was weaving me ever deeper into the deeper, "darker" process of magic. I had a strong sense that Freyja was an intermediary with the dragon, and it was this fear-ful creature that was demanding more of me through some form of initia-tion. If I could survive the primal wildness that ensued, I thought that it would bring me to an altogether different understanding, and hopefully, a far-reaching comprehension, of some of the intense intricacies of magical consciousness. It felt like Freyja in her cat aspect, as well as a Valkyrie horse, was taking me deeper into the knowledge of magical wildness. I had to face my fear of what I knew would come, which was some form of initiation with the dragon. The Austrian poet Rainer Maria Rilke said, "Perhaps all the dragons in our lives are princesses who are only waiting to see us act, just once, with beauty and courage."[1] Although Rilke's work has sometimes been dismissed as overly simplistic,[2] his association of dragons with fear and acts of courage strikes a deeper chord that is far from naive. I could reframe Rilke's words into "Perhaps the dragon in my life was a goddess who was waiting to see me act with beauty and courage?" This chapter recounts how I developed a particular relationship with Níðhöggr, the dragon of northern European mythology, and how he would introduce me to the cosmic tree Yggdrasil, whose name comes from a horse that takes its rider to the gal-lows. From here I was drawn into the classic epic poem *Beowulf* as part of my own fearful discovery of a wild, elemental knowing of the dragon.

NÍÐHÖGGR THE DRAGON

In order to engage more fully with this confrontational process, I did some research on dragons. Tim Ingold re-tells a cautionary medieval tale by

Gregory the Great (circa 594 CE) from the *Life of St. Benedict of Nursia*, in which traditional monastic narratives proceeded along trajectories of movement, seen as paths or ways, in which the medieval thinker was a wayfarer whose mind would travel from place to place. Fear was a form of control, while the dragon represented a loss of bearings from the known path of the monastic life. The dragon was not an objective cause of fear—it was visceral fear itself. The tale goes that a monk was itching to escape from the close confines of the cloistered monastic life. Father Benedict, becoming fed up with the monk's continual whining, eventually ordered him to leave the monastery. When the monk eventually stepped outside the monastery, a fearsome dragon blocked his path. Terrified, the monk called to his brethren for help and they accompanied him back inside the institution, which he never left again. According to Ingold, the vision of the dragon was recognised by medieval people as the form of the monk's otherwise unarticulated agitation—he was at the point of being consumed by fear and showing symptoms of personal disintegration. In the medieval monastic tradition, dragons and other terrifying monsters were used to control novices by instilling fear in them.[3]

One dragon that spoke to me particularly was the northern European Níðhöggr. Northern European mythology speaks the cultural language of the Icelanders, Norwegians, Danes, Swedes, and Germans who came to settle in England. This area has hosted many peoples, all bringing different myths and legends that have become embedded in folklore. The land of the south, which was part of the ancient kingdom of the southern Saxons since the fifth century, appears to hold many different memories. It is my experience that these memories are not exclusive and the land will transmit sensory experiences in varying ways, depending on the individual and the context. Northern European mythology has been associated with extreme nationalism, but the dragon that I experienced will communicate with whoever will listen, regardless of origins, ethnicity, or place. I imagined that Níðhöggr was like the spirit of a wider elemental nature that had been ignored, denied, or repressed in Western cultures, and it was this aspect that made it especially fearful. If I was going to really come to know this dragon, I knew that I would have to learn more about the dark and subjugated part of its transformation capabilities.

Níðhöggr manifests part of an ongoing process of destruction and growth. In the mythology, Níðhöggr is continually associated with death. In magical thought, of course, death does not mean what it does in the analytical mode. Death in the magical mode means transformation, and is always followed by rebirth. It is interesting to note that Níðhöggr is described as living "in" the great well of Hvergelmir, the "boiling cauldron," from which originates fate, memory, and all creation. Ymir, the primordial giant, emerged from Ginnungagap from beneath this well, and Odin, king of the gods, learned the secrets of the runes while hanging from Yggdrasil, which has this well at its roots. This dense imagery gives us a glimpse at the many

non-verbal, highly associational and emotional meanings of the relationships between the tree of life, creation, memory, fate, the gods, the mysteries, and the dragon.

My communication with Níðhöggr started at a particularly stunning
beech tree that was growing in a copse at the bottom of the steep escarpment leading up to Chanctonbury Ring, an Iron Age hill fort on the Sussex
Downs. Although this was a relatively small tree, which at first sight did
not look as majestic as some others that I had seen, it did feel as though
it was magically powerful, as it had a large cavern beneath its roots. Even
though it was not a traditional ash, I felt that this tree was Yggdrasil-like
in its otherworldly presence. The tree's roots grappled for footings in the
chalky escarpment, spreading outwards like a crinoline skirt of knuckled
fingers, the roots searched for a hold in the disappearing earth. The tree had
only partly succeeded, for part of the slope had eroded away, leaving the
underside exposed like a dark cave. As I climbed right under the tree it felt
like I was entering an underworld of Yggrasil; my mind seemed to expand,
and I imagined that I was entering a different time and place. As I looked
upwards between the gnarled root-fingers along the trunk, my eyes reached
up past a lovers' heart, with initials entwined in undying love carved into
the smooth bark, to the branches—then green with new leaves—and beyond
to the sky. Crawling deeper until I was right under the trunk of the tree,
I imagined the almond tree of my childhood, when the lightning had transformed the tree into a dragon. In the root-enclosed darkness, I got a sense
of the presence of Níðhöggr. This tree did seem like a manifestation of Yggdrasil, containing all worlds of the mythological imagination. I focused on
Níðhöggr lurking at the bottom of Yggdrasil, in the realm of Hel, bringing
about death through his gnawing of the tree roots, and so creating life anew.
Life and death, light and dark, order and chaos, a stable pattern and transforming energy are part of an ongoing, cyclical spiral through time.

As I became more accustomed to the heavy presence of the chalky earth
and the roots surrounding me, I remembered that Yggdrasil's name comes
from a god called Ygg, who rides drasil, the tree that is magically also a
horse. The name *Yggr* means "terrifying" and is another name for the god
Odin, while *drasil* is associated with both horses and gallows, referring to
"one who walks" or rides, often on horseback.[4] Odin rides a grey horse
called *Sleipnir*, the name of which comes from the Old Norse and means
"slippery." This horse has eight legs, four legs for each world he traverses,
signifying his "slipping" into the otherworlds: a magical, shape-shifting
horse! And so the meaning of the name of Yggdrasil is the horse or gallows
of Odin. The tree was the horse that took Odin into the realm of death, for
Odin hung on Yggdrasil, sacrificing "himself to himself" for nine days and
nights to receive wisdom. The horse takes its rider to his gallows, and so
the fearful Níðhöggr, the glittering dragon, slithered into my imagination.
Odin's initiation would also be my initiation into the deeper recesses and
depths of magical consciousness. I would gain insight from the reptilian

inhabitant of the deepest depths of one of the roots of Yggdrasil. This seemed to be the first part of my growing awareness of the fearful aspect of the dragon. As I climbed up from under the roots of the Chanctonbury tree and made my way homewards, the process had already started, though more in my unconscious than conscious mind.

INCUBATING THE DRAGON: BEOWULF

Hoping to find a way to fathom the deeper elements of what all this could mean, I turned to *Beowulf*, an Anglo-Saxon heroic-elegiac poem[5] about a confrontation with a dragon. Here, I thought I might find synchronous clues to the destructive aspect of the dragon. *Beowulf* comes from the minds of the people of southern Saxony, those who inhabited the area of southern England named Sussex. The southern Saxons came originally from an area south of Denmark around 450 CE, and established settlements all along the Cuckmere Valley on the south coast of England, an area that I knew well and that felt deeply magical to me. These Saxon people were pagan when they arrived, but converted to Christianity due to the influence of St. Wilfrid in the seventh century.[6] Thus, the tale was in the cultural memory of the people who inhabited the south of England, Sussex in particular. The words of the poem seemed to echo in the land, in the call of the seabirds, and in the rhythm of the waves as they pounded on the shingled coastline. *Beowulf* was originally told orally by bards, but was first written down in verse by Christian scribes towards the end of the seventh century in Rendlesham, East Anglia, a bit further around the coast of England from Sussex. The formal act of writing it down preserved it for future generations, but it was the version told by the Christian scribes, who saw the dragon as a monster, as evil and an adversary of God to be vanquished,[7] and also as an aspect of fear to preserve the monastic tradition.[8] This was the dragon that prowled the margins of the monks' minds, keeping them on the straight and narrow. The dragon was fear itself, fear of personal disintegration and of primordial chaos. Even still, however, there are many subtleties to the poem that reveal a poet who, though nominally Christian, incorporated a great deal of pagan elements.[9] Despite the Christian overlay of several elements of the story, it is plain that the poet deliberately universalised the story of the great king and his monstrous foes to be applicable to pagan and Christian alike. Though there is by no means any consensus on the meaning of the highly ambiguous nature of the relationship between Beowulf and the dragon, many scholars of the poem have seen the dragon fight, for example, not as a mere vanquishing of an enemy of God, but as a union of two mighty forces[10] and a symbol of the (Jungian) Self archetype—meaning a symbol of a great union of life and death, light and dark, and a unifying force in the universe. In this reading, Beowulf's "battle" with the dragon signifies the hero's confrontation with death itself, which, through his union with the dragon, shows his transformation into something transcendent.[11]

We are already close to the idea of a confrontation as I am describing here, a repetitive theme colourfully imagined by the *Beowulf* poet. But what if there was more to the story? What if the dragon told another story? What would happen if I deliberately chose to go beyond the bounds of the known, to place myself directly in some sort of encounter with the dragon? I wondered if I might go mad. On the other hand, perhaps there were truths of spirit to be found in the dark primal and elemental wildness. There was only one way to find out. It would be my task to sense the silence in between the words; this might give me clues to an older, deeper meaning that would help to structure my quest. The poem, I thought, might provide me with a start to take my exploration of the dragon further, for in the culmination of *Beowulf*, a dragon is killed, a momentous event! In this sense, *Beowulf* is a mark in the landscape of the magical imagination, a fusion at a given point in time between the old pagan and new Christian modes of thought. The story is set a long time ago, in an ancestral past. According to Tolkien, *Beowulf* is a "product of thought and deep emotion" that marked a long process of conversion from pagan to Christianity and in which some effects were immediate. An "alchemy of change" producing "the mediaeval" was at once at work: "One does not have to wait until all the native traditions of the older world have been replaced or forgotten; for the minds which still retain them are changed, and the memory viewed in a different perspective: *at once they become more ancient and remote, and in a sense darker.*"[12] The author of the poem sets out a new faith, new learning, and also a body of a native tradition for "the changed mind to contemplate together;" it is a new perspective in an ancient theme, a heroic legend set amid historic allusions.[13]

The narrative describes events in Scandinavia when Beowulf, a prince of goodness who lives in Geatland (now southern Sweden), travels to Denmark to King Hrothgar's mead-hall, the place where his warriors gathered to eat, drink, and hear stories, to rid the Danes of the terror of a fiend called Grendel, a wasteland-stalker and an alien spirit from an "unnatural birth." The Danes have suffered twelve winters of fear and death due to attacks by Grendel who, according to the author of the poem, walks with a baleful tread and dwells among wolves, demons, and ghosts in the nearby swamplands. Not long after the hero Beowulf arrives in Denmark, the wasteland-stalker attacks the barricaded night house, as predicted. Beowulf retaliates and fights Grendel, tearing his arm off in the clash. Mortally wounded, the monster slinks back into the swamp to die. The severed arm is hung high in the mead-hall as a trophy of victory. Grendel's mother, described as a monstrous Hell bride who lives in a mere overhung with trees and infested with serpents and sea dragons, goes to Heorot to seek revenge for her son. She kills Aeschere, one of Hrothgar's most trusted advisers, while Beowulf is away and then grabs Grendel's bloody arm before returning to her underwater lair. To avenge Aeschere's death, the company travels to her watery abode, whereupon Beowulf dives into the blood-filled water and fights Grendel's mother in her subterranean cave. Beowulf kills the mother of the wasteland-stalker by sheering though her neck. Her end is swift and sudden, wrought by a magical sword. Beowulf then finds Grendel's corpse, cuts the head off and presents it as a trophy to Hrothgar, before eventually returning once more to Geatland as a hero.

After Beowulf's return to his homeland, he eventually becomes king and rules wisely for fifty years until he is called back to Denmark for a final confrontation, this time with a dragon. All had been well until a thief disturbed a burial mound where a dragon was guarding a hoard of treasure. The dragon emerged from the burial mound in a blaze of fury and began a terrorising campaign—his precious treasure had been stolen and he sought retribution. Beowulf confronts the dragon, and its death was certain as he hacked the creature in half. In the process, Beowulf was wounded from a venomous bite on the neck. His fate was unknowable but still certain, according to the Anglo-Saxon author of the poem. Both must die, for this is the course of their destiny. However, we can see the deeper symbolism of the return of things back to the primordial, fertile wildness of the dark chaotic unconsciousness from whence everything comes. For in the end, Beowulf is immortalised in the very poem itself, for it is through narrative that Beowulf achieves his apotheosis. Again, despite the nominal Christianity of the author (who never mentions Christ once in the poem), we are given to understand that Beowulf's spirit is given to God to receive the "doom of the just," despite the fact that Beowulf is himself a pagan, which should, according to dogma, consign him to the flames for eternity. Not so for Beowulf: here the poet ignores dogma and tells a tale truer to the pagan spirit of the poem, which is that Beowulf, through facing the horror of death itself, and in fact dying with the dragon—his spiritual opposite—he conquers death itself and is able to return to the primordium.

Tolkien refers to certain critics of *Beowulf* who want to dissect the meaning from the historical, philosophical, archaeological, and mythological aspects of the poem, but ignore "Poesis" the poetic journey through the narrative. Poesis was "usually forgotten; occasionally admitted by a side-door; sometimes dismissed upon the door-step," but rarely seen as poetry with a message so powerful that it overshadowed the historical content.[14] The poetic message concerns an encounter with the dark: Grendel, his mother, and the dragon. The real battle is between the soul and its adversaries.[15] The poetic meaning of the story is magical. Michael Alexander, a translator of the poem, describes Old English poetry as "cunning, non-straightforward and peculiar." In particular, "kennings," an Old Norse term, were used as a specialised form of metaphor whereby two words were put together to form a poetic image, and poetry was a source of wisdom.[16]

GUARDIANS OF WILD, POETIC WISDOM

I wanted to find out more about the poetic wisdom of Grendel and his mother, for I sensed that they were all finally connected with the death of the dragon. Grendel is an expression of lots of different things all at once, of many understandings that reawaken things in us.[17] Grendel and his mother are raw, elemental beings of the wild; they are the all-consuming, marauding elemental spirits of the mere, the river, the haunted marsh, where all-powerful deities live in places that were once regarded as sacred in pagan, pre-Christian times. Here, certain lakes, like springs and wells, were the haunts of female fertility deities. In antiquity, humans were sacrificed to them in lakes. Death was thought to bring about fertility and new life for the good of the community as far back as the Neolithic period. A goddess plays the leading role in a great ritual drama to ensure the increase in cattle, as well as the rhythm of the crops: "the seed is buried, and sleeps in the earth the sleep of the dead; but in the spring it awakes and springs up to a new life and the promise of rich harvest."[18] Tacitus, in *Germania*, tells of the goddess Nerthus, the mother of Freyja, who is worshipped by seven peoples living between the rivers and the forests:

> In an island of the ocean is a holy grove, and in it a consecrated chariot, covered in robes. A single priest is permitted to touch it: he interprets the presence of the goddess in her shrine and follows with deep reverence as she rides away drawn by cows: then come days of rejoicing and all places keep holiday, as many as she thinks worthy to receive and entertain her. . . until the same priest returns the goddess to her temple, when she has had her fill of the society of mortals. After this the chariot and the robes, and, if you will believe it, the goddess herself, are washed in a sequestered lake: slaves are the ministrants and are straight-away swallowed by that same lake. Hence a mysterious terror and an ignorance full of piety as to what that may be which men only behold to die.[19]

Beowulf speaks of a fusion at a given point in time between the old pagan ways and the new religion of Christianity. Tolkien's "alchemy of change" does not have to wait for the pagan traditions to be replaced or forgotten; for the minds which still retain them are changed, and memories become more ancient, more remote, and darker. The once revered and sacred water monsters in the form of Grendel, his mother, and the dragon become evil adversaries. The author of *Beowulf* sets out the new faith, a new learning, and also a body of a native tradition demonised for the changed mind to contemplate together.[20] It is interesting to note, though, that like the *Beowulf* poet himself, this demonisation is, despite itself, never complete, never entirely convinced. Tolkien's own translation of the poem, for example, translates a famous line describing the descendants of Cain; in Old English, the list is given as "eotanas ond ylfe ond orcneas" or "giants, elves, and orcs." Tolkien, however, is unable to translate elves as the descendants of Cain and translates this line as "ogres, goblins, and haunting shapes of hell."[21] As others have shown,[22] the *Beowulf* poet's attempt at demonising "elves" was isolated and unsuccessful, and the ambiguous, largely native, and pagan concept remained long after, even into Tolkien's own famous fantasy works.

Beowulf, through his encounter with the monsters of the dark mere, and through mortal combat and death, comes to know the dragon. In the process, the dragon dies too, but rather than being the end of the story, as the Christian scribes wrote down in their interpretation, the dragon embodies a potentiality of fertile transmutation from death to life, as with the sacrifice of the devotees of Nerthus. The kernel of this idea survives even the Christianising of the poem. At the heart of this story is an ancient alchemy of transformation, not a battle of good over evil, or of staying within safe boundaries, as a clear-cut monastery version would indicate. Everything transforms: the dragon is the ultimate symbol of mutability and change. The dragon is an elemental creature that contains the mysterious process of transformation. I sensed that this was the hoard of treasure that it was guarding, and so its death must be a powerful aspect of this process. Grendel, as a force of darkness rather than evil, attacks the hall, and this comes as a stark reminder that death occurs in the midst of life. Beowulf kills Grendel, who is in turn avenged by his mother, before Beowulf kills her too. The final encounter between Beowulf and the dragon, many years later, completes the process: even the hero Beowulf and the anti-hero, the dragon, cannot escape the inevitable. Hereon what was once sacred becomes increasingly monstrous; the elemental spirits of water once venerated have become demonised. In my continuing quest for the fearful aspect of the dragon I would have to feel out the less-than-obvious places, in the watery, fluid associations formed in my mind shaped by my intuition.

Grendel and his mother have a lupine nature, and are described as *werga, werhtho, heorowearh, brimwylf, grundwyrgenne*, all of which contain the elements *wearg/wearh* or *wylf*. Grendel is also demonised by being called a *scucca*, which means "demon," and he and his mother are both seen as the haunters and guardians of the burial mounds in marshland, and are given an aquatic aspect to match—*brimwylf*, for instance, means "water-wolf."[23] Dogs have long been viewed as guardians of the underworld, psychopomps and agents of the spirit world. These canines have a long history in mythology, from the Egyptian Anubis, the jackal-headed god of death and judgement that guides lost souls to the underworld, and the Greek dog Cerberus with his three heads, also guarding the entrance to the underworld, to the Black Dog mythology amongst the Celts expressed in the Morrigan, a goddess of death that occasionally appeared in the form of an enormous black hound.[24] Countless Celtic gods are associated with loyal, often divine, canines as well.

Canines were a gateway into the deeper mysteries of the dragon, as I already knew. Having lived and done fieldwork in East Anglia, I had heard the fearsome tales of Black Shuck, a ghostly dog encountered by nocturnal travellers, which were widespread in the area. Grendel and Black Shuck were both demonised by being called a *scucca*, a "demon," as it is from *scucca* that the second element of the name of Black Shuck is derived. The area was on the north coast of a wild and rather remote, windswept part of north Norfolk, and to get anywhere it was necessary to travel for miles along narrow hedge-lined roads that all looked the same. At night, driving for hours along these highways in the monotony of the view through the windscreen, lit only from the headlights of the car, I would sometimes imagine Black Shuck lurking in the mist drifting across the road from the fields. It was said that the black dog was a portent of death. The myth of the Wild Hunt, a cavalcade of the spectral dead attended by baying hounds, was also common in the area, and an encounter with the Wild Hunt would form an introduction into the realm of death for me, preparatory to the death-realm of the dragon. Often it is a goddess Holda, known as Frau Wode, a derivative of Freyja, a protector of souls, who leads the Wild Hunt on her white mount attended by dogs and wild beasts. In other versions, it is the god Odin who gallops on the ghost-like, eight-legged Sleipnir though the woods at night with a phantom train of baying dogs. Whoever leads the hunt is the spirit being that speaks to the particular area where the myth is being told. When I was in Switzerland, visiting Braunwald in the Swiss Alps, after giving a lecture on magical consciousness at the Migros Museum für Gegenwartskunst in Zurich, I noted that Perchta, "The Shining One," was the southern equivalent of Holda, who had been replaced by Berchtold, a male leader of the Hunt. The point, I realised, was that the folklore adapted to the specific changing times and politics of the region. In this sense, it was not so much universal, but highly particular and localised.

This was never truer for me than when I participated in a "Wild Hunt Challenge" organised by a pagan group that ran pub moots in Holt, a small town on the north East Anglian coast, and each person picked up their own messages from the Hunt. Each participant of the Challenge was required to walk alone through a wood outside Norwich at night during Samhain, the Celtic festival marking the end of the lighter period of the year and the beginning of the dark, to invite an encounter with the phantom spirits of the Hunt, as I have fully described elsewhere.[25] When I completed the Challenge, it was my first encounter with the fearful hounds of the Wild Hunt. I was realising that the hunt marks a ritualised cycle of life and death whereby the living, by joining with the spirit train, participate in the realm of the dead in the imagination. To encounter the Wild Hunt was like an initiation into fear, and I found that my mind was expanding into other experiences. Rather than a form of seeming madness, this primal chaos seemed like an incredible insight into other modes of being that transcended my usual ways of thinking.

It felt like one of the hounds of the Wild Hunt challenge visited me some time later. I was walking near my ancestor tree, where I had scattered my mother's ashes, and where my spirit ancestors had come to me after my shamanic healing ritual as recounted in Chapter 6. By synchronicity, it was also Samhain, the time of year when the ancestor spirits are said to come close, and a windswept day. I could feel the ancestors with every step. As I watched the dog walkers of material reality, I felt the ghostly hounds of the Wild Hunt accompany me, and these words found their way into my consciousness:

> Walking between the worlds,
> the wind blows the leaves
> *helter skelter,*
> *they cross my path,*
> *blowing topsy turvy,*
> *red and yellow.*
> *Each footstep takes me deeper*
> *into another way of knowing.*
> *But I can see other realities dancing*
> *between the leaves.*
> *I follow the path,*
> *and the wildness brings*
> *the hounds of the chase;*
> *they know me and I sidestep through their being*
> *into the now.*
> *For now is not the time,*
> Yet.

I knew that at some point, I would join the hunt for lost souls, but not yet. It felt as though my skeleton was walking in the breeze as I sensed the wild hounds, felt their teeth on the back of my neck. I could feel another awareness and, for what seemed like an instant, I was between the worlds of the living and the dead. I sensed that I knew both:

> *My footsteps fall between the leaves,*
> *inside I am white Bone.*
> *The hounds have taken me as one of their own.*
> *Skeletal remains still walk,*
> *between the leaves that flutter down*
> *in between the worlds.*
> *The past is gone clean away,*
> *I am left free to fly amongst the spirits.*
> *My life is here now,*
> *I breathe deeply.*
> *Joy.*

The wild death hounds were there at that moment, in the park, amidst the dog walkers of the everyday world. I could feel their presence. It was exhilarating and comforting, all at the same time. For a split second, a moment in time, I was given a glimpse of the Ride and my soul could fly on rushing currents in my mind. The full force of my confrontation with the elemental dragon was yet to come, but I would not have long to wait.

WILD, ELEMENTAL DRAGON

My confrontational encounter with the wild dragon would happen while I was conducting fieldwork with Mad Shamans, an eclectic group of practitioners of magic, at Cae Mabon, a retreat space of several indigenous dwellings situated in a clearing amid an oak forest in the foothills of Mount Snowdon, north Wales. Organised by environmental educator, dancer, and shaman Gordon MacLellan, or Creeping Toad, as he is commonly known, this group positively invited discussion, especially of the more challenging kind. In fact, the group had developed quite a reputation in pagan circles for being challenging and taking a provocative and questioning stance on matters of a shamanic or pagan nature. To join Mad Shamans was considered an honour in the pagan world that I inhabited at the time. A person had to be invited by a member and, having been invited once, there had to be general approval for subsequent invitations. Upon receiving the first invitation to a Mad Shaman gathering, one was made very aware that it was a trial for suitability, and there were many tales told, recounted time and time again as group folklore, of invitees that had fled at the first encounter due to the fierceness and apparent turpitude of some of the members. Mad Shamans was a group that liked to push boundaries, a good place to go beyond the known. When a friend, a member of the Mad Shamans, invited Gordon and myself to dinner, we had the chance to talk. Before long, I was on my way to London for a meeting with another member of the Mad Shamans for further assessment and questioning. An invitation to join the group at their next meeting followed shortly after. Gordon and I became close friends. Many years after our first meeting, he gave me this sacred underworld spirit denizen that he had crafted. She stands about a foot tall, has tattoos all over her face, holds a bear drum, a bag of shamanic paraphernalia, and is covered in beautiful beadwork and feathers (see Figure 12.1).

During the course of my Mad Shamans days, we visited Cae Mabon many times. Here I found a freedom of spirit and easiness, once I was accepted. This was never more true for me on a personal level than when I was exploring my dragon sensory awareness, for the dragon was taking me into unexplored regions, the like of which I had never before known. Cae Mabon is in the land of the red dragon. Although the lands of Wales are associated with Celtic mythology, nonetheless in my mind, there is an underlying magical truth that underpins all mythologies. The experiences that they induce are similar, despite the social, cultural, and political divisions that emphasise difference. These tribal differences are symbolised in a battle between the red dragon of Wales (*Y Ddraig Goch*) and the English white dragon. In Arthurian legend, the wizard Merlin had a vision of a red dragon, symbolic of the Celtic British people, and a white dragon, representative of the invading Anglo-Saxons, fighting beneath the hill fort of Ambrosious Dinas Emrys in northwest Wales. Níðhöggr, for all intents and purposes an Anglo-Saxon dragon, is only one manifestation of the dragon—nothing is fixed when it

Figure 12.1   The Anthropologist's Sacred Underworld Denizen

comes to dragons! Subconsciously, I knew that the dark dragon was calling me into the realm of Hel, or the Celtic underworld of Gwyn ap Nudd, a spirit being that I had already encountered during the Wild Hunt Challenge in Norfolk. My task in confronting my fear was to go deeper into the realm of the primordial, elemental dragon, deeper than the red dragon and deeper than the white dragon, to a place where tribal battles have no significance. I sensed I had to face the primal wild dragon within. In characteristic form, the dragon shifts into many dragons and much else, including manifesting as the goddess Freyja. However, underlying all dragons is the magical truth that lies within the primordial, raw elements of place, the wild spirits of nature.

I elected to sleep alone in a black shavan, an Iranian canvas tent designed for the nomadic life of the desert, at Cae Mabon. I wanted to know what it would feel like to be so directly alone with the wild in this most elemental of places. Erected under a small copse of trees by the side of a fast-flowing river whose waters came thundering down from the mountainside, the shavan had steam-bent oak laths fitting into a central dome-shaped wheel; it was anchored to the ground by a rope and held together with a large peg driven into the earth. It was the dark womb of the black dragon. That night in the womb of the dragon was like no other I have ever experienced. The sound of the water was deafening: it drove my numbed mind into spiralling eddies of whirlpools and underground currents.

In the all-consuming, marauding blackness, I was visited by the wild spirits of the river, the trees, and the earth, and beings that were so totally non-human that they took me to a place of extreme terror. I experienced myself being engulfed and consumed by what felt like an alien, elemental otherness. No words can fully express the feeling, but bare, cold, desolate, exposed, and stark come close to the experience of having all security of life removed in a confrontation with the waters of this place as they crashed down the mountainside.

I was surprised to realise that I was still alive when I eventually woke as dawn was breaking. My tongue had erupted in mouth ulcers from the trauma. I felt totally exhilarated that I had undergone what seemed to me as an initiation into death and life itself. My fear of being alone with the wild spirits had led me into a direct confrontation with the unknown. It is this confrontation that has the potential to give deeper understanding. I realised that when I had faced my fear, the alien, spirit elements of nature—the fear-some beast of the dragon—became a force within nature that would give me strength and knowing. Fear had been replaced by a sense of my own courage to stray beyond the boundaries of the known. The dragon had shown me something of the continuity between life and death. Paradoxically, I found that the most fearful thing is that which ultimately heals fear. The dragon is the beast of fearful nightmares, a monster that haunts the imagination in the night, but an understanding of the dragon offers a way out of the same nightmares, for the dragon is not an objective cause of fear: it is the emotion of fear itself.[26] This was indeed the hoard of gold that the *Beowulf* dragon was guarding—this was the synchronous connection with Freyja's wildness. The goddess was part of the pattern of interlinking mythological threads, and her quest for the gold would take me further in my understanding.

NOTES

1. Rainer Maria Rilke *Letters To A Young Poet* (Portland, Oregon: Scriptor Press, 1929): 31.
2. Nicholas Lezard Review of Rilke's *Letters To A Young Poet*, in *The Guardian* newspaper of May 12, 2011. Accessed February 24, 2011, http://www.theguardian.com/books/2011/may/12/letters-rainer-maria-rilke-review?commentpage=1
3. Tim Ingold 'Dreaming of Dragons: On the Imagination of Real Life' *Journal of the Royal Anthropological Institute* 19 (2013): 735–737.
4. Henning Kure 'Hanging on the World Tree' in *Old Norse Religion in Long-Term Perspectives: Origins, Changes and Interactions* Anders Andrén, Kristina Jennbert, and Catharina Raudvere (eds.) (Lund, Sweden: Nordic Academic Press, 2007): 68–71.
5. J.R.R Tokien 'Beowulf: The Monsters and the Critics' *Proceedings of the British Academy* 22 (1936): 275.
6. Patrick Coulcher *A Natural History of the Cuckmere Valley* (Lewes, England: Book Guild, 1997): 4–5.
7. John Grigsby *Beowulf & Grendel: The Truth Behind England's Oldest Legend* (London: Watkins Publishing, 2005).
8. Tim Ingold 'Dreaming of Dragons: On the Imagination of Real Life' *Journal of the Royal Anthropological Institute* 19 (2013): 735–737.
9. Erik Goodwyn *A Psychological Reading of the Anglo-Saxon Poem Beowulf* (New York: Mellen Press, 2014): *passim*.
10. Goodwyn *Psychological Reading*, 211–270.
11. Ibid., 260–270.
12. J.R.R Tokien 'Beowulf: the Monsters and the Critics' *Proceedings of the British Academy* 22 (1936): 262–263 (original emphasis).
13. Tokien "Beowulf", 248, 265.
14. Ibid., 246–247.
15. Ibid., 265.
16. Michael Alexander at a lecture on *Early English Poetry*, Sutton Hoo, Suffolk, May 18, 2013.
17. Ibid.
18. P.V. Glob *The Bog People: Iron Age Man Preserved* (London: Faber & Faber, 1969): 156–159.
19. Ibid., 161–162.
20. Tokien "Beowulf", 265.
21. Ibid., 16.
22. Alaric Hall *Elves in Anglo-Saxon England* (Suffolk, UK: The Boydell Press, 2007).
23. Alby Stone 'Hellhounds, Werewolves and the Germanic Underground' http://www.primitivism.com/hellhounds.htm
24. David Waldron and Christopher Reeve *Shock! The Black Dog of Bungay* (Harpenden, UK: Hidden Publishing, 2010): 13–14.
25. Susan Greenwood *The Nature of Magic* (Oxford: Berg, 2005): Chapter 6.
26. Ingold "Dreaming", 19, 734–752.

13 Forging Anew

To illustrate the power of an alchemical transmutation of understanding, the essence of this chapter concerns the deep shifts in meaning that can occur deep within the psyche during an initiatory experience. My confrontation with the dragon showed me that it was possible to transcend fear, to "find the gold hoard held in the wild lair of the dragon," but my initiatory process was not over. And, more importantly, Freyja had not disappeared. She transmuted once again in my mind. The dragon gold was a synchronous mythological link to this goddess and her gold necklace referred to in *Beowulf* as the Brisings' Necklace, a magical talisman forged by four *dvergr* or dwarfs who lived and worked deep in the earth. Freyja was enchanted with the golden Necklace of Brisingamen, as it is also known. Feeling that she had to possess it, she visited the dwarfs that had crafted it within a deep cavern in the earth, sleeping one night with each of the four of them to obtain its precious gold in an alchemical wildness that transmutes analytical understanding. Magically speaking, the dwarfs are smiths, as they transform metal through fire; they are also associated with light, having taken glowing cinders and sparks from Muspelheim and thrown them into the Yawning Gulf to bring light to heaven and earth. The dwarfs were formed in the carcass of Ymir, an old giant who arose from Icywaves, a place associated with Yawning Gulf, which is in turn connected with Ginnungagap, the mighty primal void. The dwarfs were first like maggots, but under the order of the gods they became conscious, had human form and intelligence. Each of the primal dwarfs held the skull of Ymir, holding it aloft: in the East it was the dwarf Austri, in the West, Vestri, while in the North it was Norðri, and Suðri in the South.[1] Thus, they are important creative forces that represent different aspects from the four quarters of the cosmos in the magical imagination: the dwarfs can bring illumination from darkness.

* * *

My own talismanic necklace that I had made in honour of Freyja connected me in spirit to the goddess. This necklace was itself forged in its own manner through the action of photosynthesis on tree resin to form its own shining golden amber. The necklace would play a significant part in another initiatory experience that was frightening for me in a different way. In my field notes I wrote: *One night as I lay in bed, I felt as though I was in a space between sleeping and waking. I had woken up feeling very cold. It was quiet and dark—eerily dark as moonlight, or the ice-dark of Helheim, the dark realm of ice at the base of Yggdrasil, shone through the bedroom curtains. I felt as if I was walking through the land of death, alone. It was stark, relentless, inevitable, cold, hard, bleak, and I was filled with hopelessness and a sense of despair. What was the point of life? Death was always so close—everyday, every minute, every second. I was aware that I had been to that place before when my horse Cielle died. That was the place of my depression. There was no warmth, no colour, it was barren and deserted yet everyone went there. . . I felt that I just needed to be with the feeling for a moment. Then the realisation came to me that not everyone comes here. That felt like a relief, as I did not want people I cared for and loved to feel so alone, so dark, and so beyond hope. Then I felt a voice that I knew was Freyja's telling me that I was a Valkyrie, I had mastery over the realm of death, and Death was my ally. That felt better and I intuitively searched for a necklace around my neck, the amber and bone necklace. I felt the light of the amber; its golden glow transmitted light and warmth, it seemed from the primal void of Ginnungagap. I knew that Freyja had come to me—I felt her as a shaman, she was teaching me about death and rebirth. Death—the place of barren wasteland was not the end. I felt warmth and hope return to my body. Ice had met with fire in the eternal return.*

I sensed that I had been through a double initiation: once with the elemental otherness of the dragon, and now with Freyja, who had come to teach me a different type of wild, elemental knowing. The dragon's gold hoard, as told in *Beowulf*, would come to me through Freyja as an elemental recapitulation, a reclaiming of energies from my past life in order to channel them into the present. This involved delving into my memories in order to connect with the elements: I had to *feel* the dragon in a different manner to make it personally meaningful.

* * *

As I fingered the amber beads, cowrie shells, and the bone of my Freyja necklace (see Figure 11.1 in Chapter 11), I could feel my awareness shifting. In my imagination, Freyja was staring into the flames of a fire deep within a cave. She was a goddess who loved gold; she lusted after it and she could feel the presence of it as she felt the presence of her own heart beating. As she stared into the fire, she started to feel the pull of the wild gold deep within the earth, like liquid amber. It made music to her ears and the sound was like a drum beat pulling her into another rhythm, a heartbeat rhythm. The beating grew louder and she found it impossible to resist the urge to follow the sound to its source. The goddess stood up and tuned her senses inwards to follow the beat, her heart resonating with the throb of the gold. Making her way to a deep crevice at the back of the cave, she slid between two rocks that were jutting out. Once inside the crevice, she had to feel her way with her hands and feet. It was dark and the walls of stone pressed ever inwards upon her. Freyja's lust for the gold drove her onwards and downwards into the cold, dark crack deep into the earth. The darkness shrouded her, and all that drove her onwards was the beating of her heart linked with the pull of the gold. An age passed but eventually, Freyja came to an opening, and the rock crevice slowly opened out into a large underground chamber. Her ears picked up the sound of tapping, and as her eyes slowly adjusted to the dim light, she made out an underground smithy with four diminutive figures silhouetted in shadows working around a fire. As she moved closer to the fire, she saw that the shady shapes were four dwarfs intent on fashioning a beautiful gold necklace. The necklace gleamed and sparkled; it had a divine presence, for it was no ordinary necklace. Forged by the magical smiths, it embodied the creative force of the cosmos in its glowing lustre.

As Freyja's eyes focused on the necklace, she felt the pull of the gold in her heart more strongly than ever. It was the most exquisite necklace that she had ever seen and she saw it was made of gold; she had a passion for gold. Taking the shape of coiled golden snakes with aquamarines, quartz, and garnets encrusted into its twisting, slithering strands, the necklace called to her and she knew she had to have it, no matter what it cost. Not able to take her eyes off its gleaming lustre, she told the four dwarfs, who had now stopped working to look at her, that she would buy the piece of jewellery. However, the dwarfs shook their heads and told her that it was not for sale. Freyja wouldn't hear of it; she had to have the necklace, at any price. The dwarfs looked at the goddess and they sensed her great desire to possess the gold necklace; they also saw her great beauty. Speaking in one voice, they told her that she could have it if she slept with each one of them in turn, one night after the other. Freyja looked at the dwarfs and she did not savour the thought for a moment, but her desire for the gold necklace was so strong that she agreed to their demand.

* * *

AIR: BE INSPIRED

The first dwarf, the nature of air, was Freyja's companion on the first night. She was sky-winging as she rode on the breeze high in the air, flying as a falcon. Freyja looked down on all below her—the rivers and seas in which she had swum the previous night, and all the fields lined with hedgerows, which formed a patchwork lit by the light of the moon. She felt the air fill her until she became air . . . And then I felt the goddess Freyja in her falcon aspect: I become full of the bird. Insight—the sharp realisation of knowing; my beak hard and relentless, my bones light, my talons sharp for killing. The drawing shows the shape-shifting:

Figure 13.1   Freyja Falcon

I move effortlessly through the air, wind on feather, sculpted movements. Hunter searching for hunted—I hover, then pounce! I kill. Flesh is
transformed once more, again and again. Blood must be spilt for life to
continue—death into life. The blood is the mystery, the mystery of life.

Memories of encounters with air come to me, although I am aware that
every single moment of my life has been an encounter with air as I breathe.
The day I stop completely, I will be dead. Air is the element of inspiration. The meaning of inspiration is to inspire, inflame, or blow into. The
word inspiration dates from the early fourteenth century, coming from the
Old French *enspirer* via the Latin *inspirare*—from *spirare*, "to breathe."
That probably came from the prehistoric Indo-European base *spies*—or
peis, an imitation of the sound of blowing or breathing out. The power
of inspiration involves being open to the unfamiliar—to be inspired with
the breath of life. . . Air is the element of a certain conception of the logical, thinking mind, of my analytical training in anthropology, the study
of humankind. "Analysis" is the process of separating something into its
constitutive elements . . . examination. Scrutiny. Survey. Study. Inspection.
Exploration. Evaluation. Research. Review. Investigation. Interpretation.
Probe. Dissection.

To be inspired is to fly on the wind like a bird, to look down on the earth,
to gain another perspective. As out of an aeroplane window at night when
the glistening land can be seen beneath, I can trace the golden filigree of
Freyja's sacred necklace:

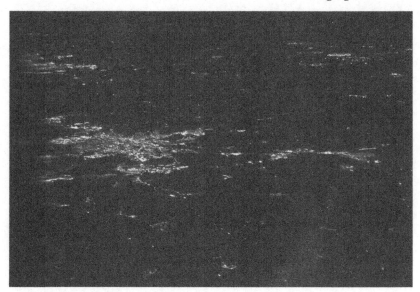

Figure 13.2   A Bird's Eye View

Here is the dragon of air: it is also within the breath of being. We can fly, but can a man really become a bird? Really? The analytical mind, the element of air, is always questioning. J.A. Baker describes in his book *The Peregrine* how he develops a ten-year relationship with a male peregrine, during which he leaves his human form to experience the wildness of the peregrine's world. Slowly, as his relationship with the falcon develops, he ponders on what the bird thinks of him. As the peregrine passes overhead, he looks sideways and down. Baker realises that the bird might watch for his arrival and might associate him with the disturbance of prey, as though he too were a species of hawk. At points, Baker found himself unconsciously turning into a bird as he watched humans dispassionately. On one occasion, he describes how he found himself crouching over a kill "like a mantling hawk," his eyes turning quickly about, looking for humans. He was imitating the movements of the hawk.[2] The falcon has a freedom of eye—he sees and remembers patterns we don't even know exist.

What did this tern (below in Figure 13.3) flying overhead think of me as I was taking its photograph as I walked along a deserted beach on the uninhabited and remote Island of Copinsay, part of the Orkney archipelago?

Oh, to be a bird! . . . I am a bird! The wind whistles through the trees, it is the spirit of the bird. I hear the trees rustling and I know the dance that makes the bird fly. Fly the dance!

Figure 13.3 Tern Over Copinsay, Orkney

WATER: LET EMOTIONS FLOW

And so it was that on the second night Freyja slept with the second dwarf, the spirit of water. On this night, the goddess sailed on the swan's road to a mere overhung with tree roots mirrored in the water. Diving down deeper, she flowed along many underground streams and rivers until they opened out into the grey-blue sea.

Plunging into the waves, she made her way through crystalline ledges and shimmering underground caves. Freyja swam through the tides of the waters where fish swam in brightly coloured shoals. As the water washed over her, she felt the pull of the moon in the watery depths; her emotions darted and swam like the shoals of fish glimmering. Her tears fell—salt meeting salt. . . (see Figure 13.4).

My memories come flooding in. I have always had a love for the sea; it has always called me. I am seven years old. I am travelling in a car to the sea on the south coast of England from our home in Surrey, fifty miles to the north. Any moment now, the blue-green watery horizon will come into view. *Who will be the first to see the sea; who will be the first to see the sea?* Finally arriving at the seaside, my whole body is transfixed with excitement—fingers stiff and toes curling (see Figure 13.5).

The sea has a vast timelessness that seems to stir the very essence of my being. Crouched over rock pools, my father is showing me hermit crabs, sea anemones with waving fronds in vibrant colours, and small shrimps. At

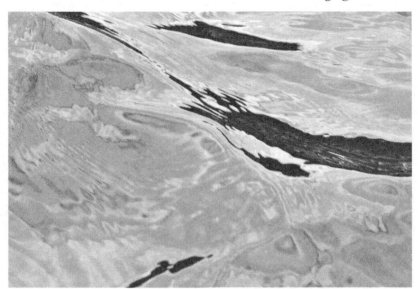

Figure 13.4 Water Flowing to Sea

Figure 13.5 Anthropologist as Child on Beach (Source: Photograph by E.G. Duparcq, the anthropologist's late father)

first I can't see them, they're invisible to the eye, darting in the water, then I see them! Dad always shows me things in nature; there is a whole world contained in that small pool oasis, until the tide comes in once more and they become covered by the waves. . . Water is exciting!

The next memory I have of water is about connection. I am in California, at Esalen in Big Sur where Gregory Bateson spent the last months of his life. I feel that Gregory's spirit lives here in the sparkling water flowing under the bridge, so symbolic of his ideas about looking for the patterns that connect. . . The Pacific Ocean is so ever-present, so charismatic with its crashing waves, craggy rocks, seals, sea lions, whales. The ocean comes swirling into the small bay at Esalen, a haven for the monarch butterflies that dip gracefully into the rock pools to sip a drink, but I'm drawn to the quieter spring that flows down a canyon from Cone Peak in the Santa Lucia Mountains, the highest point in the lower United States. The spring gushes down the canyon into the land at Esalen. It's the bridge that stands over the spring that flows past the beautiful timbered meditation roundhouse that captures my fascination. The bridge connects Murphy House, the erstwhile home of Michael Murphy, one of the founders of Esalen, with the Lodge, the communal meetinghouse. The bridge also connects me with the water underneath (see Figure 13.6). Gregory Bateson was a "bridge" between different forms of information for me. I stand on its wooden planks and look between the boards. I feel a shiver of the spirits of water as they flow beneath as words come:

> Sunlight reflecting, sparkling
> through Crystal glass recollecting.
> Another time, another place, a world away.
> Same meaning.
> Going deeper.
> Connection, past into future,

Figure 13.6　Esalen Spring Water

through now.
Sunlight rippling.
Ancestors, faces, shapes, shifting, coming through . . .
Just connect. . .

The water reminds me of another river, this time in Kolkata, India. The Hooghly is the most westerly river of the Ganges delta in West Bengal and one of the mouths of the Ganges. It's a very different river. The Hooghly runs alongside the Botanical Gardens, the home of one of the world's largest banyan trees, said to be the resting place of Krishna and representative of eternal life due to its seemingly unending ability to produce roots and still more roots, extending ever outward. This river is polluted and it stinks, a far cry from the sparkling clearness of the spring at Esalen, but it is a sacred tributary of the Ganges. Remnants of past festivals linger in its waters: images of the Hindu elephant god Ganesha, the "remover of obstacles," can be seen on its muddy banks in Figure 13.7.

Further along the river, children play in its brown water, while some old men wash themselves and *dhobi wallah* washerwomen clean clothes. A few days before I had been on a ferry across the Hooghly to visit the Ramakrisnu Temple, a place with the Vedanta philosophy that we have to transform our base human nature into the divine within; here lies the unity of all humankind. The waters, wide and misty, carry all soul trackways. On the other bank to the Temple, a man hacked the top off coconuts, then split the top so that I could sip the sweet water as a refreshing drink. . . Water connects all.

Figure 13.7   Ganesha

FIRE: FEEL THE PASSION

The third night, Freyja was taken into the very heart of the blood-red garnets in the necklace. As she went into the deep crimson stone, she felt a strong rush of wild energy up her spine and she knew that this was the flame of her passion, the very will of her being. She knew that she was taking a journey to her heart's desire. This was fire! Following the course of her blood, she came to a chamber wherein lay the source of her enthusiasm: the fire, her inspiration. Freyja looked deep into the fire and at that moment she saw her life force and she sensed this was also her integrity: she was the judge and she was the jury of her own experience. . . She is said to be turpitudinous, Freyja is the scarlet woman:

I feel the fire of enthusiasm. The word *enthusiasm* originally meant to be inspired by a god and was first used in English in 1603, coming from the Latin *enthsiasmus*, to be "possessed by a god." I feel possessed by a god as I recall reading about Little Red Riding Hood, a fairy story about a wolf that eats a grandmother and granddaughter. A girl walks through some woods to deliver food to her grandmother, who is ill. On her journey through the wood, she encounters a wolf. The girl tells the wolf where she is going, and on his suggestion, picks some flowers in the wood before proceeding to her grandmother's house. In the meantime, the wolf goes to the house, pretends to be the girl so the old woman lets him in, and eats the grandmother. The wolf disguises himself as the grandmother and waits for the girl. When Little Red Riding Hood arrives, the wolf eats her too. The

Figure 13.8   Freyja as the Scarlet Woman

shamanic meaning of the tale is one of transformation—from life to death and rebirth to discover the passionate *enthusiastic* wild within, the dark, the unconscious, and the lupine. Wolf. . .!

I become possessed by the spirit of wolf while trance dancing in the middle of the Dovedale valley, Derbyshire, in England. The valley sits surrounded by peaks where ravens fly and can be approached via a long, winding, snake-like drive down the dale. Sheep graze on the surrounding hillside, which is intersected by dry-stone walls, the type that crisscross over all the dales. Past the single farmhouse, on the left and further down, past a barn that nestles in the fields of the dale, the River Dove threads its way through the bottom of the fields on its way towards Milldale. A spring bubbles in one direction and a dewpond broods quiet in the other. In the distance is the seemingly enchanted earthwork ruins of Pilsbury Castle, an eleventh-century wooden Norman castle that stood on an earlier Saxon or Iron-Age earthwork that once guarded the passageway through the valley. The spirit of the land comes through me, releasing the wild fire of my spirit. Tears come to my eyes. I swirl round and round and experience the music of the dale: the long valley with its winding river, the womb of the dragon, the rhythm of life and death, and fear and happiness. . . Then I become a wolf. Lupine and wild, I feel the fire come into me as I throw back my head and howl:

> Around and around
> from deep inside
> a long mournful growling,
> night is dark,
> moon three-quarters full.
> Twenty-four hours pass
> the moon is fuller.
> Time waits in eternity
> like a hungry lover.
> Time stands still.
> Music inside pulses,
> heart quickens,
> feel the stirring
> of the growling.
> Inside.
> Hairy grey, growing shaggier
> meets the call, growls inside
> Beckoning in.
> Moon's embrace, wanting, needing,
> call to call.
> Head back howling
> deep inside the growl of time
> passes into
> Now.
> The scarlet wolf emerges.

Figure 13.9   The Scarlet Wolf Emerges

EARTH: HOLD FIRM

On the final night, Freyja slept with the dwarf element of earth. Earth holds; earth is the mountain and it is also the cave. Eventually, it led her back to the slit in the rock. Once more she follows the way inside, the rock closing after her. . . deep inside the earth she can feel the earth. . . A cave deep in the earth, a sea cave, comes to mind. Travelling on a small boat, we eventually come to a sea cave on the coast of East Mainland Orkney, an island off the furthest tip of Scotland. The name "Mainland" comes from Old Norse "Meginland" and formerly, the island, the largest in the island archipelago that comprises Orkney, was known as "Hrossey" or "Horse Island." The cave can hardly be seen from the seaward side of the coast. It lies like a slit in the rock face, but as we get closer, as the waves lap the sides of the boat, its darkness beckons. We move inside the dark stone, segmented in layer after layer, the colour of grey-magenta gradually fading into grey and then black as we travel deeper into the dark earth, the waves now rippling petrol-green and raven-black. Emerging from the tunnel, we reach an opening where a waterfall gushes, casting spray onto my face as I look upwards into the brightness of day, once more. . .

Back into the past, an oil painting hung on the wall when I was a child. It depicted a boy lying on his back on a grassy hillock. His arm is over his eyes shielding them from the sunlight, and his arms and legs are bare. There was a sense of relaxation and contentment in this picture. My mother painted

Figure 13.10   Orkney Sea Cave

the picture of the boy and that is why it is so familiar to me. I saw it being created as she painted it. It now hangs on my wall (see Figure 13.11).

The picture reminds me of the writing of the nineteenth-century nature mystic Richard Jefferies, who describes how in "the glow of his youth" he used to walk to a hill during periods of when he needed soul-thought. At the top of the hill, he had forgotten the petty circumstances of existence and felt himself to be himself. It was there that he had deep experiences of nature, feeling himself to be utterly alone with the sun and the earth. Lying down on the grass, he spoke in his soul to the earth, the sun, the air, and the distant sea. He felt as though the earth was speaking to him. Sometimes, when lying down on the grass looking up at the sky, gazing at it until he felt he could see deep into the azure, Jefferies felt his eyes to be full of the colour. He would turn his face into the grass and thyme and become lost and absorbed into the being or existence of the universe: "I felt down deep into the earth under and high above into the sky, and farther still to the sun and stars. Still farther beyond the stars into the hollow of space, and losing thus my separateness of being came to seem like a part of the whole."[3]

It was my fiftieth birthday and I was climbing up Mount Snowdon or *Yr Wyddfa*, meaning the burial place in Welsh. Snowdon is 1,085 metres or 3,560 feet above sea level. I was tricked up Snowdon. I would never have agreed to go right to the top if it hadn't been for a friend who lied to me that the summit was just around the next corner. I am grateful to that friend. Otherwise, I would never have had the experience of climbing a mountain. At the summit, I was disorientated and experienced vertigo, but the feeling

Figure 13.11   Boy on Grassy Hillock (Source: Painted by B.V. Duparcq)

of actually standing on the top of the mountain was incredible. It is said that you can see Wales, Ireland, Scotland, and England (including the Peak District the South Pennines, as well as the Isle of Man) from the top. It was too cloudy to see far, but I could feel the majesty of the earth, deep, deep, deep beneath. . .

* * *

Freyja returned home, but she kept quiet about her initiation into the elements. She knew that she had seen the hollow of space as a star. Meanwhile, I knew that what Freyja had helped me experience was a form of recapitulation, a magical process of gathering in the golden energy from my memories of the elements, each part of which was significant and added to the meaning of my connection with a trackway of my being.

NOTES

1. Brian Branson *Gods of the North* (London: Thames & Hudson, 1970): 52–60.
2. J.A. Baker *The Peregrine* (New York: New York Review Books, 2005): 95, 125.
3. Richard Jefferies *The Story of My Heart* (London: Macmillan, [1883] 1968): 1, 6–7.

14 Cyclical Return

James Frazer famously described an underlying magical cyclical pattern through death and rebirth in his classic *The Golden Bough* (1921). Although Frazer's work is not without its critics (as I have elaborated elsewhere),[1] it does clearly point out the essential cyclical quality of magical consciousness. Inspired by English Romantic artist Joseph Mallord William Turner's painting of a sacred grove and sanctuary of the goddess Diana in Nemi, Italy, Frazer described how a tree in the grove, the embodiment of Diana, was guarded by a succession of priest Kings of the Wood. Frazer noted that a candidate for the priesthood could only succeed to the office of King of the Wood by slaying the current incumbent, and he retained office until he himself was slain. Frazer claimed that such a cyclical, recurring theme underpinned all myth. This is indeed an important feature of a magical orientation of mind, as demonstrated by what happened next in the mythological story of Freyja and the sacred golden necklace of the Brisings, in which Loki, a trickster god, brings about death and dissolution. In this chapter, I recount how I learned about my own sense of the magical cycles of life through a reading of this myth. I came to an understanding of their meaning through various experiences, particularly a visit to see a Bronze Age mare pulling a sun disc in the Danish National Museum, sensing the spirit of my grandfather by the visiting some Great War battlefields in Flanders, and walking along the "death path" taken by Virginia Woolf as she walked to the River Ouse in Sussex to sadly drown herself. My experiences culminate in the creation of a shamanic rattle in the spirit of my dead horse Cielle, who becomes a "Valkyrie dragon-horse" as I ride into the realm of death in my magical imagination.

* * *

Unbeknownst to Freyja, Loki, the trickster god, had followed her when she had visited the dwarfs. Loki, like Níðhöggr the dragon biting the roots of Yggdrasil, brings change, and change is necessary in the cyclical mythological round. So, Loki played a key part in what happened next in the narrative of the golden necklace. Loki is the father of the goddess Hel, after whom

Helheim, the realm under the roots of the cosmic tree Yggdrasil, is named, and Fenrir, the wolf that bit Tyr's hand off, and after whom the magical sword Tyrfing is named, as well as Jörmungandr, the serpent that encircles the world. Loki also gave birth—while shape-shifted into a mare—to Sleipnir, Odin's eight-legged horse.

Loki had seen Freyja return with the necklace hidden under her cloak, and he told Odin, Freyja's lover, that Freyja had slept with the dwarfs. Odin was jealous and told Loki to take the necklace from her. Changing himself into a fly to get into her hall, Loki saw the goddess asleep wearing the necklace. Shape-shifting into a flea, he bit her and she moved so he could release the clasp of the necklace and remove it from her. When faced with the loss of her necklace, Freyja knew at once that Odin was responsible. Freyja confronted Odin, who challenged her to use enchantments to maintain the cycle of life and death. Odin set Freyja a task: she was to make king Högni and king Heðinn, plus their retinue of twenty kings each, battle for one hundred and forty-three years. As they were killed in battle each day, Freyja must bring them back from the dead overnight to fight again in the morning through her magic. This mythological story about Freyja and the necklace is found in the *Flateyjarbok* (literally, the *Book of the Flat Island*), a medieval Icelandic manuscript compilation. It was compiled by two Christian priests in late 14th century, and the end of the tale is signalled by the victorious arrival of the King Olaf, who dissolves the curse, resulting in the final death of all those killed by Christians. Thus, the interaction of light and dark, life and death, and the relationship of interconnection between them is largely lost to the meaning.

* * *

The issue was how to find my own sense of cyclicity. With Frazer's cyclical return fresh in my mind, I recalled once again the ghost ship in the National Museum of Denmark, the one that had made such an impact on me, as described in Chapter 5. Looking at that ethereal vessel, I had started to feel patterns of connections to the cyclical space of the ancestors that had passed that way and to sense an ancient magical rhythm of life and death. There, in the museum, bound by the rhythm, I remembered that I had wandering into a room adjacent to the ghost ship. In front of me was a small Bronze Age model of a mare pulling a bronze disc representing the sun, the so-called Trundholm Horse Chariot, found in Zealand in 1902. This small model was an incredible eighteen to twenty centuries old: it was dated at 600 BCE. Both the chariot and the horse were mounted on four-spoke wheels, and on one side the sun was gilded, marking the passage of the sun across the sky from east to west, while the other side of the disc was dark, signifying its nighttime return journey from west to east. In a mythological understanding, the mare transports the sun through each day, and also through each solar year. Each day the sun is born and dies, as each year it is also reborn and dies. The journey reflects the sun's daily movement, but it also represents the annual cycle of the seasons of growing and waning light. It also symbolises the rhythm of an individual's life and death. It is notoriously difficult to impute meaning onto such ancient artefacts, to try and comprehend what was in the minds of people such a long time ago, but this cyclical meaning surely seems to be beyond doubt. Northern tales about the sun tell of how a man called Mundilfari had two children, a boy Máni (moon) and a girl Sól (sun). The girl was given in marriage, but the gods snatched away both brother and sister and set them to work in the heavens instead. Sun was pulled in a chariot drawn by two horses called Arvakr (Early-Wake) and Alsviðr (Supreme-in-Strength). The roots of the horse, chariot, and sun myth are deep in Indo-European soil and might be connected to ancient Greece, and further back still to a source in Pharaoh Amenhotep IV's reformation of sun worship in Egypt circa 1400 BCE.[2]

Whatever the actual history of the sun myth, the cyclical return of the sun lays deep in Scandinavian cultural memory. The ship, like the mare pulling the chariot, creates motion—a shift from one place to another that represents time. The sun in ancient Nordic cultures was the goddess Sol or Sunna, and, more latterly, her manifestation as Freyja, who in her solar aspect was carved on cave wall images. These images show the passage of the sun as being taken through the waters by a fish, and then flown through the air by a bird, before being transported by a horse and then a snake before the fish completed the cycle once again. Each creature was a part of the movement from dark into light, and back again into dark as the sun made its way across the firmament. This theme is also familiar in many cyclical myths that arose out of the syncretism of the Mediterranean melting pot of Egyptian, Greek, and Roman ideas about solar deities moving through the cosmos, examples being the Egyptian Amun Ra, the Greek and Roman Apollo, and the Romani gypsy Kam, with whom I became familiar during rituals with Jardani the gypsy shaman, as described previously. As this mythological cycle flows from one aspect to another, it marks the connections that each aspect has with the whole; it symbolises a turning whereby everything in the cosmos is connected. A returning solar theme was common in the ancient world and incorporated light and dark each day and through the year as the sun moved through the celestial realms in ancient minds, and also through an individual's life journey.

Themes of cyclic renewal of life and death find their climax in Ragnarok, the so-called twilight of the gods. Belonging to a finite race, the gods bore within them the germ of death. The whole scheme of Northern mythology was a drama, leading to a climatic battle. Ragnarok was a huge turning point that brought about death and destruction before a rebirth of a new cycle of life. The general disintegrative process starts with the ripples caused by Jörmungandr, the disturbed encircling world serpent and one of Loki's progeny; his writhing causes huge waves in the depths of the ocean. One of the great waves stirred up by Jörmungandr's struggles sets afloat a ship that was boarded by Loki and the fiery host from Muspelheim. Loki steered the ship boldly over the stormy waters into conflict with another ship holding all the frost giants. At the same time, one of his other offspring, Hel, the goddess of death, crept through a crevice in the earth out of her underground home, closely followed by the Hel-hound Garm, and the dragon Níðhöggr, who flew over the battlefield bearing corpses upon his wings. All the while, the giantess Angurboda fed the wolves Hati, Sköll, and Managarm, the progeny of Fenrir, with the marrow of murderers' and adulterers' bones. These wolves pursued Máni, the moon, and Sól, the sun, and devoured them. As soon as he landed, Loki welcomed these reinforcements with joy, and placing himself at their head he marched with them to the fight. The gods knew full well that their end was near. Odin rode down to the Urdr fountain, where, under the toppling Yggdrasil, the Norns sat silent with veiled faces, their web lying torn at their feet. Once more the father of the gods whispered a mysterious communication to Mimir, after which he remounted Sleipnir and rejoined the waiting host to engage in the battle with Loki.

Reading and feeling the state of Ragnarok, I could sense a liminal decentred place of dissolution. This recurring theme, incorporating death as a part of returning life, was hard to grasp, and death, as part of a life journey, seemed so final at that point. How could I comprehend a cyclical dynamic underpinning to such a seemingly final and destructive state as death? I needed to return to my own spirit ancestor, my grandfather, in the hope of some other form of comprehension.

* * *

Taking care not to trip up the stairs, I always used to take Grandpa a cup of tea each morning in a delicate rose-covered and gold-rimmed bone china cup on a matching saucer. One day, my father stopped me, saying that Grandpa had had a heart attack in the night and died. I was eight years old at the time, and this was my first real encounter with death. After my grandfather passed away I moved into his bedroom, but did not think much more about our relationship until I became an anthropologist many years later. Our early attachment had lain dormant like a seed in the earth, waiting for the right time to sprout. I would find that an unfolding pattern of events and realisations would reconnect me with the spirit of my grandfather. After my experiences with Jardani, I felt much closer to Grandpa and I wanted to understand more about his war experience, the unspoken parts of his life. When an opportunity came for me to visit Flanders and some World War I battlefields, I took it, and that is how I came to be in the Ypres Sanctuary Wood Museum.

The museum has many small wooden boxes with holes in the side for viewing old photographic images of Great War battles that happened in the area. If you turn the handle on the side, a sepia projection slide comes into view, showing the reality. Slide after slide reveals the monochrome atrocities that were enacted in the name of war; each wooden box holds different flickering moments of carnage. The walls of the museum room house cabinets of helmets (one with a skull and cross bone), photos, military badges, guns, and letters. On the walls there are more photos: there is not an inch to spare. In the middle of the room, amid dummies wearing dusty uniforms, lie three saddles—testimony to the role that the cavalry and mounted infantry played during the early years of the war. The saddles, leather stiff with age and heavy with memories, sit like a symbol of the past connection with horses, one long since a distant memory among the trenches. The shift from cavalry to infantry was made in 1914, at the beginning of the war, to accommodate changing military procedures. The use of trenches made it impossible to use mounted infantry and cavalry (although horses were used to pull gun and artillery carriages). This explained to me how my grandfather had fought in the Second Boer War as mounted infantry and also as mounted infantry at the beginning of the Great War, and then foot infantry. As explained in Chapter 7, my grandfather was in the Second Dragoon Guards (The Queen's Bays) and this regiment, part of this First Cavalry Brigade based at Aldershot, was formed from the Second Dragoon Guards, the Fifth Dragoon Guards, and the Eleventh Hussars. Each regiment served in the trenches as infantry once they dismounted, under the command of a brigadier.

There is so much death and destruction in war. It is hard to comprehend for someone not immediately involved. I want to feel it because it will bring me closer to my grandfather. I walk through another room stacked full of empty shells, more memorabilia, and I smell the stink of mud and death. Some sweet machines stand by the doorway, inappropriately. I feel nauseated. I have to go outside into a small wood of downy and silver birch, elder and sweet chestnuts. I feel the place. It cries out to my senses and I feel overwhelmed with what has happened here—the place feels haunted by spirits. There are trenches that are about a man's chest in height reinforced with corrugated iron shuttering and protected on the outer topside by fences of barbed wire. Inside they are muddy, very muddy, and there are planked runways that give a grip on the mud. Every so often there is an enclosed passing/collection point that is covered with an iron roof. The tunnels have corrugated bridges to enable crossing on the top surface. The trenches are interspersed with deep bomb craters. The place feels eerie. The sound of a lone bagpipe sounds, a recording, and the sound of the music is drowned by groups of laughing English and German school children of about fourteen or fifteen years old; they walk down the trenches and the girls squeal at the mud. There seems to be little respect. Maybe laughing is their way of dealing with the multitude of horror. Maybe this is how things move on for later generations (there is always a playfulness in the ritual approach to death, one that recognises the boundaries and then toys with them with ornament and ambiguity.)[3] I pick up a sweet chestnut seed and look at it. Is there any way that I can find an explanation for what has happened here? I can understand the historical events in material reality, but is it possible to understand the human carnage in terms of the life of the spirit? The chestnut seed represents the renewal of life in another aspect: a new start, fertility, and life after death. It helps me to think in this way, but what does it mean for those that have fallen? They gave their lives. Why? Because they had to, or they were shot; maybe they did not think about it, perhaps they could not. It is only us who have the time to ponder on these things, to see things from the present perspective, to view the situation with the benefit of hindsight. When they were in the present they just had to do what they had to do and not question: "Your country needs you!" It is we who need the explanation for such waste of human life: son, husband, brother or fiancée . . .

Some time later, after visiting a couple of cemeteries—where white grave stone after white gravestone, most bearing crosses and giving name and regiment, is lined up to ordered, pristine attention—I arrive at Passchendaele Tyne Cot Cemetery, the largest in the world. In the visitors' centre the faces of the fallen are projected large on a wall while their names and ages are announced. Look into each face and see the person—the life that has ended here in this place. Once again, the reality hits. Looking out of the window—with houses, fields, trees, the flint wall of the cemetery in view—I can see the scene of the Battle of Passchendaele. Tens of thousands of soldiers died here in 1917. Below the window is a map of the exact view out of the window, as it was in the time of the battle. There is total desolation—craters, tree stumps, and ruins. The faces of the soldiers keep staring out of the wall behind me and their names continue to ring out in a haunting, ghostly rhythm. There is a peculiar emptiness. This war was a pointless loss of life. Maybe all wars are ultimately pointless in terms of the loss of life, but some wars, on some level, might be more justified as defence against an aggressor. How to justify what happened here? Impossible. How to repay the life that was lost here? Impossible. The souls of the dead wander on these battlefields, but now there is an eerie peace. The red poppies, springing up from the devastation of the battlegrounds on the Flanders fields, signify life after death, the spirit that lives on even through the death of the body. Maybe there is heaven in this place now, or a place of peace for the dead in the aspen poplar trees. Said to be the trees of heroes, they are clonal organisms that grow from a single root network that can be literally tens of thousands of years old. Thriving on forest fires, which clear out everything and make way for new aspen trees to grow, the root network survives, in some cases up to a million years by some estimates, suggesting that as the tree lives on, so the dead live on too. The trees have protective powers. It feels as though they are protecting the souls of the fallen; the shimmering leaves in spring and summer enable the souls of the dead to be fly free with the wind. The soul flies free, untouched by earth and sea. The spirits of the dead, man and horse, move on the land, in and out of the trees; present and alarming to those who do not want to know. The spirit treads the land.

After a night of sleeplessness, feeling the weight of sadness, loss, and pain—the weight—I realise I have to let the spirit go . . . like the soul, I must let it resound and ring, run free and not hold it in my body. The body needs to breathe—let it go—like the wind rushing through—let the breath take the pain away. Understanding about death and mortality of the body is essential for the journey of the soul. The soul has to fly, as in this Anglo-Saxon riddle:

> My gown is silent as I thread the seas,
> Haunt old buildings or tread the land.
> Sometimes my song-coat and the supple wind.
> Cradle me high over the homes of men,
> And the power of clouds carried me
> Windward over cities.
> Then my bright silks
> Start to sing, whistle, roar,
> Resound and ring, while I
> Sail on untouched by earth and sea,
> A spirit, ghost and guest, on wing.

The spirit is not killed, only the physical body. It flies on, as I imagine it in this photograph that I took of an ancient Sussex yew tree (see Figure 14.1 on the following page):

That is some consolation, but I still feel pain for those killed—the wasted lives in a pointless war—and for Grandpa. My grandfather was not killed during this war, he survived, but it was said that he was never the same after the shell shock. How did he cope with witnessing horrifying scenes of war, if even just a fraction of the destruction? I feel connected to the carnage because he was my flesh and blood; I lived with him for eight years. My grandfather is my direct blood connection to this atrocity. I touched death when I held his hand, sat on his knee. I can look at a photograph of him taken much later in his life and see the sadness in his eyes. He told me stories about the horses. Not about how millions of horses died here. I was spared this pain, until now. In life, death is so close. Never have I been so aware of mortality.

* * *

Thinking more on the issue of death, I decided to engage with my feelings as I walked along a path just along the coast from Cuckmere Haven. It was not a coincidence that this was a path that Virginia Woolf had walked when she took her own life. The path led from Monk's House in Rodmell, Woolf's country home, to the Ouse, the river that runs from Lower Beeding in West Sussex to New Haven on the English Channel. Virginia and her husband Leonard Woolf bought Monk's House in 1919 as a retreat from London; they could see the River Ouse from the window. It was by drowning in the Ouse that Virginia Woolf lost her life due to mental instability. Fields of cows and winter crops, made possible by the drainage of the tidal inlet of the Ouse Valley, lay on either side of the walkway. The day was cold and I imagined what it would have been like for the novelist as she walked to

Figure 14.1   Ancient Yew Tree in East Chiltington, East Sussex

her death in 1941. Plagued by mental torture, it is said that she picked up stones to put in her pocket, the stones that would take her down into the Ouse's watery depths. The day that I walked the wintry air was cold, the colours of the downs muted and veiled in haze. The path seemed long, for it lay between so-called madness and sanity. For Virginia it was the path of no return when her depression claimed her. The stones had done their tragic and grim job.

I felt the chill in the air. As I approached the small rounded culvert where she drowned, there was a palpable calmness. Reeds surrounded the pool; they trembled slightly. On the surface, a thin layer of ice held the duck-weed in suspended animation. I imagined her lying face down in the water and then slowly sinking; it was three weeks later that they found her body. The inquest on Virginia's death found that the balance of her mind was disturbed. She walked a path between worlds of rich imagination and the literary and artistic world of Europe between the two world wars. Virginia Woolf was haunted by mental fragility, first from the death of her mother when she was thirteen, and then when her father died in 1904. The following years were marked by recurring depression. Maybe she needed to write to make sense of her internal life. Perhaps her genius came from bringing through the otherworld, but in the end it took her in the process. Her ashes were scattered on the downs, beyond the Monk's House garden and under an elm tree, since fallen. Virginia Woolf could be said to have a type of pain of the soul, and her death made me think more about the cycle of life. I needed to go more into the process to feel the pattern of light and dark, life and death.

By synchrony, after my walk along Virginia Woolf's path of death and my visit to Flanders, both emotional events, Cielle, my deceased bay Arab mare, came into my mind. It had been in the period directly after Cielle's death that my emotion about the horse increased through the grieving process. At this time Jo Crow, a close friend from the Mad Shamans (the group that I had belonged to when I went to Cae Mabon and had my initiation into the elemental dragon) invited me to join her rattle-making workshop. Held at Ridge Farm, a sixteenth-century farmhouse surrounded by fifteen acres of woods and fields in Sussex, with a sound studio where the likes of Jimi Hendrix and the Rolling Stones recorded their music, the place held a lot of energy. Shamans use rattles to contact magical realms, and I knew intuitively that the rattle I was to make would be a horse rattle. It was Cielle's rattle, which would connect me to her even though she was dead. And so it was that I came to be lying on the floor and, fuelled by my grief for the horse, journeying to find the spirit of the rattle:

When I entered the cave in my journey in the imagination I saw Cielle's colour—her bay coat gleaming; I felt her warmness and her spirit enter me: Cielle's spirit went right through me, and as she came out of me I started riding her and she became a snake-dragon turning into snake vertebra—she was the snake's vertebra white and glistening.

> We moved down
> and through,
> and around,
> spiralling
> downwards.

The journey was short but very powerful, and I knew intuitively what it was about. Afterwards, all the participants of the workshop went out into the grounds of Ridge Farm to find significant parts for their rattles. I needed to find some stones or other materials to put inside to make the rattling sounds.

As I walked out into the daylight along a small path, I felt myself drawn towards a small horse chestnut sapling. It felt right to take one of its five-fingered leaves to put inside the rattle. The horse chestnut was the connection in everyday reality with the spirit horse. Other things came to me too. It was at this time that I became aware that this rattle was to be an intensely private rattle; it was only to be used for the deepest of deep occasions. I felt in awe of the feeling that it brought up in me. Once I was back inside the farmhouse, it was time to construct the rattle. First, the design of the horse head had to be drawn on paper to make a template; then the template image was transposed onto rawhide and cut out. After a period of soaking, the leather became soft enough to sew around the edges. It was stuffed with sand to get the right shape, and, after drying overnight, the horse head was ready to be emptied of the sand and filled with objects, such as small stones from the beach or seeds, to make it rattle before having the handle inserted. This was the stage when the rattle started to feel as though it was coming alive. I put the horse chestnut leaf inside, along with several other things that rattled, and bound the handle in place. I now had a working rattle to connect with Cielle in the spirit world.

However, the rattle making was not finished by a long shot. The following week when I returned home, it felt as if I was kept in the service of the rattle; it seemed to demand that I paint it in a certain way. Somewhat to my surprise, the horse's head became dark blue and there were black and red dotted lines running through the blue. She was the blue of twilight: the in-between colour of the sky betwixt day and night. She had no eyes but she was touched with gold: her bridle was bright royal blue and was adorned with gold and silver bells that tinkled at the slightest movement; red ribbons also hung from her bridle. Where I had joined the wooden handle to the rattle was bound in soft chamois leather and over the leather was stitched five gold and silver periwinkle shells; falcon and pigeon feathers were attached. The woman who had loaned Cielle from me had sent me some of Cielle's mane and I added this to the rattle. When I rattled her, the sound was the sound of her hooves, and the bells tinkled like the bells on the saddles and bridles of the Shetland ponies that I had ridden as a child in the arcade of a department store in Croydon many years ago. Below is a photograph of the silver periwinkle part of the rattle that shows the cyclic swirl of the shell:

Figure 14.2   Part of Cielle Rattle

For me, Cielle had become a Valkyrie dragon-horse, a blue-black night-mare, as my initiation with Freyja had foretold. With the help of the rattle, awareness slowly dawned on me that Cielle was a magical horse that could help me to know more about death as a shaman. As a mare in this reality, she had lost her offspring. This is the worst thing that can befall a mother, equine or human. As a magical horse, I felt that Cielle knew about death and that she would travel with me. My Cielle horse-dragon rattle would accompany me, but it was not to be viewed directly by others. It works in the realm of the in between, through shadows, out of the corner of an eye, in the silences of the liminal. It can be glimpsed to the left in Figure 14.3 and as a shadow in Figure 14.4.

For it was through a glimpse and through shadows that I would travel along the path of the slain to find the meaning of the dragon. Cielle felt like a warm presence that would help me overcome my fears, as I had helped her overcome her fears when she was alive in everyday reality. As a dragon-horse she would help me go deeper into magical consciousness along the path of the slain.

Everything had to go. It was dark and cold but I was aware of my pulse of life—of my fire of life. I was alive! The pulse of life was within. My heart-beat kept me moving along the path of the slain. I felt the need to protect my aliveness, and so in my imagination I wrapped around me a black robe to keep the pulse vibrant. Time is a snake-like spiral, as light moves through dark into light. Feeling a ringing sensation in my ears and a tingling all over, I slid onto the bay mare's back. Time spirals downwards like a snake,

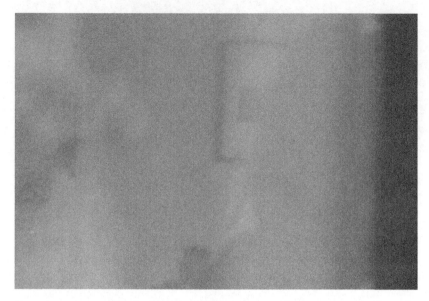

Figure 14.3 Reflection of Cielle Rattle on the Left

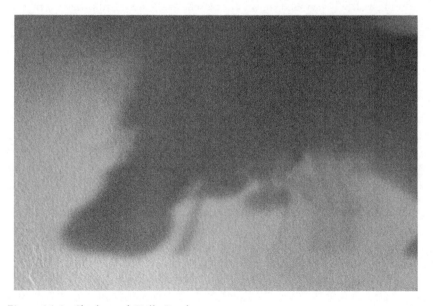

Figure 14.4 Shadow of Cielle Rattle

winding backwards. The mare and I melt into one as vertebra dissolves into vertebra; to let everything go, all containment of shape. We hold onto life, but one day we have to let it go and slip into death. This is the death mare, the nightmare. She gently takes us into the unknown. The realisation that one thing glides into another. Eternity is now. We walk into darkness, everything has rolled past; we hold on to nothing. There is nothing except a feeling inside that rises up through the blackness. At first it is barely felt, hardly audible. The tingling becomes stronger—the dragon turns. My awareness changes and I become conscious of being part of a pattern of interrelationships, a dance of the cycle of life and death.

NOTES

1. Susan Greenwood *The Anthropology of Magic* (Oxford: Berg, 2009): 75–76.
2. Brian Branson *Gods of the North* (London: Thames and Hudson, [1955] 1970): 67, 69.
3. Adam Seligman, Robert Weller, Michael Puett and Bennett Simon *Ritual and Its Consequences* (New York: Oxford University Press, 2008).

15 Ancestors

The Old Ones, whispering.
The blood runs down our limbs.
The sap rises, and falls.
Time stands still.
Quiet.
Ours is the knowing
that time passes through lifetimes.
Life and death are One.

As I look back, the dragon has taken me to the vortex of the between. It has been a voyage through ghosts of memories, on the water of emotion. I have been meandering along the tide line in my memory. The waves lap the shingle seashore, leaving smooth, glistening sand in their wake. As the tide turns, there is just enough time to walk on its even, sparkling flatness before the water covers the stones once more. The moments between—where my footprints last for seconds—is a time betwixt and between, before the incoming waves rear upward, turquoise-green, a translucent invitation to the deep fathoms below, descend crashing again into lace-edged froth on the beach. The dragon is in the stones, and in a reflection of the moving waters; a chimera that exists in the space between the waves of my awareness, it is here and not here at the same time. This is the in between, the liminal, the expansive space of magical consciousness. Life is a cyclical dance of inter-connectedness of the past, present, and future in the mythical imagination of magical consciousness.

Here we see the particular connectedness of magical thought "from the inside"—meaning this is what the interconnectedness, spoken of abstractly when viewing magical thought from the perspective of analytical thought, looks like. Viewing magical thought from within itself, however, we have images, feelings, and above all, intentionality—that is, the dragon. But I have had to suspend questions to learn the process of a cultivation of a knowing relationship. My journey was not quite complete. I have to return to the lair of the dragon one more time to find its golden hoard among the realm of the ancestors. A sense of "Ancestors" or "ancestral knowledge" is important in magical thinking, for it provides a sense of foundation, of security, and location—meaning is thereby located in a cyclical time and place. As my shamanic healing ritual with the Gypsy *chovihano* had taught me, death in the form of ancestors was a part of life. This chapter shows, once again, the importance of myth as a framework for understanding the language of magical consciousness, and how it helps to shape and give meaning to individual experience.

* * *

The importance of ancestry in particular is demonstrated in an Anglo-Saxon myth called the "Poem of Hyndla" (Hyndlujoth). The narrative tells how Freyja travelled along the path of the slain to teach her lover Ottar his ancestry. Ottar must know his lineage so that he might avenge the dwarfs in a battle with Angantyr, the owner of Tyrfing, a cursed sword that was gained by tricking the dwarfs. Freyja, as we have seen, has deep reciprocal associations with the dwarfs through the golden Necklace of Brisingamen, and so she is party to their adversary's retribution. The "Poem of Hyndla" is a compilation of two much older, poorly preserved poems in the *Flateyjarbok*. The first part of this narrative is a collection of semi-historical names of heroes in the sagas of the Norse tradition, and the second is a fragment, a record in *Voluspo* of a seeress's divinatory journey by Snorri Sturleson in the twelfth century. Having lost much of its original meaning, and not valued as either mythology or poetry, scholars have thought this poem is confused, according to Henry Adams Bellows, translator of a 1923 version of the *Poetic Edda*. However, if read from a magical perspective, it is not confused, but rather infused with meaning. This myth can be read as a narrative about a journey along the path of the slain to Odin's hall Valhalla, and it concerns a forthcoming battle of worldviews fought between Ottar, a protagonist of the dwarfs, and Angantyr, who represents the forces of destruction. It involves the mediations of Hyndla, a seeress giantess who will recite for Ottar his genealogy.

At the centre of the myth is Tyrfing, a golden-hilted magical sword forged by the dwarfs. Tyrfing reputably would never miss a stroke, and would easily cut through stone and iron. It is mentioned in the poem Hervararkviða in the *Poetic Edda*, and Tyrfing was originally made for king Svafrlami, Odin's grandson, who had trapped the dwarfs Dvalinn and Durin and forced them to forge the weapon. The dwarfs did as bidden, but cursed the sword so that it would kill a man every time it was drawn, cause three great evils, and kill Svafrlami himself. Svafrlami was indeed killed when he fought Arngrim, who took the sword. And so it passed into the possession of Angantyr who, along with his eleven brothers, spread fear and destruction. The name of the sword comes from Tyr, a Norse god associated with war, battle, and sacrifice, and *fingr* is Old Norse for "finger." The sword is "Tyr's finger," and this has an extreme magical meaning when one realises that Tyr is the god who had his hand bitten off by Fenrir, a wolf who embodied the forces of chaos. The gods Thor, Odin, and Tyr became alarmed by Fenrir's increasing size. Fearing that the wolf's wildness would destroy the cosmos, they tried to bind him with chains. Seeking to appeal to the wolf's vanity, the gods offered Fenrir a challenge to see if he was stronger than the fetter. The first chain snapped easily, and so did the second, which burst so violently that the metal shot into the universe and became the stars. Rather alarmed, the gods then approached the dwarfs and asked them to make a silken thread. Agreeing to this request, the dwarfs made Gleipnir from the sound of a cat's footfall, the beard of a woman, and the roots of a mountain, a bear's sinews, a fish's breath, and a bird's spittle. By this time, Fenrir was becoming suspicious, and would only agree to be bound if one of the gods put a hand in his mouth. To this request the gods agreed, and the dwarfs' thread bound Fenrir. And so Tyr had his right hand bitten off, and the sword Tyrfing was named after a god without a hand. Or perhaps, a bit more prosaically, the tyr of Tyrfing could simply mean "god-finger," and not refer to any particular god. The sword is indeed a weapon imbued with the dwarfs' wild magical power.

Freyja travels to Valhalla, the hall of the slain, on behalf of Ottar, whom she has shape-shifted into the golden-bristled boar Hildisvini, her "battle-swine," to fight Angantyr, who had tricked the dwarfs and brought fear and destruction. It is significant that she rides the golden-bristled boar, as the dwarfs made him and it shows her magical affiliation. Hildisvini is described thus in the *Poetic Edda*:

> Wild dreams methinks, are thine when thou sayest.
> My lover is with me on the way of the slain;
> There shines the boar with bristles of gold,
> Hildisvini, he who was made by the cunning dwarfs.[1]

Boars represent courage, fertility, bravery, and intuition, the qualities of a successful warrior. The boar was a sacred animal in early Scandinavian and Germanic countries and the emblem of the Vanir tribe of fertility deities, of whom Freyja is a principle goddess. Freyja is empowering her warrior through wild dreams on the journey on the way of the slain.

The goddess enlists the help of Hyndla, a giant ancestress, one of the first living beings and an elemental force of nature, to teach her protégé about his lineage to empower him in his battle with Angantyr. Hyndla, after being cajoled by Freyja, reluctantly agrees to accompany the goddess on the path of the slain and rides a wolf. The name "Hyndla" means "the dog," and when the giantess yawned the sound was said to be like a dog howling at the moon. Freyja travels along on her battle-boar while Hyndla rides the canine from which all dogs are descended. Dogs are guardians of thresholds, and Hyndla, like Freyja, is a prophetess, a seeress or volva, and knows the ancient magic. As we have already seen in relation to the mythological poem *Beowulf*, Grendel and his mother had a lupine nature, and wolves and dogs are guardians of the magical gateways of the mind. Often, such seeresses would perform *seiðr*, a practice that involved entering an alternative state of consciousness and either travelling to spirit realms or calling in spirits from non-material worlds to gain information. Sometimes seeresses sought to change the patterns of events through chanting runes, or perhaps using enchantment through spells. At the gates of Valhalla, Hyndla recounts Ottar's lineage as a form of such ritual ancestral enchantment. She also gives him memory beer so he might be able to remember and recite his ancestry in the forthcoming confrontation with Angantyr. A brief synopsis of the myth follows:

The giantess Hyndla was asleep. She was growling in her cave, and it was not a pleasant sound. The goddess Freyja and her boar stood in the cave's mouth, listening. Then Freyja called out: "Hyndla, my friend! Hyndla, my sister! Wake up! Come out of your hole in the hill." The growling gave way to a sound like a bitch howling at the moon. The giantess was yawning. The goddess Freyja was trying to persuade Hyndla to go to win the god Odin's favour in his hall at Valhalla, the hall of the slain, but she had to persuade the giantess. Eventually, Freyja's persistence paid off and after wrangling, wheedling, cajoling, and threatening, she won the giantess's half-hearted agreement to journey to Valhalla. Hyndla knew that Freyja had turned her lover Ottar into a golden-bristled boar whose bristles showed him the way in the dark. The giantess rode a wolf and the goddess mounted her boar; the two animals ran in harness and at last the travelers reached the gates of Valhalla. Freyja and Hyndla dismounted. Freyja asked Hyndla about the ancestry of Ottar, the lover whom she had turned into a boar. She also asked about Angantyr, the owner of the magical sword Tyrfing. The giantess reluctantly recounted the ancestry, knowing that the boar was listening. When the ancestry was told, Freyja looked at the giantess in triumph and told her how Ottar had made a wager with Angantyr, staking their whole inheritance of the matter of their lineage. Then Freyja told Hyndla to give her boar memory-beer so that when he met with Angantyr in three days' time, he would remember every word of the lineage that Hyndla had recited. The giantess opened her rotting cavernous mouth and yawned. "Go away!" she said. "I want to sleep again. I'm not doing you any more favours." She gave Freyja a withering look. "My noble goddess," she said, "you leap around at night like Heidrun (a goat outside Valhalla) cavorting with a herd of goats." Freyja slowly raised her arms. "I will girdle you with flames so you cannot leave this place without catching fire." Hyndla laughed in contempt. "You've gone running to Od," she said, "who always loved you; and many another has wormed his way under your apron." A band of flame, a quivering halo, surrounded the giantess. Her limbs tightened; she pressed her arms against her side. "Flames about me!" cried the giantess. "The earth is on fire, and I must pay the full price or forfeit my life." Hyndla flinched as the girdle began to tighten. "Ottar's draught of memory-beer," she called.

"Take it! It's full of venom. It will bring him to an evil end." "Stuff!" said Freyja. "Nonsense! It is you who are full of bitterness and rancour. Your threats will do no harm, though." The goddess was smiling as she trailed her fingers down the boar's back. "Ottar will drink nothing but the best if I get my way with the gods. Ottar will prosper."[2]

Hyndla, being a giantess and a seeress, knows the deep ancestry that goes back to the beginning of cosmic creation, and Freyja has to work to empower Ottar with this information. I sense that I need to reconnect with my own ancestral spirit.

*　*　*

Exmoor ponies were grazing on Castle Hill on the Sussex Downs, an undisturbed chalk grassland known for its profusion of wildflowers, especially a variety of orchids and butterflies. As I walk on the down land, I notice that a herd of twenty-one mealy mouthed Exmoor ponies are grazing amongst the yellow-tipped gorse bushes. Britain's oldest breed of native pony, the Exmoor is the breed closest to prehistoric horses; the ponies have been put here to keep down encroaching scrub. I watch the ponies, their brown barrel bodies gleam in the early spring sun. The ponies take me to another place in my mind, as horses always do. The ponies are like the small horses that I have seen in pictures of the Chauvet cave in southern France. Jean-Marie Chauvet and his two friends, Éliette Brunel and Christian Hillaire, happened upon this cave in December 1994. Behind some fallen rocks, they dug a passage and found themselves inside a fallen shaft leading to a network of chambers and galleries with wonderful paintings over 30,000 years old. There were herds of small horses, so similar to Exmoor ponies, pictured galloping along the walls in the cave. Time has no meaning in magical consciousness. I could be there in the cave. Time is a snake-like spiral; as light moves through dark into light, it spirals downwards like a snake, winding backwards as I had found when my dragon-horse Cielle and I had melted into one another, as each vertebra had dissolved into each vertebra, and I had let everything go. The gentle death mare that was so timid in material reality had bravely taken me into the unknown. As Freyja, a Valkyrie, riding my nightmare we had entered the darkness to meet the dragon dance of life and death. But there was more to learn about the ancestors and one particular myth about a journey along the path of the slain seemed to arise from a golden thread of synchronous connections in my mind.

As I walk along the beach on the south coast of England once again, I find fossils of sea urchins, and within them I see with the dragon as an earth-star, a chimera that exists in the space between the waves of my awareness. I know that within material reality the fossil dates from the Cretaceous period, between 66 and 145 million years ago on a geological timescale, and that deep within its lifespan is the process of metamorphosis. All sea urchins begin life as microscopic larvae that feed on plankton, but in time, a juvenile sea urchin develops inside. By taking over the body of its larval host, it eventually emerges completely transformed. Sea urchins are "direct cousins" of human beings.[3] In material reality we are connected: we all had a common life in the sea. Metamorphosis means to "change shape," and in my imagination, the fossil holds the creative process of metamorphosis in magical consciousness. This is another important aspect of magical consciousness: that of its ever-changing nature. Analytical thinking breaks things down into static, interacting parts; magical thought, since it must deal with things that cannot be so dealt with, resorts to seeing the "essence" of things that are ever changing, in an effort to connect with them. Just as children instinctively will tell you that a tadpole and a frog are "the same thing," and just as an acorn and an oak tree are "the same thing," so magical consciousness holds the essence within ever-changing things as real and infused with meaning and intent. Hence the dragon, in analytical thought, does not exist, but in magical thought, it is plain as the hand in front of one's face, or alternately, and paradoxically, can be felt through the senses but not seen. The ability to deal with rapidly changing factors, shapes, senses, contexts, etc., is the strength of magical thought, and even the most analytically framed argument will often resort to it when pushed, because often, true understanding of a situation cannot be grasped without the holistic "magical" and interconnected, ever-shifting quality that resists reduction.

Some time later, I feel a stone on the shingle; somehow it feels like a special stone and I realise that it is indeed a sea urchin fossil.

Figure 15.1   Dragon Sea Urchin Fossil

The stone has been shorn in half: one side is sea-worn, smoothed by the constant coming and going of the tide, while the other side reveals its glistening, inviting surface (see Figure 15.2).

As I hold the dragon stone, I look into the silence to find the magic of a different perception—the space betwixt-and-between. I sense myself expand into sea, cliffs, birds, and the pulse of life. I feel my awareness deep inside the dragon:

> Scaled creature of times past,
> and times to come. . .
> The beat of the drum calls me
> into
> the dragon's furnace
> Blazing.

There is another knowing deep within this fossil. The stone seems to hold the moment, the stillness, the expanse of time in metamorphosis. New patterns of being emerge. It seems that everything is possible within a creative stillness that has engulfed me as the waves lap the shore and the cry

Figure 15.2 Shorn Dragon Fossil Showing Underside

of seabirds fills my ears. This feels like a primordial place where anything can happen. I know the fossil is ancient; it has been formed over the millennia from climate changes, and the sea level rise in 5000 BCE that separated England from the rest of the continent.

Looking again at the fossil of the sea urchin, I think about how this creature, now immortalised in stone, lived in the sea here when the water levels were higher, the weather was warm, and dinosaurs roamed on the land. Looking up at the brilliant blue sky, made even more vibrant by the stunning whiteness of the Seven Sisters chalk cliffs behind, I notice that the descendants of the dinosaurs—herring gulls, fulmars, and jackdaws—are nesting in small holes and cracks on the sheer cliff surface. My mind enters a different place as I hold the fossil; it feels like I can enter into a vast stillness in which everything is connected in magical consciousness. I see the dragon in the stone—the urchin has become a dragon in my imagination. Nostrils flaring, its gape is wide and flames bellow from within the cave of its mouth. The dragon is like the guardian of the Underworld cave, through which I must pass if I am to find out more about the ancestors, but somehow, it does not scare me. It feels inevitable. This stone connects me with other fossils that I have collected along this beach.

Many of these fossils have what seem like trackways—parallel lines of small white dots. Going back in time thousands of years in my imagination, I sense that the trackways on the fossils will take me deeper into magic. Like in the *Ancient Mariner* poem, they are like water snakes as they move in tracks of shining white, with a flash of golden fire beckoning the dragon's hoard of treasure (see Figures 15.3 and 15.4).

These fossil trackways remind me of the trackways painted deep within caves used by Stone Age peoples. As the Stone Age painted lines on cave walls weave in and out of the rock face, so they lead to other worlds in the imagination. Perhaps human beings have always used such natural features of their environments to encapsulate this change of perception? It seems so. Some contemporary Kalahari San people interpret the painted lines in prehistoric cave paintings in South Africa as "threads of light" that come down from the sky to take shamans in a trance upwards to the ancestral spirit realm. So might I travel along the path of the slain in these earth-stars to the skies, and down below deep into caves of the earth? The fossil pathways take me deeper in my imagination to a cave: the cave of forgotten dreams emerging. I feel as if I am being led along the white dot patterns, as the markings on a cave wall. I am being led into the cave of the ancestors, but I sense the timing is not right. I have to be patient and allow the opportunities and feelings to arise by synchronicity and not force the pace.

* * *

The River Dove, which flows along a limestone valley in the Peak District of Derbyshire, eventually makes its way through Milldale, a sleepy hamlet,

Figure 15.3   Fossil Trackways

and onwards past the caves that arise out of the limestone in this area. Some months later, I returned to a trance state of magical consciousness while walking alongside the Dove. I felt the rush of the clear water as it cascaded down over stones, leaving trails of green-tendrilled water plant leaves shimmering underneath. The pull of the water drew me on, and the sound was deafening as it led me to the approach to Reynard's Cave. Ancient peoples used this cave. I learned recently that archaeologists discovered a gold and silver hoard here of Late Iron Age coins, thought to belong to the Corieltavi tribe, and Roman coins, that pre-date the invasion of Britain in 43 CE. Humans have used the cave for over two thousand years. Seated high up on the rocks of the limestone gorge, the cave is approached by a steep climb. I battle with my feelings of fear: I have vertigo and as I start to make my way upward I know that if I look backwards, I will become disorientated. Taking a quick look, I test my balance; I know that I had to stay centred in myself and then I will be able to make it to the top. Beckoned by the dragon, I look upwards and I see the cave welcoming me. The path is uneven. It has been raining and it is very slippery. The stones make footholds so I can ease my way up. *Why didn't I wear the shoes with more tread? I always forget to*

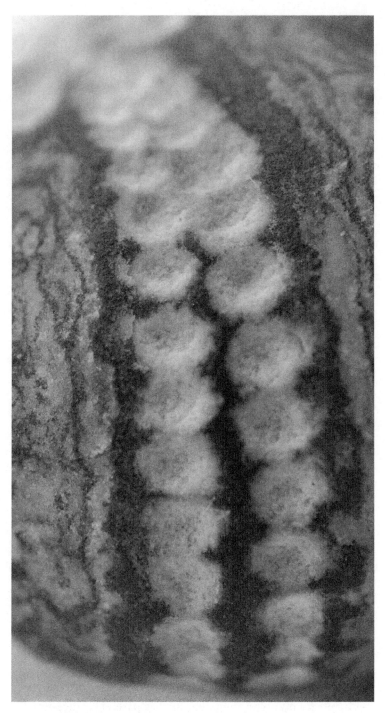

Figure 15.4   Fossil Trackways (Detail)

wear the right shoes! Telling myself not to look down, I will myself into the cave. Slowly, I make my way up. The fear is still with me but contained. Up and up—too far up to give up, must go on, only a little bit further. Sudden waves of disorientation come over me. Panic takes control. Upward, it is only a few more steps, one last step into the cave.

As I climb inside the cave, it is like entering the skeletal remains of a giant dragon. Along the top of the cave runs an enormous stone vertebra; ribs curve downwards, forming an arch. It is dark on the inside and water trickles down through the ceiling. A sense of exhilaration—I have overcome my fear about the steep climb to get up here and I am sitting in the cave at last! The cave is the skeletal remains of the dragon. The experience of being physically in this cave takes me into another time in my mind. I realise that the actual moment is but a flash in eternity, but that the flash does not have a beginning or an end. It is a totally different perspective. The end is the beginning, time winds around and around in a snake-like spiral, ever moving and ever changing. I feel I have come home. I feel a connection with a different reality:

> Backwards through time
> falling back
> deep into darkness
> time of the other ones.
> Another place, another time.
> The water drips from the ceiling of the cave,
> time passes.
> Another life, another time.
> Cold earth, cold stone
> the drip of water
> cold,
> dark,
> drip.
> Time passes,
> one moment leads into eternity.
> Eternity of the moment.
> Back into the dark
> skeletal cave.
> Bone on bone,
> time disintegrates.
> New beginnings
> emerge gently
> out of the darkness.
> Darkness gives way to the new born.

The dragon is here in the rhythm of eternity and rebirth, the place of the ancient ancestral spirit. I sense the ancestors.

I slowly retrace my steps down the slippery path. The ancestors in magical consciousness are close. The synchronous associations of ancestors,

Figure 15.5   Dancing the Dragon

horses, a goddess of life and death, and the dancing chimera of the dragon have brought me full circle in this ethnography of my mind, as seen in Figure 15.5 of a fossil photographed through a reflection of a window to show the "looking-through" aspect of magical consciousness.

NOTES

1. The *Poetic Edda* translated from the Icelandic by Henry Adams Bellows in 1923 and published in New York by The American-Scandinavian Foundation.
2. Adapted from Kevin Crossley-Holland's *The Norse Myths* (London: Penguin): 100–103.
3. *Metamorphosis: The Science of Change*, BBC Four, England, March 13, 2013.

Part Three
Conclusions

16 A Creative Synthesis
Analysing the Magical Mode

As the foregoing chapters have highlighted, a magical "ethnography of mind" is an individual process that occurs through metaphorical and synchronistic patterns of meaning. The previous experiential chapters have shown how the anthropologist derived magical meanings from events, feelings, and relationships that surrounded her within her environment. They demonstrate how a train of events leading from a shamanic healing could instigate a pattern of understandings outside the more conventional anthropological field. In this respect, they show a "wild," untrained, and formulised mind in action as it searched for synchronistic significance. An understanding of this magical procedure provides an important link between magic as a primary panhuman mode of thought and the instrumental magic more commonly understood, characterised, and studied in academia, such as collective ritual, or spell making. Researchers most often identify this latter form by its effects rather than through manner in which it occurs. It has been a purpose of this work to illustrate and analyse magic as a process of thinking that has its own form of analogical reasoning. However, the experiential reports of the previous chapters can still pose a challenge to logical analysis, and this final chapter offers an analytical response to the experiential section of this volume. Our aim is a creative synthesis whereby we can reach a place of being able to recognise both analytical and magical orientation parameters in a way that is complementary rather than oppositional.

In this ethnography of mind, Greenwood presents a deeply emotional, subjectively powerful, and at times phantasmagoric vision of gods, goddesses, dragons, ghosts, and ancestral spirits. She reports a number of experiences that threatened to shatter her own sense of self and personal grounding. Linear, causal relationships were abandoned and it seems the imagination was left to run amok, giving the analytical mind a narrative that could strain logical comprehension. Yet for all the reasons given in the previous chapters, we know that it simply will not do to disregard such reports, as to do so would be to apply analytical frame to a phenomenal set in which it simply does not apply. The temptation would be to ignore it as a mere series of "random" images or fragmentary reports related to the subject's personal life, with the implication that it can tell us nothing of use.

This, however, would be to grossly oversimplify the situation, for much of this report has a strongly collective character to it, and we of course have no evidence whatsoever that it is "random," nor what "random" should even mean when it comes to imagery.

Furthermore, we know the problems that arise when we fail to recognise the commonly encountered bias that favours the analytical mode as the sole arbiter and only truly "rational" approach to understanding the ontological relevance of a given experience. Nor, as we have argued throughout, can it be dismissed as "purely imaginary," as if that somehow equates the vision with nothing at all. At the heart of this dismissal is the fundamental division between what is felt to be *real* and what is dubbed *imaginary* in the first place. Hidden within the analytical mode's dismissal is a choice of axiomata: those of the analytical mode. Yet we have already established that this particular dichotomy is only valid in the analytical mode of thinking. Within this mode, it is fully correct to say the experiential data is imaginary and hence "unreal," as reality is measured by that mode. In the magical mode of thought, however, reality is adjudicated by other criteria. The analytical division between real and imaginary originates from a division between externally derived and internally derived imagery; that which comes externally is "real," whereas internally derived imagery is "imaginary" (i.e., unreal), as discussed in Chapters 9 and 12. In the magical mode, however, the boundary of the shape-shifting self is not well drawn; hence, this division breaks down. What would be labelled real and imaginary becomes blurred because the sense of self is expansive; ideas, images, feelings, and impressions simply *emerge* in phenomenal awareness, with no differentiation between "real/imaginary" accompanying the analysis. In this purely magical mode, everything experienced becomes "subjectively real" to the experiencer.

That said, such phenomenal impressions, because they are acquired while in a magical mode of thought, cannot be easily compared to the impressions that have been framed by the analytical mode of thought without potentially making a number of serious category errors. Nevertheless, it is easy to see that these two modes need each other! Stripped of the analytical mode, the ego becomes lost in a sea of impressions; our very identity risks annihilation. This, of course, precisely occurs in more severe cases of mental illness, such as schizophrenia, bipolar disorder, or severe posttraumatic stress disorder, just to name a few examples. In less severe clinical examples, subjects can present as being lost in the world of fantasy and imagination, unable to connect with others or with the physical world in any lasting or substantive way. Such people have a very poorly developed sense of self and often complain of life feeling empty, or they hide such feelings with excessive flight into fantasy. Without the analytical mode, convergent thinking is lost, and chaos reigns. Equally, however, without the magical modality, divergent thinking becomes lost. Thinking becomes rigid, and "the forest is lost for the trees." Patterns are never observed, connection is lost, and solipsism, alienation, and arid, sterile rootlessness reigns. The universe becomes mechanical and devoid of meaning, feeling, and emotion. This is no less a dangerous realm than the realm of unfettered magical thought. As ever, a balance is called for; both modalities are our inherited birthright. Both work better as a team than as opponents.

For the sake of clarity, let us reiterate the (admittedly somewhat artificial but illuminating) proposed division of thinking into its two fundamental modalities, recalling the thought experiment using Bozo, reflected in Table 16.1.

As it stands, all the considerations thus far have led us to argue that the mind appears to have two primary modes of thinking and being that it uses that do not necessarily oppose one another, but instead seem to complement one another. When thinking more analytically, the psyche takes physical matter as primary and seeks to explain, understand, and compose thought in terms of reduction—that is, when looking at a complex, chaotic array of events, the analytical mode seeks to simplify, to break down into components that one can then subsequently analyse in isolation. It seeks to formulate firm, strongly drawn boundaries for entities that are clearly separated in time and space and interact only under specific conditions of variably defined "contact." Verbal and written reasoning is strongly favoured, and everything that cannot be explicitly verbalised or written is considered suspect, and possibly muddying the waters, as in the case of oral versus historical accounts. Causality is of the physical, efficient variety only, with the processing of experience biased in the direction of convergent paths—i.e., A leads to B leads to C. Finally, the analytical mode, when viewing the mind itself, does what it always does: it draws distinctions and makes simplifications. In this case, it draws a deep line between what is "objective" versus what is "subjective." This leads to a potential pitfall: the designation of the subjective as ontologically inferior to the objective. Strictly speaking, it is

Table 16.1 Two Fundamental Modalities

Analytical	Magical
mechanistic cause (bozo's neural firing)	animistic causes (bozo's intent)
objective vs. subjective division	experiential
logical reasoning	analogical reasoning
isolated context	irreducible context
rigid boundaries	shape-shifting
non-participation	participation
strong locality	non-local and/or local
strong, linear temporality	atemporality and/or cyclical temporality
verbal	nonverbal/sensory/metaphorical
aims toward clarity of understanding	aims toward emotional integration
convergent	divergent

most analytically correct to rather make the distinction only and leave the value judgement out of it.

By contrast, the magical modality is altogether different—in no small way first because it is largely non-verbal. Images, emotional impressions, and symbols are its method of communication, representation, and re-description. This may very well be the single most important difference between the two modes, because a literary society that can spend sometimes decades indoctrinating its young with verbal learning will favour the analytical over the magical as a result of this profound but hidden bias. This distinction also means that there will always be a certain ineffable quality to all magical pronouncements. This drives the more analytically minded among us crazy, but it does not have to. It is simply a necessary aspect of this mode of thinking, and is a consequence of the preverbal layers of the mind in action. These are layers we share with other animals.

The magical modality starts not with matter, but with minds. Such minds are not entirely distinct, but exhibit a unity-in-multiplicity that is common in the magical mode. Divisions between objective and subjective are blurry at best, as the rule in magical thought is participation rather than reduction. It does not ask, "What are the interacting parts of this system?" Instead it "feels for" the bigger picture. This, as well as the non-locality (although in some cases, it can be very specific and local), atemporality, non-distinction, and irreducible context are all part of the regnant *holism* of the magical mode. In this mode, events and experiences are never parsed into component parts to be isolated, studied, simplified, and so forth. Everything forms a complete whole that is greater than any sum of its parts because of the importance of **context**. *This* particular granary fell on *this particular* day and killed *this particular* person because of *this particular* person's malicious thoughts. All of these things work together to form a unified whole in thought. Remove any part of it, and the whole ceases to exist. Finally, magical thinking is not convergent but divergent—one utilises such thinking when one is given a brick, say, and asked "How many different uses for this thing are there?" The question that requires convergent thinking might be, "What is the best way to use this brick to make a house?" In divergent thinking, there are many answers, including, "What is my feeling regarding this brick, from whence did its parts—stone, sand, or clay—come?" Convergent thinking, however, narrows on *the* answer: the *correct* answer.

HOW NOT TO ASK THE WRONG QUESTIONS

Having reiterated the two modalities of thought, it is clear that the particular mode of processing will *in itself* generate the kinds of questions asked and guide the direction of understanding in very different directions. One can clearly see, also, that to take a narrative that was composed in a heavily magical mode of consciousness, such as the various experiential materials offered by the ethnography in the previous chapters and to subject it to an analytical type of treatment is to invite category errors, as well as put us at risk of asking nonsense questions. To subject an argument for how one should engineer the strongest castle, or devise the most effective method of hunting antelope, or throw the strongest roundhouse kick to an analytical treatment requires the proper kinds of questions: *What is the best material and technique to build a wall? Where are antelopes usually seen during the hunting season? Which weapon is most likely to take them down? How do I move my hip to generate the most power in my kick?*

The magical modality, however, asks entirely different questions: *What do the gods of war wish of me, and how can I convince them to favour me in the upcoming siege? What was written in the portents? What is my enemy thinking?* For hunting, one might ask, *Which place feels right? How might I convince the forest spirit to sacrifice itself to feed my family?* Concerning martial arts, *What is the "energy" (or Chi) of this movement? What animal spirit (crane, cobra, etc.) am I adopting? How do I become one with my opponent (such questions are indeed asked by martial artists of advanced skill)?* When crossing modalities, it is important to keep in mind the correct questions for assessing the various strengths and weaknesses of each mode.

WHAT IS THE DRAGON?

The purpose of this long preamble is to highlight the reader to all the potential logical pitfalls that exist when we are asked to interpret a particular narrative, like that of the participatory and sensory ethnography of the mind in the previous chapters. It is to serve as a warning to the potential problems that might arise when we ask, for example, what is the dragon? We have argued for balance between the modes throughout this work—now it is time to make good on that promise. The question emerges: is there a way to understand Greenwood's dragon from the analytical mode?

From Greenwood's detached perspective, she was struck by four key factors when analysing the material from her dragon experience. Firstly, that she experienced the dragon as a process, not a material reality, or a being, or even an end "result." The dragon was a symbol for a creative space of connections in the mind. Greenwood experienced this as another reality intimately connected with the present, but also markedly different—it was "misty," difficult to grasp unless she "just went with it" and waited for the mist to clear. When she first started anthropological fieldwork on magic, she likened the feelings to "schizophrenia," being in two places at once: a magical and an analytical modality. In time she learned how to control each, and even bring an analytical mode into the magical and vice versa. From discussion with Goodwyn, Greenwood came to realise the extent to which the process of deep magical consciousness was potentially unbalancing due to the lack of tight social controls usually found in the more embedded traditional contexts. In the absence of such control in these research circumstances, Goodwyn held the space of analytical thought while Greenwood could explore the deeper recesses of "the analogical reasoning of magic." A central tenet of what Greenwood was learning about the dragon was the cycles of life and death as part of a dense and tangled cluster of interlaced threads of magical associations. Conceptually, this appeared to be similar to what Tim Ingold, drawing on Deleuze and Guattari's notion of a rhizome,[1] writes about "antigenealogy" as a "continually ravelling and unravelling relational manifold."[2] Secondly, the dragon was found within ritual and ritualised process, such at that instigated by the Gypsy shaman's healing, and in the Odin and Freyja mythodrama. More diffusely, it was contained in the finding of synchronous links through fossils, while the mythological language of Freyja's necklace shaped the experience. Thirdly, the dragon was located in places and landscape: for example, in the waters at Carshalton, the Taff River in Wales, in Felpham with the ghost of William Blake as a locus for connections, and in Cae Mabon amid the elemental Snowdonian mountainside. The dragon was symbolic of the elemental connection between deep caves within the earth and sky-winging flight into the firmament. Fourthly, the dragon's hoard of gold represented ancestral memory, of making connections with the past through cyclical notions of time—spiralling into "deep time" wherein some sense of eternal "essence" could be felt, as in Hesse's novel *Steppenwolf*. Here, the protagonist finds the living heart of the world in a divine and golden track—similar to the goddess Freyja's desire to follow the gold into the dwarfs' cave—experienced at a concert of old music, whereby a door was opened to the other world. During this episode, Steppenwolf dropped all his defences, was afraid of nothing, accepted all things, and "to all things gave up his heart." This feeling came again while reading poetry and pondering philosophical thoughts: it shone out and drove its gold track far into the sky.[3] Steppenwolf finally enters a magical theatre advertised "FOR MADMEN ONLY" with the "PRICE OF ADMITTANCE YOUR MIND" and the caution "NOT FOR EVERYBODY,"[4] and it is here that he finds the immortal world of the soul. Much of this resonated with Greenwood's experience of the process of magical consciousness. Ancient artefacts prompted the imagination and memories of Greenwood's own "golden track" connection, specifically at the Danish National Museum with the Iron Age ship and the Trundholm Horse Chariot and the Flanders Great War battlefield museum. She could sense the depth of experiential memory, as located within the objects and their synchronous associations.

Might we *also* be able to understand Greenwood's narrative in terms of neuroscience, often a subset of the analytical mode? We should immediately be aware of the scope of this question; too rarely in the past when one asks what the "meaning" of a particular narrative, vision, or experience have the limits of the analytical mode been considered. Too easily it has normally been to dismiss such narratives as superstition, illusion, or worse, pseudoscientific explanations such as "random neural firings"—whatever such explanations are supposed to really mean. Hopefully, now, we are well enough equipped to ask such a question as what neurobiologically might be happening during one of Greenwood's experiences and to provide an analytical answer that does not commit any category errors or non sequiturs. The answer we obtain will be an analytical one that is quite different from the magical one. The magical answer is one that would require a direct engagement with one of the nonphysical beings Greenwood encountered, to which she could ask, "What are you?" Even in such cases, the answer is often enough "I am what I am"—the magical mode is nonverbal and imagistic. As the very question "What are you?" is asking for a verbal translation of images and feelings, it is unlikely to yield much while *using* magical thought except *more* images, symbols, and metaphors. However, answers may come as feelings or insights into verbalised material, conversations, or situations, showing that both modalities often operate simultaneously. As the Talmud states on the subject of dream interpretation: "the dream is its own interpretation." If it could simply be verbally thought, then one would think it in the analytical mode. But some experiences cannot be expressed fully in words without losing the holism that encompasses the magical modality—and that is "the dragon."

MAGIC AND SELF: ANALYSING THE ANALYTICAL AND MAGICAL MODES

The first observation we can make when analysing the ethnography of mind in the previous chapters is: what is the brain is doing during states that are predominantly magical rather than analytical? To do this, we have to link one or the other modality to some kind of physical process somehow. The easiest way to do this is to use what is most different between the modalities—the self/non-self boundary. The relaxing of this boundary is behind much of the characteristic shape-shifting of magical thought in general, and as we will see, the other characteristics appear to follow. Understanding "the self" is of course a huge philosophical area of debate, as we discussed in Chapter 2. For Frederic Myers, the mind was both a unity and a multiplicity: there was a larger individuality or Superliminal Self, a subliminal self that underlay personality, an infinite reservoir of psychical unity. The personality or self (with a small "s") was more external and transitory, and was located in the chains of memory that formed "character."[5] Indeed, Myers, as we have already seen, saw human individuality as a practically infinite reservoir of personal states, a kaleidoscope that could be "shaken into a thousand patterns," but with no pattern being able to utilise all the pieces contained in the tube.[6] Myers had a "filter interpretation" of the mind-body correlation: the biological organism was an adaptive mechanism that limited and shaped ordinary waking consciousness out of a larger, mostly latent, Self. The mind was not a producer of consciousness. Here we have an expanded view of consciousness: out of innumerable potential sensory or psychological processes only the most useful for survival have emerged, determined by natural selection. The ordinary waking self was not the only possible self that could have developed out of latent Self.[7]

What are the neurobiological and cognitive correlates of a well-defined versus ill-defined self? We must know the answer to this question if we are to provide an analytical understanding of the two modes. This will then help us understand what is going on neurobiologically in the brain when we are in the analytical or magical modes. Since the brain and mind are so tightly linked, knowing one helps us to understand the other. The work of neuroscientist Patrick McNamara is relevant here.[8] McNamara, building on the work of numerous studies of the brain engaging in religious experiences, defines the Executive Self (or simply the self) as a construct that evolved to bring order to the chaotic interplay of various unconscious impulses and drives. It is essential for good functioning from day to day, and appears to consist of autobiographical memory, agency, personality, bodily awareness, intentionality, and a sense of unity of awareness; these aspects of cognition self-organise during development, to varying degrees, and are essential for everyday activity. Each person, however, always has more than one self operating at once—whereas one self will be the primary self, other selves will always be floating about the mind as "possible selves," which includes the hated, admired, ideal, feared, past, and alternate selves. The primary self emerges from the fertile chaos of the mind and organises[9] selves spontaneously through its interaction with the environment over time, typically with one primary self and many other secondary, "possible selves." In general, an easy way to understand the function of the self is to consider its primary goal: to ask and define, "Who am I?"

NEUROBIOLOGICAL CORRELATES OF THE SELF

McNamara shows that there are a number of brain regions whose actions correlate with the processing associated with the self: primarily, the neural networks that mediate the executive self include the right sided orbitofrontal, dorsomedial, dorsolateral prefrontal, and anterior temporal cortices. Other regions known to be involved to varying degrees in mediating the executive self include the anterior cingulate, the insula, and the posterior cingulate cortices. These cortices are tightly interconnected and exert inhibitory action on practically everything else in the brain,[10] a fact which emphasises the way the self acts as a constraining "master-control" network that reigns in the chaos and promotes a coherent, centralised process that encourages the integration of wide arrays of input and coordinates behavior based on a unified vision of cross-modality inputs.

We know that these brain regions are active in self-functioning from studies of pathology: the characteristics of a well-functioning self are *interrupted* when the functioning of these brain regions is disrupted. Such pathological functioning can be seen in various psychiatric disorders such as schizophrenia, multiple personality disorder, bipolar disorder, obsessive-compulsive disorder, and many other mental illnesses. All of these disorders can be viewed as disorders of self-functioning.

Note that the self, as described here, is not a "thing" but a process, subject to dynamic changes over time. As it so happens, furthermore, there is an innate "push" that serves to improve the overall functioning of the self over time; this occurs through what McNamara calls "decentring": during decentring, the self is dismantled and agentive volition is inhibited. Once this happens, the subject is immersed in a fertile "wild" chaos of possible selves. Ideal selves that are more integrated, wider in scope, more flexible in functioning, better integrated, and in general more expansive are linked to the destabilised old self and (presuming the process occurs properly) this linkage allows a new self to organise and form, emerging from the primordium in a more functional form.[11]

McNamara describes the various ways in which this potent transformative process can go wrong, such that the self can wind up split, disintegrated, or inflated (such as can be seen in pathological narcissism or fanaticism), highlighting that decentring is not always a benign process of self-actualisation and "inner growth." It can be terrifying, life altering, and it can go horribly wrong. Decentring furthermore often involves highly culturally refined techniques to induce such a state, during which time the neurobiological regions that mediate the self are deliberately down-modulated by the culture to help the individual transition from an immature to a more mature state (as seen in the various rites of passage documented worldwide), or from one sort of social setting to another. Transforming the self to accommodate the new setting is part of smoothing out the adjustments needed for the subject. In these situations, decentring is induced, which places the subject in a chaotic world of creative and destructive mental chaos. The subject is then flooded with images, emotions, and ideal (meaning angelic and/or demonic) forms. It is in this state that magical consciousness dominates the mind.

Decentring can be achieved through a variety of methods ranging cross-culturally from the use of entheogens, mantic techniques such as chanting, deep meditation, intense focusing activity, privations and various physical tortures, to, in the Western traditions, a number of psychotherapeutic techniques, including free association, active imagination, and some kinds of dream interpretation. While decentred, the subject is in an essentially magical state of mind, as the boundary of the self is nearly destroyed (but in an ideally highly controlled setting), permitting an engagement with other possible selves, including godlike selves. The process, when functioning properly, has the ability to restructure the self into a stronger self with a number of altered functions and improved abilities. A rebuilt, stronger self normally leads to a greater sense of unity in experience, persisting positive affects and attitudes, a feeling of deep insight and recognition of the profoundly ineffable aspects of phenomenal experience. Furthermore, a strong self has an enhanced sense of personal power, empathy, and the ability to contextualise primitive emotional drives such as sex, fear, and anger, as well as an enhanced ability to appreciate complex metaphorical imagery. These benefits have been noted by the study of the development of the self[12] and point to the likely *function* of decentring in general: a powerful, likely evolved process that (when functioning properly!) promotes the integrated and sophisticated coordination of behaviour and emotional responses.

WHENCE COMES THE DRAGON?

As we examine the experiential data in the preceding chapters from the analytical perspective, it is likely that Greenwood's various encounters with the dragon she is encountering are an alternate self of among the highest ideal forms. All of the above aspects of self-functioning can be found in her experiential account—the sense of unity, ineffable connection, contextualisation, and control of primitive emotional drives, and an ever-expanding view of herself and her consciousness are recurrent themes in the experiential narrative. Furthermore, it is obvious that there are several points at which she experienced decentring to varying degrees, not only with the shamans, but on her own at various points—particularly in the water cave. Given what we have reviewed concerning the potential dangers of decentring gone awry, we know that Greenwood went into this exercise with an already strengthened sense of self, bolstered by her many previous decentring experiences and her strong family bonds and connections. A similar exercise in decentring in someone with a severe mental illness such as anxiety, depression, or a history of trauma, however, could have easily lead to disastrous results.

FERTILE CHAOS AND CREATIVE MADNESS

The ability to create a newer, stronger, progressively more expanded self-network is dependent upon the nascent creative capacity of the mind. We see this as we look at some of the neuroscience of creativity.[13] Briefly, when viewed by neuroimaging, we know that creative activities such as art, music, and divergent problem solving are correlated with intense activity in the association cortices, particularly in the right hemisphere. As researchers in the field of creativity have noted, there is a typical process that is followed. First, the mind is prepared by gathering relevant data for the creative task at hand. This is followed by a period in which this data is taken "offline" and allowed to "incubate" in the unconscious—in our terminology, meaning taken up by non-self processing. This incubation is then followed by sudden bursts of inspiration that enter consciousness as if from out of nowhere, sometimes nearly fully formed (a famous example are the symphonies that sometimes spontaneously occurred to Mozart, which he could then write down as if taking dictation).

The brain regions that appear to mediate intense creative activity include the bilateral, medial and inferior frontal, left mediotemporal, parietal, and retrosplenial cingulate cortices.[14] These regions exhibit a particular physiology that is especially well suited to self-organizing behaviour.[15] Such behaviour is typical of nonlinear, dynamic systems where there is no centralised control centre, but control of the behaviour of the system is rather decentralised and distributed throughout the entire system—examples of this sort of behaviour can be found in flocking birds, protein folding, global weather patterns, cellular genesis, and brain development. In such systems, historical and spatial changes get quickly blurred due to the ability of small perturbations to spread changes throughout the entire system—this also adds to the overall *holism* of such systems, which can behave in unison. Notice the important qualities of such systems include lack of central organisation, and nonlocal and nontemporal interconnected and holistic qualities. It is these conditions, however, that are conducive to self-organising behaviours that are precisely the conditions present in magical (i.e., decentred) thinking.

The numerous links between madness and highly creative individuals[16] suggests that the common element between them is the relative intensity of the above creative activity—in the highly gifted and creative, the individual is able to master the continual upsurge of creative influx into consciousness, whereas the mentally ill become overwhelmed by it, leading to disorders of the self. For it is the self that must contend with this non-self creative activity; controlled and properly applied, decentring can allow the self to grow and expand, accommodating this upsurge mediated by the association cortices and transforming it into a more balanced, integrated, and functional self, which *is* the central organiser. Here, we see the reason behind the need for decentring in the first place: only with a relatively weak controller can we foster new self-organisation in the system. On the other hand, the continual pressure from this aspect of the mind may threaten to shatter, divide, or otherwise disrupt the self for the worse outside of a controlled decentring to produce uncontrolled decentring—a potential disaster for the subject.

DRAGONS AND PROCESSES

The dragon, then, can be likened to an attractor point in this chaotic non-self system; a point of stable flow amid this torrent of creative forces within the non-self mind that, when viewed by the self from a properly prepared perspective, can flow into it and bring enlightenment, balance, strength, and expansion. The experiential narratives give us a detailed description of Greenwood's encounter with this attractor point (what might be termed an archetypal image in Jungian thought)[17] from the point of view not only of a highly decentred self, in which we see the purely overwhelming magical thought inherent in this state, but also afterward, which sees a binding of the analytical with magical thought into an analytical-magical alloy, a creative synthesis, working through various decentrings and forging newer, more sophisticated, and refined selves along the way through exposure to the creative fire of the fertile chaos that underlies the self.

That, at least, is what the dragon looks like when viewed from the analytical mode. Are we surprised that the dragon, in this mode, is treated like a mechanical process, operating like interacting particles in a chaotic system? Of course not. That is how the analytical mode views everything—but this is not the whole story, nor should it be, lest we ignore the necessary creative power of an ability to see things from the magical perspective. Against the strong reductionist temptation to say, "That's all there is with zero remainder!" we must remember that that assertion only applies if all the facts are accounted for. They are not; the subjective impression and aspect of this brain activity cannot be accounted for by a purely analytical analysis, as we have already discussed.

Therefore, to see the dragon in its full, hybrid light, we have to contend with the animistic magical mode, which as its first principle views things not as mechanisms, but as inspirited minds. From the magical mode, which is the nascent mode when the self is decentred, the dragon is an inspirited mind—and a powerful, godlike mind at that. Since minds, as coherent wholes, are generally foreign to the analytical mode, but inherent in the magical mode, it makes no sense to ask which is "correct," or whether or not the dragon is "real," for the strictly analytical answer will diametrically oppose the strictly magical answer. It is the hybrid answer we are arguing for throughout this volume. Under this perspective, which recognises the two modalities and ways in which they interact, we must say each has a certain measure of truth within its own context and perspective.

A CONTINUOUS UNIVERSE

As we have consistently emphasised in this work, the two orientations of analytical and magical modes of thinking interrelate continuously one with the other. The issue remaining is how to gain some sense of cohesion between the two domains that we have outlined as ideal types. Here, we need an encompassing theory that allows for both modes in a creative synthesis, without reduction to either. Once again, we can find insight in the work of Myers, who had a belief in the scientific method, and in the continuity of the universe whereby all phenomena, mental and physical, were continuous, coherent, and amenable to the rational and empirical methods of science. For Myers, consciousness was not singular; it had its roots in a transcendental environment, an overarching unity of the psyche.[18] It will be recalled that Myers searched for a comparative model of the human psyche that could make sense of specific occurrences under whatever cultural and historical guise they were expressed: beyond A and B, there was also an X.[19] We propose that this X could be imagined as similar to a Buddhist underlying non-dualistic divine reality that is ordinarily concealed, but exists within all phenomena. As in Tantric Buddhism, in particular, with its many deities, there are centres of consciousness that have many complex automatic actions and perceptions outside the awareness of primary consciousness. For Myers, these centres of consciousness were regarded as personalities or selves—intelligent sources of thoughts, feelings, and actions, but not necessarily alternative states—that interacted with each other, much as in Tantric Buddhist practice whereby a practitioner meditates with various aspects of divinity that at some point reflect the non-dualistic divine reality. It is interesting to view Greenwood's experience of the dragon in this light. In this case, the dragon becomes a powerful attractor mind that in magical consciousness connects with other significant divine aspects of reality, specifically, in Greenwood's case, the goddess Freyja, to create a sense of connection and meaning focused on the "wild," deeper aspects of the psyche.

As we saw in Chapter 4, Gregory Bateson was interested in the knowledge gained through "abduction," the intuitive process of reasoning through metaphor, as he explored though a reading of Jung's "Seven Sermons to the Dead." Bateson's work on metaphorical patterns that form a matrix through which the individual is related—as creatura to pleroma—is useful for thinking about creating a sense of wholeness that at some level can encompass different types of knowledge. Where Abraxas was a transpersonal metaphor for the unity of mind in nature for Bateson, we suggest that "the dragon" in our example of an ethnography of mind works as a metaphorical attractor point for the feeling, structuring, and classifying meaning process of magical consciousness. This meaning has important individual, social, and environmental aspects that, in a modern, Western context, help relieve fragmentation and isolation and help bring the individual together with his/her specific lived context. Many authors have sensed the magical "truth" of this process—William Blake, Samuel Taylor Coleridge, and Herman Hesse being obvious examples in point—and so have all the various world mythologies that speak to the creative Imagination. They all reveal and engage on some level with the process of magical consciousness. This is the ultimate primary reason and the ultimate rationality of the "mystical mentality" of magic.

NOTES

1. G. Deleuze and F. Guattari *A Thousand Plateaus: Capitalism and Schizophrenia* B. Massumi (trans.) (London: Athlone Press, 1988): 15.
2. Tim Ingold *The Perception of the Environment* (London: Routledge, 2000): 140.
3. Hermann Hesse *Steppenwolf*, translated by Basil Crighton and updated by Joseph Mileck (New York: Bantam Books [1969] 1929): 34–35.
4. Ibid., 187.

5. Emily Williams Kelly 'F.W.H. Myers and the Empirical Study of the Mind-Body Problem' in *Irreducible Mind*, Edward F. Kelly, Emily Williams Kelly, Adam Crabtree, Alan Gauld, Michael Grosso and Bruce Greyson (eds.) (Lanham, Maryland: Rowman & Littlefield Publishers, 2010): 82.
6. F.W.H. Myers 'The Subliminal Consciousness' (Chapter 4: Hypermnesic Dreams. *Proceedings of the Society for Psychical Research*, 8, 1892): 363, quoted in *Williams Kelly* 'F.W.H. Myers' in *Irreducible*, 82.
7. Williams Kelly, 'F.W.H. Myers' in *Irreducible*, 73–82, 95.
8. Patrick McNamara *The Neuroscience of Religious Experience* (New York: Oxford University Press, 2009).
9. J.A. Scott Kelso *Dynamic Patterns: The Self-Organization of Brain and Behavior* (New York: Bradford, 1995). Also Walter Freeman *How Brains Make Up Their Minds* (New York: Columbia University Press, 2001).
10. McNamara *Religious Experience*, 46.
11. Ibid., 46–57.
12. Ibid., 53.
13. Reviewed in N.C. Andreasen 'A Journey into Chaos: Creativity and the Unconscious' *Mens Sana Monographs* 9(1) (2011): 41–48.
14. Ibid.
15. Olaf Sporns *Networks of the Brain* (Boston: MIT Press, 2010).
16. A. Juda 'The Relationship Between Highest Mental Capacity and Psychic Abnormalities' *American Journal of Psychiatry* 106 (1949): 296–307. A.M. Ludwig 'Creative Achievement and Psychopathology—Comparison Among Professions *American Journal of Psychotherapy* 46 (1992): 330–356. Simeonova et al. 'Creativity in Familial Bipolar Disorder' *Journal of Psychiatric Research* 39 (2005): 623–631. Kyaga et al. 'Creativity and Mental Disorder' *British Journal of Psychiatry* 199 (2011): 373–379.
17. Erik Goodwyn 'Recurrent Motifs as Resonant Attractor States in the Narrative Field: A Testable Model of Archetype' *Journal of Analytical Psychology* 58 (2013): 58, 387–408.
18. Adam Crabtree 'Automatism and Secondary Centers of Consciousness' in *Irreducible*, 57.
19. Williams Kelly, 'F.W.H. Myers' in *Irreducible*, 332–334.
20. Jeffrey J. Kripal *Authors of the Impossible: The Paranormal and the Sacred* (Chicago: University of Chicago Press, 2011): 43.

Index

Printed in Great Britain
by Amazon

24406172R00156